You've Gone Too Far This Time, Sir!

by

Danny Bent

ISBN   1456550306

EAN   978-1456550301

'You've Gone Too Far This Time, Sir!' was first published by Night Publishing, a trading name of Valley Strategies Ltd., a UK-registered private limited-liability company, registration number 5796186. Night Publishing can be contacted at: http://www.nightpublishing.com.

'You've Gone Too Far This Time, Sir!' is the copyright of the author, Danny Bent, 2011. All rights are reserved.

All illustrations and the cover design are the copyright of the artist, Sandra Rivaud, 2011. All rights are reserved.

Proofread by Luke Woolnough

Danny Bent's website can be found at:

http://www.dannybent.com/

S

I met Danny Bent at Heathrow Airport where a large reception committee was welcoming him back from his epic cycling trip to India which he undertook to raise significant amounts of money for charity, and to prove that some people still have a sense of adventure even if that adventure might end up killing them.

He was also keeping faith with the pupils at the school where he had been teaching. He had preached long and hard that cycling was more environmentally friendly than flying or driving so, when he decided to work in a school in India, that is how he was committed to getting out there.

The title of his book is 'You've Gone Too Far This Time, Sir', which is what one of his pupils used to say to him on a regular basis as she admired the daring of his exploits, and at several points in his 9,000 mile journey it appeared to him, as it appears to us, that he had indeed taken too much of a risk. In the scorching heat of a Uzbek desert, for instance he says,

"I could feel my cheeks sucking against my skull. My eyes were sunken and dark. My suntanned skin was pulling taut across my muscles. My tongue was stuck to the top of my mouth. I was dizzy from dehydration and my speed had reduced to 10km/h, about the pace of a brisk walk.

As time went on I began to get really desperate. I was burning up. My body had stopped sweating; it had no liquid to spare. My cheeks were salt-encrusted.

I didn't see the point in stopping and waiting, I might have waited for days for someone to help me so I just kept plodding onwards. I knew there was a village ahead and if I kept rotating my scorched legs I hoped to get there eventually. Surely they'd be able to spare some water and food. Head down.

I couldn't see in front of me, but I was travelling so slowly there was no risk of crashing into anyone.

Suddenly two hands were resting on my handle bars ...."

This is a fearsome tale of endurance, but it is above all a story of friendship, of the simple kindness and openness of the people he met as he crossed the world. Without their help he might well have died; without his presence, their lives would have been that much less eventful.

In short, this book is a timely reminder of the good in humankind and a testament to the faith that with the help of such goodness we can conquer all adversity.

The Duchess of York

Live your dream!

This book is dedicated to everyone who's ever had a dream.

Chapter 1

The rhythmic hum of wings beating as birds fly overhead fills my ears. I can hear the sea breeze blowing up the valley, playing with the leaves on the trees, and the pounding of the waves beneath me slowly eating away at the rock formations. I can hear the terrified screams of my friends echoing around the mountainside and I can see their tear-stained faces peering over the thirty foot vertical cliff.

I'm at the bottom of the cliff. I can't speak and I can't feel my body.

Thirty seconds ago I had been cycling with friends on the Côte d'Azur in France, climbing from turquoise blue sea to snow-capped peak repeatedly to train both legs and lungs to cope with the pain during the racing season. My cleanly shaven, white, freckled legs were becoming honed machines, pistons that fired without the slightest effort. My lungs were able to suck in and process litres of the thin mountain air with each gasp. I was feeling strong, pushing harder with thoughts of glory in the back of my mind.

Suddenly, my super light carbon wheel clipped a rider in front, my best friend and arch-enemy on the bike, Stephen Bell. If ever there was a man built for cycling it was Steve. Arched back, narrow piercing eyes, thighs like tree trunks and a competitive edge that could slice diamonds. We had been rivals since my introduction to cycling with the advantage switching from one to the other as the years passed by. We had crossed the finish line with exactly the same time in our previous race and I was starting to feel the balance tipping in my favour again.

The contact flipped my bike, throwing it to the right, towards the cliff edge, catapulting me and the bike clear off the road, down the vertical face of the abyss.

I remember the fall in slow motion. The first moment as I left the road, the faintest smell of burning rubber, the floating sensation, reaching to grab a lone, straggly weed growing between the cracks in the limestone rocks, the sight of it coming free in my hand with only the tiniest amount of force, the sensation of falling forever. And then nothing.

There are more eyes looking down on me now. Some I recognise, some I don't. The screams are still ringing in my ears. A single tear falls through the air. The sun reflects off the shimmering surface as it falls to earth like a tear from heaven. It lands on my left shoe, triggering a tingling in my big toe. Initially the sensation just sits in my toe wondering what to do next, contemplating its options, then it spreads up my right leg and down the left. *I can move my legs again!* It rushes up my spine, splits and zips down both my arms. My fingers are wiggling. With an almighty bang this sensation explodes in my brain and voice box. My mouth opens and I shout back at the onlookers, "I THINK I'M ALIVE".

* * *

This is a story about love and adventure. It is also a true story. Our main character is a boy born in the Peak District amongst the bubbling Buxton springs. Nestled in a green and thriving valley, he was born into a simple household where his cot lies. Two pairs of eyes look on him from above, one set blue, the other hazel brown.

The eyes belong to his parents, two people who formed a bond and gave their genetic structure to our boy and then their lives. They were struggling to afford to furnish their flat, yet they lavished him with undivided love, attention and care. Albino blond, spattered with freckles, ears that his head will eventually grow into, his mother's blue eyes and a strong jaw line adorned with a cheeky grin, he lays quietly like a bomb waiting to detonate.

Placing him in a backpack, his Dad - an international athlete - would take him orienteering before he could walk. Running from point to point, through rivers, over fells, climbing rocks, how could our boy not pick up a bit of this adventurous spirit along the way? An attitude was shaped that no experience was a bad experience. His mum found him drinking from the toilet bowl at the age of one. Rather than tell him off, she asked what it tasted like, whilst reassuring him that the water from the taps was nicer.

As soon as he could walk, he would climb tables, leap off sofas, clamber into streams, chase frogs. He'd run up and down the almost vertical steps outside their house. When he was two years old his family finally had the money to see what was outside of Great Britain and they all went camping in France. On the ferry crossing, a wise man in a dark overcoat with a fashionable moustache watched him running around, overexcited and without a care in the world, and stated, "He's like an accident waiting to happen."

At four years old he undertook his first adventure on his bicycle. Having just removed the stabilisers he decided this was it; no more help. He opened the front door, sat on the stairs that led from the hallway, and mounted his bike. He wobbled at first but then cheered wildly as he managed to stay on, gripping the handlebars so that his knuckles were as white as his legs were shaky. He passed the dressing table and the chest of drawers containing all the muddy shoes and maps. The coat stand whizzed by as he picked up speed, passing through the front door. He didn't want to stop and proceeded to cycle down the steep steps before flying over the handlebars.

The 'poorlies' on his knees and the lump on his head did nothing to deaden his adventurous spirit which was nurtured and allowed to grow with time. The scars that remained were treasured - he was the first boy in his class to ride a bike without stabilisers. He was back on in no time and he was fast, the fastest kid in the street. But he couldn't turn corners and wasn't much good at stopping.

When the family moved to a house just up the road from their flat, a cycle workshop was created in the cellar. His dad would use parts of wrecked old bicycles to fix his wrecked new ones.

At eleven, during a junior school leavers' assembly in front of all the mums and dads, his headmistress asked his classmates what they wanted to do when they left school. Footballer, doctor, film star, politician they replied one by one. His answer was no surprise to the audience who had grown used to his quirky optimism and spirit. "I want to cycle round the world and raise money for charity". A big 'Ahhhhh' resounded around the school hall, "so sweet."

However, before he could start realising dreams, he had a few more lessons to learn.

He graduated and left Southampton University with the highest honours in tomfoolery, indulgent buffoonery and mathematics. Educational establishments had wrapped him in cotton wool for the past fifteen years, protected him from growing up and armed him with a solitary piece of paper rolled and tied with a ribbon - a degree certificate - and told him to get out there in the real world, find a job, build a life, start a pension, acquire life insurance, get married and start a family.

"What?" he remembers thinking, "I didn't sign up for this!"

He was lost in the big grown-up world. Friends' values and opinions changed overnight, about turns were made but he didn't hear the sergeant give the order. No one wanted to be silly any more. Trips to Toys R Us to check out the cool toys Geoffrey the Giraffe had released this month seemed to be over. Cycling to work in the same clothes you went out in the previous night was deemed a no-no. Protesting against the violation of human rights was out the window. Trying to outdo each other with bad taste outfits from the local Oxfam shop no longer added to your street credentials. It was all designer frocks, Chelsea tractors, mobile phones, 2.4 children and that inevitable second house in the country. Under friends' arms he saw briefcases not surf boards. Suits were the new shorts, consumerism the new Marxism.

Lost and disorientated, he was like a child ripped from its mother's bosom and left in the heat of the savannah. Out there he was easy pickings for the predators, those that stop at nothing until you are between their jaws as they tear the life from you. Financial institution after financial institution snapped, gulped and dived - he had to leap high to keep out of their reach. He did his best but was no match for their craftiness, their cunning. In the end his world became part of their world, the trading floor. He was told to 'get up to speed fast' so that they could start 'singing from the same hymn sheet'. Moving at speed and singing were things he enjoyed; working in an office was not.

Without the slightest interest in what he was doing, and without a single care for the money that was mounting up in his bank account, he was promoted to supervisor and then manager. With his tie slung low, shirt untucked and blond shaggy hair resting on his shoulders, he would fly all over Europe telling people how they should perform, what his firm expected and the results which were fundamental to the business, when it was clear to see that he wasn't following his own advice.

Walking like a Zombie from bed, to train, to work, and then back again, he was miserable, his energy lost. His one release was his bike – taking it away on holiday and flying up and down mountains without a care in the world.

The boy in question is me, Danny Bent. Not exceptional, but not what you would call normal either.

* * *

At that exact moment, as I was falling to what should have been my certain death in the Alps, I was more alive than I'd been the past five years.

Instead of closing them for eternity, it opened my eyes. How could I have been given so much and not give something back? I didn't need to think of me - enough people were doing that already. I wanted to think of someone else, something else.

10

Back in the office one week after my fall I packed my things into a small box, told my boss I wouldn't be coming back and within another twenty-four hours was sitting in a classroom surrounded by happy, smiling faces. I was taking the next pedal rotation on my journey through life...

Chapter 2

My heart races. There is no way on earth I'd have thought I would be here, not now, not ever. A trickle of sweat sweeps down my cheek, winding in and out of the red bristles that come from days without a mirror or razor. Pakistan is laid out before me in all its splendour.

A country at war on two fronts. I didn't think this was a trip for this lifetime. The question was whether it might be the end of it.

To the west lies the border with Afghanistan where staying alive isn't easy. Residents can be ousted from their homes at breakfast by the Pakistani army which then proceeds to blow up their dwellings in search of targets. At midday they may have to dive for cover, narrowly avoiding misguided US missiles falling the wrong side of the Afghan border, only to be blown up at tea time by a suicide bomber.

To the east is India. Ever since partition sixty years ago, military conflicts and territorial disputes have been rife. A country brutally cut in two by Britain, the scar is yet to heal and blood still weeps from the wound.

Looking past all this is a country shrouded in a burka of beauty. In the south, miles of golden beaches meet hot, dry deserts etched with flowing rivers of life. The rich alluvial plains of the Punjab are joined by aquamarine rivers flowing from glaciers enveloped by the three highest mountain ranges in the world. Symbolising the war, violence and the power struggle taking place in Pakistan, the Himalayas, the Karakoram, and the Hindu Kush all collide in a monstrosity of power and grace. Pakistan has so many mountains soaring above the clouds at over six thousand metres that many of them haven't been given so much as a name.

I'm balanced on two square inch pieces of rubber. My legs are spinning at one hundred revolutions per minute. The wind is tearing at the clothes that cover all my body except my face which is decorated with sparkling crystals of frost and ice.

The mountains fill my field of vision, in front, behind, left and right. They fill my every thought, my consciousness and my subconscious. If it wasn't for a rough road following the valley I'd be lost and, without shelter, would be dead by nightfall. One lapse in concentration on the way down could see me repeating my fall in France, but this time the drop is going to be at least three hundred foot. Jagged rocks protruding from the valley floor wait to impale and smash my body to pulp. My remains would be fought over by the numerous brown bears, wolves and the rare snow leopards that frequent these mountain passes. They are my only company. Otherwise I'm alone.

How on earth did I find myself travelling alone on a bicycle in what the national press, media and travel organisations describe as the most dangerous country in the world? What possesses a man to enter such a country, to put his life on the line, to pit his wits against murderous conditions and men? Can one solitary man survive?

To start answering these questions I need, without the help of a DeLorean DMC-12 and the Doc, to take you back in time...

* * *

I became a junior school teacher in the leafy suburbs of West London. I cycled the Thames towpath to school where I'd be greeted by thirty happy, smiling faces all longing for the education I had been graced to give them. I guess I wasn't your stereotypical teacher. I didn't tell the kids off, I didn't use a marker pen and a whiteboard, didn't dress in tweed with arm pads. I drank juice not tea, hung out in the playground not the staff room, ran in corridors and played pranks on other teachers. I was affectionately known as the naughtiest kid in the school.

Consequently, I would always get allocated the box classroom farthest away from everyone else to avoid disruption. Encouraging the children to throw paint at Teacher in art, dressing in helmets and harnesses and climbing trees in maths, or creating Plasticine stop frame animations in science, I wanted my classroom to be alive. Not just a buzz or a heart beat. I liked the tiles on the roof to be vibrating. Some days I was tempted to try and blow the roof clean off (I got into trouble for that one). I was one of the pupils and they were all teachers. Their knowledge and ideas were as valuable as mine.

A particularly confident nine year old, Lucy, used to put her hand up and say, "You've gone too far this time, Sir," before the head teacher bustled in looking fraught and agitated wondering what all the commotion was about. I loved it.

So when in Geography I was struggling to make the subject of Chembakolli, a rural village in India, as exciting for the kids as it was for me, I was troubled. How could I bring this topic to life? I hoped to find a solution in my friend Louisa, a teacher who danced her way through class with smiles, laughter and enthusiasm - the perfect person to consult.

In a world of home computers, DVDs, MP3 players, the latest video games, and interactive TV, we agreed the children needed something they could relate to. After a bit of thinking and a few too many beers, she stated that kids needed to see a figure they could relate to out there - a figure they knew, respected - living in a mud hut in the village, collecting water and washing in the local stream, hunting for food with a bow and arrow, taking the long journey to school each day through the jungle, avoiding the local wildlife.

As tequila hit the back of my throat and more brain cells evaporated, an idea suddenly emerged through the dulling cloud of alcohol: "I could go out there."

Lou gave me her very best disapproving teacher face.

"You'd have to be stark raving bonkers to do that....... no shower, no hot water, no X Factor, teaching at a village school with no books, no boards, no pens. Eating brains, maggots and chicken feet." She stopped her tirade. "You're right!! You'd be perfect."

* * *

"You are what?" It was Lucy again. I was telling my class I was leaving to go and live and teach in Chembakolli. "Oh, you've gone too far this time, Sir."

The next moment will stay with me for the rest of my life, a memory burnt into my retinas. The problem with giving children an open playing field in which to work, where they are confident to speak their mind without the fear of retribution or teasing, is that sometimes they can really catch you off guard.

Jasper, a boy normally with his head in the clouds but with an amazing aptitude to relate subjects to real life, pops up his hand and asks, "How will you get there?"

In my head I'm thinking, "I'll fly, how else would I get there, silly bean?" until, following his gaze, I see where he is looking. My eyes fix on the back of the classroom. Our Green Awareness poster. I look back at his eager face waiting for an answer. The rest of the class turn in anticipation. I take two steps forward and then one back towards my desk. There's a big red cross next to the plane, partnered with a sad face and a fact card written in my own hand telling the children that air travel pollutes the world more than all the power plants in China, that it produces more CO_2 than any other business. Another smaller cross sits next to a picture of a train and a bus. The next on the list is a child on a bicycle with a big, happy face and a big tick.

I am left with a choice - unravel what I have taught them about green issues over the past year or ... the other choice is unthinkable. I shudder.

Just like a school sweater, I know that if I allow one thread to unravel, by lunchtime their whole education will be sitting at their feet like woolly spaghetti. Sarah, Jasper's seating partner, drops her pencil and, as it hits the ground, I'm brought back to reality.

One statement, five words, changed my life forever: "I'm going by bicycle".

Chapter 3

After speaking to the bewildered school in India to explain that I would be a little late, I was left with just two months to organise a trip across half the world - fifteen thousand kilometres.

I'd like to say everything was meticulously planned, with the route engrained in my mind after poring over maps into the night with only a cigar and a brandy to keep me company; with knowledge of the history, the culture, and the languages of each country I would cycle through saturating my grey matter; having erected my tent time and again whilst timing myself until I could do it blindfolded; and after spending days elbow deep in grease taking my bike and equipment to pieces and putting it back together again so I knew exactly how each and every bit should be used. However, every night until the end of term I had commitments. An open evening for new parents, class performances, orchestra, sports days, cross country club, drama club. I had no time to plan anything ... so I didn't ...

Cotswold kindly offered to organise all my camping gear. *Bicycle* built me a bike that we hoped could cross mountain ranges and deserts, and handle forest floors, roads and tracks. I had some peace of mind.

* * *

On the 17th July all the teachers at school were drinking a glass or two of wine to celebrate the end of the school year, exhausted and suffering from the illnesses that a thousand sneezes and snotty noses generate. It was time for teachers to put their feet up, relax, time for holidays, lie-ins, and catching up with friends. That was all teachers but me. I was drinking to forget. I was leaving bright and early tomorrow on the expedition of a lifetime. I'd organised to meet friends at my local café at 7.30 the next morning for coffee and cakes which I hoped would power me on my way.

When I staggered back to my flat too many glasses of wine later, the front door lay slightly ajar. Pushing through I should have been greeted by four panniers neatly packed, my bike, and a fresh pile of clothes all ready for tomorrow. Instead, my possessions were everywhere, boxes had been turned upside down, drawers hung open, belongings were scattered about the floor crunching under my feet as I ventured further in. As I switched on the light I could see that my most expensive piece of kit, my tent, was missing. I held my head in my hands.

Burglary? Oh no, no, no. Sorry to worry you. This was just the state of my affairs the night before I left. I was surrounded by unopened boxes, papers, and equipment. My tent hadn't arrived yet. Some problems with deliveries meant it was still in the post to the Cotswold store. They were hoping it'd arrive tomorrow and then be delivered somehow to me whilst I cycled to Dover.

By midnight nothing had moved. I was sitting on my bed, sewing a present onto my shirt that a girl at school had given me. It was a tiny silver lucky star. It had already become significant to me – a symbol of hope, new beginnings, faith. For someone devoid of religious and spiritual beliefs it was strange to be putting so much trust into such a little thing. By the time the sun was rising the my first day of my new life, I decided it was best to shove everything into my panniers and hope for the best, an emotion I would learn to rely on quite heavily over future days, weeks and months. I was setting off in three hours' time.

* * *

I woke after a couple of hours' sleep to my screaming alarm. I rolled over and pulled my pillow over my head.

I wanted to hide, ignore the fact that a steal-framed bike christened Shirley, packed with what I hoped were all the basics that a man needed to survive any situation, was sitting at the bottom of my bed. She was chewing at my toes, ready to get on the road for the first time. I was chewing my bottom lip hoping that Scotty would beam me up.

Pulling on the Lycra I would soon become attached to – literally – I pulled the bike upright and made for the exit. I lived on the second floor and had to get Shirley down two flights of stairs. With all the baggage, it weighed about fifty kilograms - not far off my own weight. I tentatively dropped the front wheel over the first step before being dragged down the rest of the flight by my feisty companion, falling to a crumpled heap at the front door. My concerned neighbours opened their own doors to find out what the commotion was about. Lying at their feet was a thirty-year-old man pinned underneath a bicycle. Laughing, they said, "Good luck, Dan", opened the front door and shooed me out.

Friends were supposed to be coming to see me off. In the café, I was alone barring a cameraman who fluttered around taking video footage of me looking awkward, scared and lonely. As the smell of roast coffee swirled through the air, my best friend from junior school arrived with a smile that lifted my heart. She was so proud of me: I realized I'd already made a difference. My chest expanded and as teachers, pupils, family and friends arrived, all dressed in pink with their bikes at the ready, I started to get excited. Could I do this?

A cheer rang through Richmond as those without bikes cheered off about fifty mad folks who'd pledged to cycle one hundred miles to Dover with me to raise awareness of the charity and show their support for what I was doing.

I'd chosen to ride the fifteen thousand kilometres for ActionAid, a charity whose pledge is to "End Poverty Together".

Within five miles we were stopping for a puncture. Not mine - my bike was still intact. I felt smug. I used the opportunity to throw sickeningly sweet energy bars and drinks down my throat, hoping these would give me the extra energy to cross the hills. Carrying all that extra weight in baggage, the hills that I'd once raced to the top of, pounding my fists as I summited first, were slow slogs. Sweat dripped off my nose onto my bike, my legs burnt as though they were laced with glass.

These, I have to mention, are hills, the highest one being two hundred metres above sea level. I would be climbing mountains more than forty times bigger than this in the coming year if everything went to plan. Friends pushed, dragged, provoked and encouraged me to get my sorry ass to the campsite where we were to rest before my ferry left in the morning.

Once there it was the first chance to air my ukulele. Others had brought guitars, drums, bells and tambourines, and we sat round a campfire playing music and singing until it was time for us all to squeeze into our tents. Mine had been handed to me as I cycled along by the wonderful people of Cotswold who'd pulled out all the stops to get it to me on time. This was convenient for all those who'd forgotten their tents and now squeezed into mine.

* * *

Sunday 19th July 2009

This was my day, the day I'd dreamed of since I was eleven, the day that changed the course of my life forever. The sun was shining, the grass shone electric green, lambs in the nearby field played gleefully under the birds that soared through the salt-drenched sea air.

I crawled out of my tent looking like a monster from the deep. Swollen eyelids, tongue lolling to one side, hair encrusted because I had not showered after the gruelling ride yesterday.

Sports coaches will tell you the best way to recover from a long hard day in the saddle is protein shakes, plenty of carbohydrates, gallons of water and electrolyte to replace the lost fluid and minerals. Possibly the worst recovery is five pints of lager, pie and chips. But, quoting Bear Grylls, "Survival means doing what you have to do".

My mouth tasted like I'd been sucking used cat litter all night and my gut rolled and gurgled. The sun's glare burnt my eyes and the beautiful noises beat against my eardrums like thrash metal. Luckily I only had a few miles to the port of Dover where my vessel awaited. She was a fine beast. The Olympic Spirit was her name, weighing in at over thirty thousand tonnes. Her spirit rubbed off on me as we dashed and dived across the English Channel to take me across the seas and to my first border, to France. The start of my solo trip!

The white cliffs of Dover were drifting away, engulfed by the sea mist and spray by the time I was up on deck. As the water spattered my face I knew that people were waving, so I shouted out goodbye. The seagulls echoed my call and carried it to my friends and loved ones waiting on the shore.

What do I do now? For the first time in two months I had nothing to do. I sat and I waited. When the boat docks my adventure really starts. I imagined the glory of it all. Riding down the plank, finding the road out of Calais and heading off into the sunset.

I did ride the plank but I couldn't find the road I needed. I just couldn't get out of the town. My pidgin French - "Où est ma route?" - whilst jabbing my finger at my map, got me nowhere. In response my French friends raised their shoulders in a shrug, held up their hands, stuck out their lower lips and said "Bof".

Round and round I went. One hour after I'd arrived I was beginning to ask myself how on earth I was going to get to India? After two hours I think I'd traversed every single road and was beginning to ask myself if I'd even make it out of Calais.

After three hours I decided to bite the bullet and rode up onto the motorway. Cars peeped their horns, drivers showed me that my understanding of French expletives was better than that of normal conversation, and I was comforted to see that hand gestures meant the same in any language.

I didn't care - I was on my way - until the police pulled me over and told me to leave at the next exit. They followed behind all the way with lights flashing. My first police escort!! Awesome.

Chapter 4

Waking in England, crossing France - albeit a very small section - and ending my first day in Belgium. Three countries in one day. I'd be in India by the end of the week at this rate. Surely you'd expect me to be feeling elated, pumping my fists in the air, cheering.

I rolled into a Bed and Breakfast in Poperinge with the weight of the world on my shoulders. I was down, already missing my friends and family, contemplating what I had taken on, wondering how on earth I'd keep this going for months on end. Belgium is flat and westernised; this is supposed to be the easy bit. My legs were tired, my back sore, my new seat had chafed places that shouldn't be rubbed. I barely spoke to the kind owner as he tried to lift my spirits.

Broken, I sat on the edge of my bed staring at my reflection in the mirror on the oak-panelled wardrobe. An ashen, grimacing face returned my gaze. I turned my attention to my panniers. I needed to do something drastic.

Tipping all the kit onto the floor in front of me, I started sorting feverishly. Within an hour I'd made two piles. To my left was a pile that I deemed essential. A toy sheep (the mascot of my school given to me in my leavers' assembly), balloons and musical instruments for the kids I would meet, ukulele, emergency chocolate, designer boxers, camera, a pick and mix of medicines and pills. To my right was the "I might need some of this, but can probably do without it" pile consisting of sections of maps, vacuum packed food, ten litre water carriers, bicycle tools and a heavy winter jacket. I gathered all of this pile in my arms and dumped it in the oh-so-small waste paper basket in my room. With my bike lighter, as the night closed in, my mood began to lift.

Embarrassed by my teenage strop the previous night, I sneaked out of the B&B without taking breakfast. A cheery wave through the double glazed window to the bemused owner of the B&B was our last interaction. I was on the road to Germany. I whizzed over a little rise (probably Belgium's biggest hill) and whooshed down the other side. It was a Monday, start of a new week, start of a new me, I needed to get some grub in my belly and to fill my water bottle and then I would be set for adventures beyond my dreams. Today was a commemoration - the ascension to the throne of Belgium's first king, Leopold I, and hence was a bank holiday.

Contrary to the consumerist markets in London, all shops were closed. I began to regret the cuts I had made last night as the sun beat down on my head and a continuous trickle of sweat dripped off my nose. I was getting very thirsty and hungry. I'd already eaten my emergency chocolate and I was dreaming of the hog we'd roasted two weeks previously to raise money for my charity at a local pub. The further I went, the tighter my tongue stuck to the top of my mouth. Streams ran alongside the road swollen from the nightly rainfall that would follow me across Europe. The water was starting to look tempting when at last I saw a neon 'open' sign in the distance. Hallelujah.

The bright, colourful lights contrasted with the secluded, traditional village setting. My mouth salivated at the thought of downing litres of fizzy, sweet drink and raiding shelves stacked with goodies. As I drew closer, I noticed that the lights not only proclaimed that the shop was open but also that it was 'erotic' and sold magazines and DVDs. I stopped far enough away for people to not confuse me with someone considering going in.

A stereotypical man left the establishment wearing a beige mac, his face adorned with thick horn-rimmed glasses that magnified his eyes giving him the look of a goggle-eyed marsupial, with his day's facial hair and a paper bag under his arm. My hunger and thirst made me question whether the shop sold chocolate willies and taurine energy drinks proclaiming that it 'keeps you up all night'. I didn't pluck up the courage to enter and find out.

Another hour of steady cycling to preserve my dwindling energy supplies and I came across a greengrocers which was open. The marrows and aubergines made me giggle after my previous experience of shops in Belgium; a good sign that my senility was already wavering. The owner filled my panniers with all sorts of sweet and savoury foods and pointed me in the direction of a campsite. I was looking forward to rustling up something special on my camp stove. I'd brought a stove that burns with any liquid fuel – at a pinch I was assured that even Russian vodka could be used to boil up a brew.

Having been told time and again to try the camp stove before I left, I found myself trying to light it for the first time. The instructions were still sitting on my sideboard at home. I'd pitched my tent between the caravans and a large tent housing a number of German families. The evergreen branches sheltered it from the setting sun, and the birds and animals in the forest gave me a real feel of wild camping. Attaching the fuel bottle, I sat the stove on the grass. This has got to be easy. Right? Turn it on and put a match to it.

Turning the nozzle I tried one match after another. I could hear the hissing of fuel. It just wouldn't go up. The German family watched on; I could feel the pressure. Maybe I'd filled it with unleaded and it was supposed to be diesel. I did that to my mum's car once and managed to get one mile down the road before the engine seized up and we (read: Mum) were slapped with a £2,000 bill for cleaning it. Back at the campsite, unbeknownst to me, the petrol was leaking all over the floor, running between my legs and over my equipment. I tried one last match which hit the right spot. A large fire ball that could have roasted another hog erupted into the air. In fact it might have done – the trees around were scorched, my maps were charred and my leg hair was burnt.

Once they'd stopped giggling, I was assured by one of the campers that it made me look more like a shaven-legged Tour de France rider. The tour was coming to a close about now and Contador had put the hammer down, leaving Lance Armstrong struggling on in the Alpine Mountains for second place.

Eating raw veggies and dipping bread into a Bolognaise tomato sauce, I made a decision not to use the stove again until I had managed to access the great World Wide Web to find instructions on how to use it. I'd had a narrow escape. I later learnt that my stove is much more effective when it is turned the right way up.

On the bike I tried to keep my spirits high by waving at anyone who passed by, encouraging the feeling that I was living my dream. The countryside also took a turn for the better. Belgium's row upon row of housing estates gave way to rows of pine trees releasing their pungent, warming holiday smell and rivers weaving in and out of fields of wheat, swaying to the beat of my pedal pushing.

These gave way to the claret red poppy fields, symbols of the bloodshed of the First World War. In these fields ninety-five years ago the German army swept through, costing the lives of hundreds of thousands of men. Many more thousands had to watch friends die, mown down by machine gun fire or picked off with primitive rifles. Their blood and guts filled the gaps between the flowers.

I tried to recite 'In Flanders Fields', a poem I studied at school, written by Colonel John McCrae after he witnessed the death of his friend Lieutenant Alexis Helmer:

> *"In Flanders fields the poppies blow,*
> *Besides the crosses, row on row..."*

I began adding the occasional made-up word or line to complete the verse and ended with some original lyrics of my own.

These men were true heroes, every one of them, giving their lives for the safety of women and children. Very different to the wars of today where families are deprived of friends, family, brothers, and lovers to aid oil prices and continue the lucrative arms trade.

* * *

A young spotted deer jumped out of the deep woodland beside me, bounding along beside my bike before turning and dashing back into the undergrowth.

I was now in Germany. I'd crossed the famous Belgium-Germany border with only a stone Belgian in uniform left to guard the crossing which had once been the most strictly enforced frontier in Europe (in the early 1900s). Europe was flying by. Looking at a map to see if it was really true that I had covered four countries in six days, it became obvious that I had barely begun. Europe is so small. Germany, the biggest country in Western Europe, is minute compared with the ex-Soviet and Asian countries I'd have to cycle through.

Once into Germany, the scenery was majestic - beautiful woodlands, blue skies, green and rugged pastures. Taking an off-road route, where I'd come across the deer, led me towards the hills. Precariously perched on top of the hills were fairytale castles, pointed spires on top of romantic towers and turrets balancing on thick stone walls. I had a feeling I'd fallen down a rabbit hole and was living in Fairyland. If the Big Bad Wolf had stopped me to ask in which direction Little Red had gone - "Wo ist mein Frau Rot?" - I wouldn't have been the least bit surprised.

What did shock me though were the speed limit signs. Famed for its no-limits autobahns, the smaller cyclable roads also had bizarre speed signs, for instance imposing a limit for tanks which was only twenty kilometres per hour slower than it was for cars. I didn't see any tanks but I did imagine one flying past me, swiftly followed by a police vehicle with flashing lights.

"Will you step out of your tank, please? Do you know what speed you were travelling?"

"Sorry, officer, I was late for church and the traffic was terrible!"

* * *

A rainbow shone in the distance, arching over the picture book scenery. I stopped to take a photograph whilst pondering the pot of gold that lay at the end. Aware that an elderly lady was standing watching me, I unclipped my shoe from the bike. My specialized MTB shoes had special toe clips that attached to the bike to stop them slipping off in the ice and wet. Using my unclipped shoe to balance myself, I took a picture. Unfortunately, just as my finger hit the trigger, the bike started to topple. With one leg strapped in, I was flung to the floor slamming my knee and elbow into the concrete, tearing the skin and revealing the flesh. The lady hobbled over and asked 'Alles gut?' I had 'studied' German at school and should have been able to string at least a few sentences together but, with blood streaming down my leg and arm, I could only remember a plangent declaration that had scraped me a pass in my final exams: "Ich habe meine Mutter verloren. Wo ist die Polizeidienststelle?" *I have lost my mum, where is the police station?*

* * *

After the fairytale beauty of the day, when I lay in my tent I couldn't help but sleep like Sleeping Beauty. I didn't wake up until nearing midday the following day when an Aussie disturbed me by wobbling my tent.

'G'day mate, sorry to wake ya'.

I unzipped my tent with one hand, holding my sleeping bag to cover my modesty and squinting against the sun which was drying the world after the night-time rains. Luckily for me there hadn't yet been a drop of rain during the day but it was still raining cats and dogs at night.

Oblivious to my lack of response, he continued, "I heard there was a crazy pommie bastard cycling these ways. You're heading off into the Ukrainian woods?"

I nodded, half asleep.

"Well here you go, bud, good on ya!" He thrust a wedge of notes into my hand that looked like an absolute fortune.

I refused to take them until he explained, "You can't change them outside the country, and I'm sure as hell not going back."

I thanked him profusely, grasping his hand with both of mine. Laughing and winking he looked down, bringing to my attention the fact that I'd dropped the sleeping bag.

I zipped up my tent as he walked away and sat rigid with shock. Then I whooped with glee, throwing the money in the air and letting it fall around me like snowflakes. I'd been handed my treasure at the end of the rainbow after all. To celebrate, I took the rest of the day off. I'd been riding for six days, my legs and butt felt swollen, and my belly was tight.

Starting a novel I'd brought with me for company, I lay on my roll mat soaking up the sun's rays until I turned the last page, before gently cycling down to a supermarket where I bought myself a feast. On my return, the children who had been pestering me to play all day returned and chatted as I cooked a one-pot gourmet dinner. I was surprised at their level of English. When I said they must be top of the class, they replied that they were actually the worst and that they were given detentions and held back regularly because of their lack of practice and pronunciation. I would be worried that, with my level of English, I'd struggle myself in such schools.

Rested and with energy levels restored, I powered through central Germany coming out the other side. Having already cycled what I guessed to be about 130 kilometres, I stopped in the afternoon at a gorgeous village café / bistro. I ordered a latte and a bowl of strawberries and cream to start. As the words left my mouth, I could feel the table next to me stop and stare. I was seated next to a tribe of German builders who were on the razz on a Friday afternoon. They were huge – well over six foot, all of them. They were looking at me as if to say '*Order anything like that again and we'll kill you*', so I quickly got the barmaid's attention and asked for a curried bratwurst and beer.

As I did so, a huge dinner plate of a hand took hold of my own and shook it with such vigour that it nearly ripped my shoulder from its socket. They wanted me to join them and, as I pulled up my chair surrounded by these man-mountains, I couldn't help but feel like Sophie in the BFG.

We played cards and drank beer - a really great way to finish my first week of cycling - then the waitress came out with a fresh round of beers. The tankards held two pints and, as I tucked into my second, I could feel my legs weakening but my tongue relaxing. My German was really starting to flow. However, on the suggestion that the drinking games should begin, I hastily said goodnight but was persuaded to take one last tipple - an apple shot that tasted like pure meths. I headed up to bed, stopping off briefly at the bathroom to bid a very close and intimate goodnight to the toilet bowl.

Chapter 5

The trouble with ending your first week with a bang is that it means you start your second week with another bang - a banging headache in my case – so I hoped that getting out on the bike might mute the bass drum beating in my head.

I was leaving Western Europe today. The border town was signposted in both directions. Two kilometres to the east or four kilometres to the north. Why would anyone choose to take the four kilometres route when you can get to the same spot in two kilometres? It seemed a no-brainer.

My question was soon answered when a signpost indicated that a twenty percent climb lay in ambush between me and Adorf. I had to grit my teeth and stand on the pedals, stomping for a good ten minutes to get myself, my bike and my luggage up there. I'd made a vow that there would be no walking my bike up hills or mountains. I hadn't imagined this would be questioned so early on in the trip.

Descending into the Czech Republic, I stopped to adjust my seat that had worked itself loose. Whilst I adjusted it, an old Czech guy came over to offer his help in the form of a bottle of potato rum. It was ten in the morning. Laughing and shaking his hand, I clapped him on the shoulder and declined his invitation. He invited me to come and stay with him whenever I wanted.

I pulled into Karlovy Vary, a town filled with gorgeous old Czech architecture. The hotels were more like palaces and had the price tag to match. I was flagged down by a passing pedestrian and convincingly told to avoid the big hotels and head up the hill for the best hostel in town. It was another knee destroyer; I could almost hear the grinding of bone on bone.

I was shown to my dorm. A typical Eastern European one, it offered a mattress that was more or less a sack filled with random lumps of foam and a bean bag pillow. That was about all there was to advertise but there were friendly faces about and young ones at that.

Sitting in the bar studying my route for the next day and making idle chit-chat over a Coke with a Spanish couple, I stood to leave when the barman called me over to offer me a herbal shot. I had to buy him one back and soon we were talking about our travels. He'd recently returned from a short trip to India. He told me about how they used poo bricks to build their houses and how many flies there were on the food. I wasn't sure whether he was joking or not. He had a false eye which meant I couldn't tell whether or not he was able to look me in the eye.

Continuing his generosity, he offered me a shot of potato rum as a photographer took some pics of us toasting the Czech liberation from communism. Most Czechs are passionate about the subject. The photographer told me that he'd had a particularly great day which he put down to carrying his Chinese lucky coin. A year ago he'd been in town when a group of gypsies came by offering lucky pendants for sale. Taking a particular liking to the coins, he bought every one she had but only had one left now, his own.

As the night continued, the manager made a potent statement. "I go walking, get stinky feet – you go cycling, get very stinky feet!!" He then ran upstairs to his lodgings and came back with a half-used fungal infection cream. He handed it to me with a big smile. There wasn't much left in the tube (his walking had obviously taken its toll) but I was thankful for the gift, and self-consciously applied it lavishly before falling asleep.

As I left the next morning, the photographer was still propped against the bar with a rum in front of him and, as I swung my leg over Shirley, he staggered over and handed me his lucky coin. "Good luck to you, Mr Cycle Man."

* * *

The barley quietly waves me through, the winds whistle and the corn pops like party poppers celebrating my arrival. A lizard scrambles out of my way. The car horns toot their approval and I savour the smell of evergreens in my nostrils...

It's the perfect setting to think about things, so I get into cruise mode and start to do just that...

The main thing I am thinking is, "Why am I doing this?" I'm not thinking it because I'm tired or in pain, even if I am. It's not because I'm not enjoying myself. I'm just kind of interested. To travel; definitely. To raise money for charity; that's a bonus. To get friggin' strong on the bike; we'll see. Hopefully I'll be kicking butt when I get back if my legs hold up. Educate myself; always handy for cocktail party chat. To allow me to get things straight in my head; nah, I'm always gonna be Bent. To meet new people? To live a simple life; it's cool knowing everything I own is in these panniers. I haven't lost anything for ten days. That's a record. To grow calves (I am eternally ribbed for having the smallest calves in cycling); I think that's the

29

one.

I am jolted from my thoughts as my wheels crunch over a particularly large lizard which has scrambled in the wrong direction and been flicked up and slapped against my panniers. My stomach lurches, but not enough to put me off my lunch.

I arrive at my favourite eating place. A scenario plays out in my mind:

"Good day, sir. I've reserved your usual seat."
"Why thank you very much - as close to the shopping trolleys as possible?"
"Of course. Would Sir like to order a drink?"
"A dram of caffeine with as much sugar as possible, please."
"As you wish. Would sir like the à la carte menu?"
"No I'll have the buffet. Anything and everything from every aisle."

1pm every day. I'm like clockwork. It's as though the supermarkets expect me. Their shelves are always full and the staff are always smiling.

* * *

I drift on. The smooth tarmac highways of Western Europe are long gone, being replaced with a rougher gravel-strewn thoroughfare, sporting a variety of potholes. These roads need concentration, especially if you're trying to read the signs!

I'd wondered in Germany whether the government spent more on signposts there than all the other countries put together. The signs seemed as though they went on forever. I could start reading a sign in the morning, continue reading until lunch (usual seat), before finally coming to an end at night.

The Czechs, on the other hand, favour a very different approach. In the middle of the night, when everyone is asleep, they sneak round houses in the same manner as the BFG but, instead of planting dreams, they look out for all the leftover games of Scrabble sitting on the dining room tables. They don't disrupt the game, so you never know they've been. They simply take all the remaining letters sitting in your letter holders. You know, the z's, c's, h's, k's. The ones you pull out when the game is almost over and curse your bad luck. Now, to save money, they use only these letters to produce all their road signs. They have developed this special machine that enlarges them appropriately before sticking them together randomly and without any thought at all as to order, forming names like *Rybna nad Zdobnici*.

It's a crazy world we live in - I don't know how I stay so normal.

Chapter 6

Hannah, the receptionist at a campsite in Jesenik, was definitely cute. With dark, flowing hair, the pale skin of the Eastern Europeans, and a body I would willingly have swapped with Shirley for a day or two, she was a sight for travel-sore eyes - the smog of the last few days had left my eyes red and puffy. So I casually hung round the reception which proved to be a little shed in the woods, and leaned nonchalantly, flexing my growing calf muscles, angling for a date the next day. Hannah was studying English and was already teaching it to both school children and adults. She smiled at my persistence and asked if I wanted to join her and her friend the next day.

My route had taken me along a busy, truck-infested highway where exhaust fumes had filled the capillaries of my lungs, clogged my nostrils and coloured my skin. Turning off this road I had to navigate the Rychleby Hills and my knees were again causing me problems. The crunching of bone and gristle on each revolution was almost audible. I needed a day's rest and here was an invite to spend it with two Eastern European girls. *Do I want to join you?* I needed to think long and hard before making a decision in a nanosecond. Hell yeah!!

I asked Hannah what they were up to. Lounging by the pool in bikinis sipping cold cocktails? Dancing at a folk festival in little black numbers? Her next words caused these images to dissipate with a distinctive cracking-popping sound only heard in the wizarding world of Harry Potter. "We're going cycling," (my knees screamed in pain), "to visit some of the lakes nearby and to do some sunbathing".

Unconvincingly, I replied, "Wonderful, that'd be great."

My day off had turned into more cycling, but at least I'd be with Hannah and her friend. Surely there'd be bikini action by the lakes.

* * *

Hannah mentioned that the fried cheese was the best thing on the menu at the campsite's café. She was right. It was the ONLY thing on the menu. Wearing a dirty apron, the cook, a curly-haired, middle-aged lady who'd had a few too many fried cheeses of her own, slopped melted cheesy batter and some greasy chips onto my plate. I ate one then, to the cook's surprise, ordered another. She was so pleased she gave me a free schnapps which tasted like it was siphoned-off cheese oil. Nasty.

* * *

Hannah's gorgeous friend turned out to be called Radim, an army lieutenant who also happened to be her boyfriend, and certainly wouldn't be looking too great in a thonged bikini.

He was competitive and wanted to show his girl that he could beat this cyclist, who she had raved about, up all the hills. I am also competitive and wanted to show his girl that I could beat some jumped-up army boy up these hills too. So at each and every hill, whilst looking calm, relaxed and composed in the face, we put the hammer down. It was a perfect rest day. He led us up alleys and through fields until everything opened up to reveal an old mine that had been flooded for safety. Cliffs of rock disappeared vertically for hundreds of feet beneath dark pools of water.

This could only mean one thing. Rock jumping! With a complexion that requires Factor Ginger sun cream at all times, I have never been one for lying on the beach. So, when I holiday with my family or girlfriends, I always seek out a spot for rock jumping which enables me to have immense amounts of fun whilst my nearest and dearest get a lovely bronzing tan.

I suddenly had that holiday feeling and a smile cut my face in two. I started with a few smaller ones – bombing in to wet the onlookers and then I moved up to about three metres, hurling myself into the depths below. To get to the bigger jumps you had to swim across the quarry and then climb the rock face. My upper body had wasted away after cycling constantly for two weeks and, when I got to the top, my arms were shaking. This was soon matched by my legs when I looked down. Oh my, that's a big drop. Surely I needed a parachute or a bungee chord for this?

I inched to the edge and stood frozen for about a minute. I went over the details in my head: feet together, arms by my side - or I could get bruising or internal bleeding, or worse. I counted down in my head. 10, 9, 8, ... , 3, 2, 1 and stepped back two paces. I couldn't do it.

I could see Hannah gazing up at me and it gave me courage. I shut my eyes and jumped. I was in the air. Memories of Nice flew through my head. This was the same height. It takes a long time to travel ten metres. Thwack! The soles of my feet hit the surface as I plummeted through it. I opened my eyes and the dark water had consumed me. I saw the bright lights coming closer and closer. I got to the top and could hear one person clapping. She was smiling and laughing. I laughed too. I'd done it. That was one big jump.

As I got out of the water, all eyes were on the rock where I'd come from. "That's right, ladies and gentlemen, I just jumped ten metres into cold dark water."

But they weren't looking where I had come from. Their eyes were higher. About thirty metres above, silhouetted in the midday sun, was a boy of no older than thirteen. He was standing up there posing for the cameras below, enjoying the attention. Then suddenly he threw himself off the cliff face and dropped to the water. How he survived I have no idea. Water from that height must be like hitting concrete.

Radim rustled us up a coffee which helped to calm my nerves which were still on full alert. He and I embraced. He appreciated my courage. He really was a very nice man and we had enormous fun all day. Hannah's a lucky girl to have him.

As night fell and we cycled back to the campsite, Hannah and Radim asked where I was going tomorrow. I mentioned that I wanted to get to Auschwitz in Poland without really knowing how far it was. They said it was impossible. One hundred and eighty kilometres in one day carrying all the kit too. Absolutely impossible.

The attitude I'd suffered when my father had proclaimed that the trip to India was impossible and that I'd get killed took over. "Anything is possible," I proclaimed, wanting to prove them wrong. They'd waved the red flag in front of a rather scrawny bull. I told them I was going for it.

The next morning I woke and I sneaked out of the campsite trying not to wake the people who had kept me awake themselves with their snoring. It was as if the people in question had stuffed their mouths and nostrils with mucus, and then fallen asleep.

As I pulled out of the gate, Radim and Hannah ran after me. "You're not getting away that easily!"

They'd decided to keep me company till the border, to try and give me some extra strength for what they were calling my pilgrimage. They would only come as far as the border as "it was the dark land" beyond. So I left my entourage behind at the border and honoured the millions of Jews who were forced to take this same route, saying goodbye to their loved ones just here - petrified, weakened by days of marching, never to be reunited.

Once in Poland, the sun beat down as I pushed on without rest to Auschwitz, the German concentration camp. The wind blew so strongly into my face that at times I was pedalling like crazy to get DOWN hill. My own three-pronged whip, my ego, beat me to go faster and get there before nightfall.

I needed food and water as I'd burnt off the *Svíčková na smetaně* (steak in sauce) we had eaten in the morning, washed down with traditional *Kofola* - Czech cola. Initially I was hopeful that I'd find a café - the shops wouldn't accept Czech money, dollars or pounds. As it was Sunday and banks were closed, I needed to withdraw money from an ATM but my bank had put my cards on hold on the grounds that money had been withdrawn abroad (because I'd been withdrawing it!).

I was really thirsty. I had one very dry, old bread roll in my bag which I tried to eat but the thick spit in my mouth wouldn't wash it down. No one offered me help, as had been the case for the Jews. They were probably scared of the consequences. I was looking quite scary and beardy at that moment. Those who offered food to the Jews as they were paraded past their houses were beaten. Those who helped them up were knocked to the ground in their place.

I tried to lighten my mood by hooting my horn, singing, whistling and being generally cheery to the Poles, but got no reaction. Those travelling in the opposite direction simply kept their heads down or looked upon me with glazed eyes without moving a single facial muscle. When I hooted my horn, their eyes narrowed. Those talking in doorways moved inside and closed their shutters when I travelled past. It was eerie.

I noticed on my map that I was getting close to the Czech Republic border again, and took an emergency turn to buy Mars bars, Coke and water. I'm sure the Jews were not allowed such luxuries!

Marching on as the sun moved to my back and then behind the horizon (I am one stubborn man), I was sure I should have been there by now. My rough estimates on the map said I'd done the required 180 kilometres, but then I realised I'd taken a wrong turn up a main road in the opposite direction. I had wondered where all those cars had come from. Turning, I trudged back the exact same way as darkness fell...

Created in 1939 after the German invasion of Poland, three million people (mostly Jews) were killed in this concentration camp, normally in gas chambers. After their arrival they lived in shacks in the camps doing hard labour under terrible conditions, with no hygiene and poor nutrition.

Describing myself as a zombie on my commute to London now seemed senseless. These people really were the living dead. No flesh hung from their bones, their eyes were sunken and dark, their clothes were shabby and torn, and insects infected their hair, clothes and bodies.

They knew they had little to no hope.

Comparing my suffering on a bike ride I'd chosen to make to what they had suffered was almost a sin. It was incredibly sad and, in my weakened state, it put a tear in my eye. I stopped twenty kilometres from the camp and checked into the only hotel I could find, a posh one with velvet bed covers, silk curtains and a mattress that caressed my body. I was hungry, so I was going to the restaurant; I was thirsty, so I'd probably sup on a soft drink or as much water as I needed, before lying down in my bed and sleeping till I fancied living my dream again...

Chapter 7

Slowing as I passed Auschwitz to think of Radim and Hannah and the fact I hadn't made it in one day, I acknowledged that they had been right. I didn't stop. After the emotions of the previous day, I didn't think I could handle it.

Yesterday was a Sunday. Polish people embrace the Catholic Church wholeheartedly.

Today was Monday - so a different day. At home I knew everyone would be sour-faced, making their way to work, squeezed into the London Tube, sitting down to the desks and computers. Here in Poland, people had spent Sunday recharging their batteries and most had taken part in religious ceremonies that had left them revitalised and invigorated. This meant smiles, laughter and inquisitiveness all day for me.

Polish girls are so utterly beautiful. It is like being a kid in a candy store. When the first one smiled at me, I almost pitched my tent at once and proposed to her right there and then, asking her to live in my tent happily ever after. If I'd continued in that vain I might have had a number of wives by now - that is assuming they'd all said 'yes', which I think a guy with my good looks, charm, wit and personality is entitled to assume (READ: ginger and quirky). One even introduced me to her grandfather, whom we happened across on one of my moments of getting myself lost, as she was leading me out of a maze on her bike.

Until now I had used the sun to navigate quite successfully. As it rises in the east pretty well everywhere, I would head towards it in the morning and, as it sets in the west equally reliably, I would continue on with it at my back. However, the clouds were so dark today I was unable to use my shadow compass. Winding through the hills there was just no way of knowing where I was. I was really pleased when I found the tiny little road I needed and continued taking hill after hill for another 1.5 hours, at which point I realised this road had taken me in a circle and I was now ten kilometres further away from my goal than when I had started.

On my way into Krakow, the former capital of Poland, I caught a bee in my teeth in such a way as would have made Mr Miyagi (from *Karate Kid I, II and III*) very proud. Either the bee was weak or I managed to spit it out just in time, because although it stung my lower lip, which swelled a bit, the pain only lasted until I pulled into a campsite in town.

On my departure, Radim had given me a bottle of potato rum which I was able to offer to four French hippies who had set up their tent just next door to my own. As I cooked some pasta and vegetables, they had divided their dinner up on four plates. It didn't look too appetising. They had five mushrooms each which comprised long thin stems and cone-like heads, grimacing as they gulped them down. My dinner was ready and I felt obliged to share it with these guys. Surely they hadn't eaten enough?

My offer was greeted by, "No thanks, we'll have our dinner later."

"I thought this was your dinner," I replied, gesturing to the empty plates.

"No, they were magic mushrooms".

On their way here, they'd taken a detour via Amsterdam and stocked up on mushrooms and a huge quantity of marijuana which they hoped would keep them going for their two weeks of travelling.

However, they were pulled over on an autobahn in Germany after sniffer dogs had smelt their weed. How slow must they have been travelling for a sniffer dog to catch a whiff? Driving along at five kilometres per hour, they were probably saying to each other '*Wow, man, slow down. Let's just chill out*'.

They spent a night in a cell, had their drugs confiscated and were then released on their not-so-merry way.

As they enjoyed their magic mushroom moment, I savoured their talking and their laughter. The French language sounded like music as I lay watching the stars and satellites move through the sky.

One of the boys looked at me suddenly and started giggling before erupting into full-blown laughter. In his strong French accent he alleged I looked like Wayne Rooney, the ugliest man in Premiership football. Why not Ronaldo, or Freddie Ljungberg even? I got him in a headlock but released him when I realised it must have been the hallucinogens leading him to make such insulting statements.

As they became more spaced out, I wandered off and met a Russian who could speak German, so I proceeded to have a Russian lesson in German. Until I hit China, Russian was going to be my only conversational option as in many areas my English would be completely useless.

* * *

More steep gradients and smog accompanied me to my last stop in Poland before crossing into the ex-Soviet nations - Prezemyls. I was feeling smug as the big mountains were to my right and I was avoiding them until a swift right-angle headed me straight at them.

On my arrival in Prezemyls, for the first time on the bike the sky opened and hurled rain down upon me, driving me to seek reasonably-priced accommodation. Everything I owned was soaked to the bone.

The hotels were extortionately expensive. Running into my last hotel and asking the price, I was greeted with the response that it would be 200z, or around £40, a night. I just couldn't afford it. My face sank and I dripped out of the front door. As I picked up my bike dejectedly, the receptionist asked if I was desperate. "Yes," I cried. He mentioned there was a dilapidated house behind the hotel that had a roof and, if I was lucky, a mattress on the floor. I was willing to give it a go. The house wasn't in very good condition and wild dogs and cats had taken up residence, but it was dry and the walls offered some protection from the wind. I lay my sleeping bag out for a night's rest.

Chapter 8

A gun is pointing at my face.

The day had started badly as I tried to leave Poland. A man had attacked me with his crutch. When I say crutch, I obviously mean one that helps a man to walk, although he didn't seem to need it as he danced around jabbing and round-housing me.

This border was also the first after crossing into France where I had to show my passport. The Schengen Agreement states that if someone is allowed into a country that has signed the treaty, then they can pass into any other member's country without impediment. The Ukraine, although still in Europe, was my first country outside the agreement, but the passport inspection had still been a formality. My passport was stamped and I was told to hold onto my exit slip. Easy.

The first difference I noticed in the Ukraine was the role of dogs in society, and with it their opinion of me. Dogs in the West are normally cute and fluffy. They like to bark at passing cyclists but only to say '*hello*'. Dogs in the Ukraine bark to let you know that they are coming after you, a point they tend to emphasise by baring their teeth to remind you to cycle like mad.

Two snarling dogs that seemed to want to tear the flesh from my bones had obviously planned their attack well. I was facing a war on two fronts, one dog on each flank. Unlike the Germans who had once suffered the same dilemma with the Russians to the east and the Brits to the west, I knew I had to squash one of my attackers. As the fiercer of the two made a lunge for my ankles, I swerved left and ran him over. He squealed as he passed under my wheel and I turned, feeling a little sorry for him. Reluctant to give chase on his own, the other dog slowed, allowing me to scamper away.

Having just survived this ordeal, I was almost impaled as a ZAZ Soviet-made mini car, drove past with a javelin sticking out of the window. I imagined a massive Soviet javelin thrower like Sergey Makarov at 6"5 and fifteen stone squeezing into this tiny car to get to his training sessions on a daily basis.

I can see along the dark barrel of the gun the finger of a blurred man whose eye is obscured by the sight.

I arrived in L'viv, the main cultural centre of today's Ukraine. The historical heart of L'viv, with its old buildings and cobblestone roads, survived World War II and the ensuing Soviet presence largely unscathed. As I took a picture of boxes of chicks being sold, I caught the eye of a guy called Georgi who said he knew just the hostel for me. He did. Apart from the machine gun behind the counter hanging below the sign asking "Have you paid?", it was fabulous.

He left me to carry my bag and bike up to the hostel and met me and some of the workers from the hostel later that night.

The cold of the metal hurts the skin on my forehead.

L'viv has a strong nationalist movement whose members side with the EU and consider themselves of Western European rather than of Russian descent. Passing through the streets, I looked at the powerful architecture which must encourage this nationalist pride. Admiring a point where Renaissance meets Art Nouveau meets Gothic, I was stopped by someone placing the muzzle of his gun against my forehead. A soldier with a sub-automatic machine gun was barring my way. My legs went weak, my throat tightened, I couldn't speak. I'm not embarrassed to say I almost wet myself with fear. I could hear the harsh Russian voice shouting at me but my brain couldn't decipher the words. His friends were laughing. I wasn't. He was thrusting something at me but my eyes were trained on the barrel of his gun. Again he thrust his hand towards me. I

41

glanced down. A shot of vodka was in his hand. I looked back at the gun, then his face, then back at the vodka. He was inviting me to share a drink with him. Why didn't he just ask?

Georgi knew a restaurant only patronised by Ukrainians. The receptionist from the hostel ordered me *vereniki*, Ukrainian dumplings, and vodka was poured. Toasts were made, each with reference to my 'unnatural', as they called it, fear of guns. The lights flickered halfway through the meal, and went out. Power cut. I'd been assured these were common in the Ukraine. Silence ensued, only broken by the girl beside me who giggled and whispered, "Now we kill a Russian".

It wasn't a very PC comment but I guessed relations weren't too sweet after many years of Soviet domination. The silence fell again before men bustled into the restaurant - the Ukrainian soldier and his colleagues. They shouted in Ukrainian and I made out "*predatel*" (traitor) and "*Ruski*" (Russian). They really were looking for a Russian. Can you believe it? They moved to the table adjacent to ours and interrogated a man right there, grabbing him and dragging him into a darkened side room. Two gun shots reverberated around the restaurant.

The Ukrainians went mental, downing vodka, cheering, laughing, saluting. My mouth was open, my pupils dilated, a piece of dumpling hung from my lip, mingling with my beard. I was assured it had all been an act, but I still couldn't believe the night I had just had.

* * *

I left the hostel still dazed from the previous night. Standing next to a group of children playing on electric cars in the town square dominated by St. George's Cathedral, I was approached by a man with his girlfriend. Both had short dark hair and she had a number of piercings in her lip. In a traditional Ukrainian accent which Sacha Baron Cohen must have borrowed for his Borat character, he said, "These children... why they not have license?" I laughed and looked at him. He laughed back, put an arm round me, introduced himself as Stuart and his girlfriend as Miker, and said in a broad Scottish accent, "Thes place is amazin', is it nae?" I couldn't disagree, although I wasn't sure I definitely liked it - the architecture, the people, the history.

At the beginning of World War II, the Russians and Germans invaded Poland and divided it into German-occupied Poland, as we know it today, and Soviet Poland, now known as the Ukraine. The plight of the Jews under the Russian occupation was terrible. They, and initially a great part of the Ukrainian population, considered the German troops as liberators from two years of a genocidal Soviet regime. However they soon changed their opinions as the Nazis started mass public executions.

The German leaders, who had thus far destroyed every city and town they had come across, ordered that L'viv be left untouched while they made it their garrison.

After a couple of days living *La Vida Loca* in L'viv, I was sitting in the hostel with Stuart and Miker, nursing pretty rotten hangovers. Rob and Till had joined us and were giggling about the size of my calves. They had deemed it impossible to cycle to the Ukraine from England, and then onto India, with legs the size of mine.

There was another groan from Stuart as his head pounded and gut lurched. Miker said, "It could be worse. We could have been drinking the local tap water." Till and Rob laughed. "We'd be glowing if we had. It's toxic." I looked down at my hands to see if there were any signs of them glowing. I'd been drinking the water as though it was going out of fashion. No one had told me. I had had no bad effects as yet.

The strength of my guts was again tested when I stopped at a truckers' refuelling station which was surrounded by men twice my size and women almost as big. I had a pig kebab that had been kept in a bucket for God knows how long and cooked on an open fire, without any adverse reactions. Who's the tough guy, man of steel. rock hard, brave soldier - me?

Apparently not.

The next day was my first taste of camping in the wild. So far I'd managed to stick to campsites and hostels. This time I could only see open countryside on all sides.

I started looking for a place to pitch my tent. I pulled into a lay-by behind some trees looking for a spot. Just as I thought I'd found somewhere suitably obscured from the road and sheltered from any wind, I saw that there was a stack of beer cans in the corner and, on closer inspection, found food packages lying in the grass. It looked as though people were living in the woods and it wasn't the normal eco stuff you might expect in the UK. I spotted a gang of men walking back over the hillside and I quickly about turned and set off down the road again.

After I had pulled over for a second time, a woman stopped and got out of her car. In perfect English she asked if I was OK. She explained she was a local English teacher. "Do you want a lift into town?"

I declined her offer saying I was happy to camp just behind these bushes. Her beautiful smile faded as she said, "It's too dangerous." She wouldn't elaborate to explain whether it was the people or the beasts who were dangerous. Dad had warned me before I had left that bears and wolves still roamed the woodlands in the Soviet countries, and Mum had sent me an email stating that she'd just been watching a programme about the number of black widow spiders now to be found in the Ukraine.

I wasn't getting in a car - not now, not ever. I was sure to face danger later on in the trip, so I had better get used to it sooner rather than later.

I put my tent up and was feeling confident that I'd found a nice spot when nightfall came. I've never been great at camping without grown-ups. As a kid we used to camp out in the garden but I'd always get too scared and end up waking Mum and Dad and sleeping in my normal bed.

Tonight was no different. My fear heightened my senses. Any noise was magnified by ten. Initially I'd hear a mouse scurry and that would sound like a body being dragged through the woods. The wind whipped through the trees.

Then I started hearing the footfalls. Thud, thud, thud. In quick succession, but regular enough for me to completely freak out. When things started being thrown at my tent, I was petrified.

My Swiss Army knife lay by my side, blade glistening. A torchlight flicked across my tent and I was preparing to fight. My heart was in my mouth until I realised I had kicked my own torch.

Slightly relieved, I was able to pull myself together. I thought I'd try to make it sound like there were more of us in the tent than me alone, so I pulled out my faithful ukulele and played a few numbers, singing as though I didn't have a care in the world, but really with my throat tighter than a camel's arse in a sandstorm. This seemed to calm the onslaught.

I lay down, and with the tiredness that ran through my legs, was able to fall asleep. Occasionally I would wake up when something crashed around me but no one was trying to enter my tent.

The next morning I woke and the sun evaporated my fears. Popping my head out to see how my neighbour's party had gone overnight, I squinted without my glasses to discover a mass of litter

44

strewn all around my tent. I rummaged around blindly for my glasses and popped them on. It wasn't litter. It was apples. Thinking *what a strange kind of party,* I realised how foolish I had been. The footsteps I had heard, and the stones that had been thrown at the tent, were all apples, big juicy red ones, matching the colour of my embarrassed face. I pulled one inside and bit down on it. The juice ran down my chin. The taste was delicious.

Chapter 9

I collected up a couple more apples and decided to celebrate the fact that I was alive. All my lucky trinkets - lucky star, stone, shell, bands, coin, fungal cream, and lamb that were now taking up at least one pannier - were invited, along with the pictures of all my family and friends. It was pretty special. Everyone had as many apples as they could eat. My lucky star had one too many and went a nasty green colour. Then the fungal cream said he had to be going otherwise his mum would be worried.

I played some rock and roll on the ukulele again. The stone, who obviously had no eyes, asked if it were an angel singing. He was impressed when I told him it was me.

The Ukraine hasn't quite cashed in on the ginger biker tourist trade, and accommodation was kinda hard to find. After cycling for six hours, I finally saw a street sign indicating that there was a hotel in one kilometre. It was perfect timing, I had started to 'bonk' - also known as 'hitting the wall' - a condition caused by the depletion of glycogen stores in the liver and muscles which manifests itself by precipitous fatigue and loss of energy. I toppled off my bike exactly where the hotel should have been, only to find a house in ruins before me. I clambered back on and further teasing signs led me to closed, ruined or full hotels for another fifty kilometres. My nerves couldn't handle another night in the tent, so when I saw a restaurant closing up I thought I'd pop in to ask where the nearest hotel was. Using English was futile, so I opened my arms wide looking left and right and used the word for hotel – *gostinitsa* - making the word rise in pitch at the end to indicate a question – an intonation used by students up and down the UK when speaking about anything.

They said no, no gostinitsa, laughing at my miserably drawn face. They then pulled a chair out from under a table and urged me to sit down. My shaky legs and gaunt face must have indicated quite obviously that I was hungry and, as they turned the lights on, they began rustling me up a feast fit for a king. As I tried to resist licking the plate, they told me "No money" and showed me to the car park where I could put up my tent.

I had assumed that as the countries got poorer as I headed east, the generosity and kindness might dwindle with it. The Ukraine proved this hypothesis entirely wrong as the next day people on the side of the road selling apples and pears tried to force me to take all their fruit for no charge. Two older ladies even got into a bit of a scuffle as they tried to fill my panniers with apples.

I was able to repay the favour the following day. An old man with a hunched back, pale skin, but a full head of blond hair, thumbed me down and asked if I'd cycle back a couple of miles to pick him up some petrol. His Lada had conked out. By the look of things it could have been many things other than lack of petrol that were stopping this car from moving. He said it was forty years old. It looked it. Which cars nowadays last that amount of time? Not many.

My father had a Lada when I was a kid and used to drive us around in it. I was a little embarrassed. Other dads had soft tops and Jaguars. What I didn't realise then, but am so thankful for now, is that he used to drive a Lada because his needs ranked far below ours. He needed the money to make sure we had everything we desired. This car still got him from A to B (usually), so he saw no point in upgrading it.

Instead of cycling back two miles, delaying him and me, I was able to offer him the petrol in my stove canister. It was finest unleaded, and somehow this Lada was able to burn whatever fuel you fed it. Once topped up with the little fuel I had, he turned the key once and vroom, the engine started first time. To repay me, he gave me four cooking apples which I wasn't able to cook because he'd taken all my fuel. They were, however, great weapons for throwing at the wild dogs.

* * *

Tooting one's car horn can mean a number of different things on the roads. A single, short, sharp toot says, 'Coming through, watch yourself there, little cyclist'. A prolonged series of toots means 'You're making me mad'. A tuneful combination of the two means 'Nice bum'. There were other variations I still needed to learn, such as the toot for. 'I'm carrying a friggin' big combine harvester behind me'. I only heard the 'I'm coming through' toot as the truck sailed past, so I relaxed until the combine harvester blades brushed past my shoulder, trimming one side of my flowing blond hair.

Of all the dangers I'd considered before coming on the trip - bandits, thieves, extremists and wild animals - combine harvesters hadn't featured too highly, and missing in its entirety was the mould that was accumulating in my water bottles, now my biggest concern as I made my way across the ex-Soviet Bloc. Having taken quite a liking to Coke, I had been pouring it into my water bottles to give me the energy to get through each day. Unfortunately, Coke seems to be a favourite of the lesser green and red mould that only toilet bleach can destroy.

When I had finished the liquid, the mould would reveal itself and I'd give it a look of revulsion and disgust. When I pulled into a hostel in Kiev after three days and 560 kilometres without a shower, the receptionist gave me a similar look. Showing me around the hostel, she paused at the shower room stating that I could use it as soon as I liked. When I did, the water came off brown.

Kiev used to be the most powerful state in Europe during the tenth and eleventh centuries. It was weakened by internecine quarrels and Mongol attacks, then ruled by Lithuania and Poland before gaining its autonomy for some time until the Russian invasion. The depth of history to Kiev is amazing but the architecture is exclusively post-war. The Germans destroyed the city in its entirety, knocking almost every building to the ground. Now it is a mix of post-war Comintern architecture intermingled with spiralling shopping centres and rings of restaurants, cafés and European boutiques. Everywhere I looked there were older Western men accompanied by Ukrainian beauties. I began to think this might be the city to grow old in.

That evening it was time to check out the best of what Eastern Europe has to offer. The club scene is renowned for being trendy, playing cutting edge tunes. It can be overly expensive and pretentious too. There was one issue: I had nothing but shorts to wear. You will remember Till and Rob from L'viv. Sitting in the hostel as I arrived in Kiev, they promptly started the jibes about the size of my legs. Till, a Swiss guy about my height, grabbed me a pair of his jeans and watched as I pulled them over my knees, realising it was impossible to get them over my thighs. I think it helped me make my point about the benefits of cycling.

As we walked towards the clubs, I continued to see older men with young girls. Till and Rob told me not to stare, "Their pimps are probably following". I looked around then realised what they'd said, and everything made sense. These girls were prostitutes that could be hired by the day, week, or month. How stupid. I had been thinking these old, ugly, greasy men were attractive beyond their wallets.

It also brought to my attention the fact that the men were probably sex tourists - an expression heard a lot in Russia and Asia - as Till and Rob had suggested. People argue that the girls are making

48

money and are funding their children's education, but these men were taking advantage of these women's position, encouraging them to do it.

Entering the club, it was clear that some of those girls were here looking for new clients. Intoxicated by the music, I made my way to the dance floor and started cutting shapes that could be used in a shape and space maths lesson. The last time I'd danced I'd been at our end of school disco. Surrounded by 7-11 year olds, in my head I was moving like Justin Timberlake. In reality, it was probably more like Brent from 'The Office'. The children around me were telling me that I was embarrassing myself. It was all the encouragement I needed. I burst into my break dance routine, popping like a worm on the floor. As I flipped to my feet in a crouched position, I found myself face-to-face with Lucy. "You've gone too far this time, Sir".

Back at the club in the Ukraine, my dancing was having the opposite reaction. Gorgeous girls came up to me and danced, but I didn't know whether they wanted my attention or my wallet. Till and Rob looked on, giving me the thumbs up. 'Go for it!'. I couldn't get out of my mind the idea that they were looking at me as if I were a bank vault. I couldn't imagine anything more insulting. People can like me for my heart, my passion, my love, my brain, dashing boy band looks (READ: ginger-bearded runt), but for my money, no way.

I moved from the dance floor and stood in a corner on my own, confused, wondering. Till and Rob had downed some vodka and were now on the dance floor surrounded by girls. A guy came up to me and said, "You're Danny, right? You're the crazy bastard who's cycling to India?" It made me happier being approached in this way than by a tight booty swinging towards me. He said word was beginning to spread and he'd spoken to a number of people in Russia about a guy who was heading their way on a bike. Awesome!

Chapter 10

The floor is throbbing beneath my feet and my ear drums are vibrating. In front of me are thousands of men jumping in unison, chanting.

Having spent the day in embassies sorting out visas, I returned and readied my panniers to leave. As I sat preparing myself for the next round, Till and Rob came in waving football tickets in my face. Ukraine were playing Turkey in an international friendly. It'd be rude to turn down the ticket, right?

The fans were hardcore, to say the least. When they bounced, so did the floor. Our allocated seats were in a quieter section but we'd made our way across barriers to get where the crowd action was.

During half time I exchanged a few words in Russian with the person whose seat I was sitting on. I used the phrases I knew, explaining that I liked the Ukraine, that I was travelling by bicycle and that I had a fondness for cheese pies. He responded asking which part of Russia I was from. Dig my pronunciation!!

* * *

As I had pulled into the hostel three days previously, I had noticed children at the window of the building opposite, an orphanage full to capacity. Their faces looked on with such longing each time I walked up and down the stairs outside the building. Leaving the hostel early in the morning on my bike, I bumped into two American couples who had formed a relationship with the orphanage through the Christian church. They were accompanied by a Ukrainian and two young children. They talked in strong Dallas accents. They were adopting the two children. What a change. Moving from a hostel, where food is scarce and hygiene limited, to Texas, the home of the cowboy hat, fake tan and shed loads of money. It was going to be a strange transition but what a transition it would be. I smiled at the couples and introduced myself.

As the young orphaned boy edged past my bike, he caught his very small suitcase on the car. His new father snapped at him to be careful, which left me wondering whether the child was so lucky after all.

With each mile I cycled away from Kiev, firstly the roads became smaller and more rural, then the housing changed to bungalows with ancient roofs and exteriors. When I stopped for food, the local shop which was selling fresh produce and a few sweets used an abacus to total up my bill. An abacus, for those of you born later than the nineteenth century, is a primitive counting frame using sliding beads on wood to perform arithmetic processes. In every small village was a church surrounded by blue crosses, symbols of the Blessed Mother worshipped in the Catholic faith. These fields of crosses were surrounded by sunflowers. In the heat they looked as though they needed a nice drink as the stems were sagging lamentably under the weight of their heads.

Outside a church, a large man came and stood by my bike. He was driving a suped-up Skoda 4WD. It looked awesome. He took tourists on adventures in the Ukraine and spoke English fluently. He insisted on giving me a lesson in Ukrainian, " ... so you don't insult us speaking Russian'. One word he said I had to know was *кайф*, pronounced 'kauf'. It has no direct translation into English but represents the feeling you have when you look at a beautiful view and think '*this is living*'.

As my first adventure unfolded before me, it wasn't long till I was feeling кайф.

The male in the leading role enters the film shot. He's riding a bike, as any great lead would in such a story, whilst carrying another bike (that's right, he's riding two bikes - one resting on the handlebars of the other).

I need to set the scene. The morning of my twenty-eighth day, after four weeks of cycling, I met a Spanish girl. Chatting, she mentioned the fact that the Ukrainians don't smile very much. I defended their corner assuring her that people had come out of their homes to give me sausages and waved to me as I went by. But in all honesty I agreed with her a little bit. Ukrainian life was all very serious.

That evening, with a row of trees hiding me from the main road, I set up my tent. The air was full of diesel and dust and the sound of passing trucks was ringing in my ears and making the ground shake ever so slightly. This was the moment our hero joined me. He was over six foot and handsome in a wrinkled George Clooney way. He was wearing a pair of illegally short denim shorts and had the physique of a man who'd spent a great deal of time working out and doing heavy labour.

Hearing him approach, as he wobbled up the lane that I had mistakenly set my tent up in the middle of, I stepped out of my tent and greeted him. He smiled. I showed him that I too had a bike, asking, "Do you speak English?"

"Yes," he replied.

He beckoned me to put my tent away and follow him to his house. Why not? It had to be better than staying by the side of the road risking another attack by a tree. It could be a malicious tree this time and then I'd be in all sorts of problems.

After I had re-attached my panniers, he forbade me to carry my own tent, adding it to his heavily over-loaded bicycle.

We set off towards his home and I began to quiz him again. "You speak English?"

"Yes."

"Are we going to your home?"

"Yes."

"Are you sure it is OK?"

"Yes."

Silence ensued.

"What's your name?"

"Yes."

"Your name is 'Yes'?"

"Yes."

"What is the name of your village"

"Yes."

I may be a little slow sometimes but it was starting to dawn on me that maybe my new friend, Yes, didn't actually speak the Queen's English. I made a mental note that if I asked someone whether they spoke English and they replied "Yes", it didn't mean 'Yes, I speak English fluently like the Queen', it meant 'Yes is the only English word I know.'

As he made a phone call – yes, he was cycling with another bike, my tent and a mobile in one hand to his ear - I looked at the sunflowers I had taken pictures of earlier, heads drooping towards the ground as if sadness was overwhelming them. I'd thought about comparing them to the Western sunflowers I'd seen - heads held high, full of colour, as if smiling. As I looked at these greying sunflowers, I noticed that every so often I saw a fantastically bright one - one that would stand out amongst their Western brothers. I wondered to myself whether this man was one of those flowers amongst Eastern men.

* * *

Passing village after village, my nerves started to tingle. This guy was thin but ripped. His every muscle bulged and rolled with each push of the pedal. *If it comes to it, can I take him?* He was definitely older than me. My knee was still troubling me - would it hold up if I had to run?

He pointed and I smiled. We were at his house. Then my smile fell away again. This was not the kind of house you find in the UK. It seemed in a permanent state of disrepair. 'Yes' was clearly a man who liked to start DIY jobs, finishing them being a different matter altogether. Litter or belongings, I couldn't quite tell, were strewn around the garden. Every corner had them built up high. The small house sat in the middle of the plot. Mildew and other mosses, plants and creepers covered the house. It was more like a hobbit's hollow but without the fantastical attention to tidiness.

My tent was no more appealing, so I stepped over the threshold. The front door opened onto a hallway. Axes hung precariously from the walls, were sat to the side and were scattered on the floor. Food sat drying on the table tops; other food was mouldering half-eaten in bowls. I stopped dead but a push in my back sent me through. Making our way along a dark corridor with drapes covering each wall, the light was so poor I could barely see where we were going. The door to the hallway was off its hinges and needed to be lifted out of the way to reveal what was behind it. The bright light in the next room blinded me. As my eyes adjusted, I emerged into an amazing ballroom-sized living room with a billiards table in the middle of it and artwork all around. How could this room be concealed inside this house? It was like a Tardis.

O to the M to the G. He started taking off his shorts. Standing in his pants, he told me to strip to my keks. He came over to help. I pushed his hand aside and did so myself. Where were we going with this? He motioned me to follow him. We left the house (axes all still in their original place, thankfully) and walked around a wall to a pond. It was full of green algae and looked radioactive. We were only a little way away from Chernobyl where the nuclear accident had happened (which the Russian government tried to cover up until the Swedish reported high levels of radioactive material flying their way on the wind.)

'Yes' dived straight in and swam a couple of lengths. This was his swimming pool. It was fairly small and green but it proved refreshing after a days cycling.

53

Getting dry, we changed and headed out. My 'being' was being forced to become liquid. I had no idea where we were going or what we were doing; I just had to go with the flow. We visited his mother's, picking up some food (peasant's opium - ground poppy seeds with sugar) and wine, and left. Next stop was a friend's. We were invited into the living room and I met Alexandre. He addressed 'Yes' as Micoli, his real name, who told him he'd brought an Englishman to visit and Alex almost exploded. He burst into English like demi-brut champagne when the cork is removed and the words were as sweet to my ears. He dashed around the house and I was told to sit and wait whilst they made dinner.

His children were home from university to mourn their grandfather's death. Yleb (his son) was a handsome chap who had a coolness about him that could have frozen vodka. His daughter Maria was so striking I was almost knocked backwards. Both had warm smiles and an excellent grasp of English.

The dinner they prepared was all home grown - vegetables, bread, meats, honey, jams and soups – and all made into traditional dishes. This was all for me. Micoli and Alexandre drank vodka with me, toasting everything British including his favourite author, John Fowles, a writer from my home town, and director Ken Loach of 'Kes' fame.

The family were passionate about philosophy and politics. Maria organised demonstrations and had been gassed by the police before now. She was a powerful, intelligent and passionate girl, and I (looking like a tramp's armpit) was smitten.

Giggling with delight as I so often do when happiness sweeps through me, my new word seemed so fitting. I pointed to my heart and said, "кайф" - This is living.

Chapter 11

Held hostage, but not against my will, Alex forbade me to leave the next day. Instead we casually cycled down to the reservoir where we swam, ate pears and lounged in the sun. Alex then took it upon himself to educate me in the reality of the fantastic lives that I had been passing all through the Ukraine. Maria sadly had to go back to university with her brother and, as they cycled off in tandem, we headed back to Micoli's to play billiards.

Micoli wasn't back from work when we arrived, which Alex assured me meant he was waltzing around the village looking handsome, meeting his girlfriends. He was the football star of the village and the girls all knew it.

Just because he wasn't home didn't mean his house was empty. It was full of semi-naked men. He had hand-built a sauna in his house which people used freely. The current occupants were slapping each other with sticks and rubbing mud onto each others' backs. It was quite a surreal moment but one that I was quick to get involved in.

Two children, Alexander and Burian, were also present. Whilst the men played billiards, I entertained the children, or was it the other way round?

Later I was solemnly warned about the dangers of travelling in Russia and, even more so, across Uzbekistan where, it seemed, the country was run by gun-wielding gangsters and corrupt police and military. Coming from a country that sells baseball bats in service stations to protect yourself, that was saying something.

The next morning Alex and his wife left for Kiev. The funeral had been taken care of and they had to get back to earning a living. So, when I woke up, Gran, Alex's mother who ran the country home, rustled me up a cracking breakfast. I think she thought I needed filling out a bit. I had eight eggs, a loaf of bread and biscuits. Whilst I was destroying what was in front of me, she gestured to offer me a drink. Wonderful. The bread had dried a little and I needed something to wash it down with. Putting a glass by my side, she began to open the vodka bottle. The look of disappointment on her face when I said no was excruciating, but I then had to stifle a laugh when she proceeded to open the wine and poured that instead (again there was disappointment when I refused a refill).

Shirley was laden with gifts of fruit and wine as I left.

* * *

To alleviate the boredom of passing through flat countryside for hours on end, I sang. I found I had forgotten the words to virtually every pop song of the past few years, so I was left with my childhood favourites from musicals such as 'Mary Poppins', 'Annie' and 'Bugsy Malone', not the most fitting songs as I passed underneath and beside huge military memorabilia. Tanks and aeroplanes were on display, accompanied by messages detailing the destruction they had caused the enemy.

I had been drinking tap water for a week and, like clockwork, my guts went from rocking out to so solid crew, to wet wet wet.

My diarrhoea was getting horrendous. I was refuelling in a café when my stomach rolled and my pupils enlarged. I had seconds to get to a toilet or I was in trouble. No toilet inside. I ran into the street. Nowhere was open. Then I noticed two mobile toilets on the road fifty metres away. I struggled there and pulled open the door. There was poo everywhere. Not one surface - sink, bowl or seat - wasn't covered in the stuff. The bowl was full to the max and people had chosen to shit anywhere but there. I shut the door as my stomach wrenched again. I pulled the door back again, took a deep breath and entered the living hell hole. It was repulsive. Luckily I didn't need a long time and was out of there in moments, but it was long enough for all my clothes to become tainted by the smell.

My change in bowel movements was almost a representation of the way the environment was changing. The smog crept up to my wheels, and then up my leg, and, like a monster from the deep, entered my body through my nose and mouth. I coughed and held a cloth to my mouth, but it made no difference. Chimneys billowing smoke showed me the way to the industrial Donetsk.

Pedalling hard to get out of this industrial area and into Russia where, I hoped, some natural beauty would reappear, the smog got so bad that I couldn't see two cyclists on the road until too late. They'd decided to do their repairs on the hard shoulder rather than the perfectly safe pavement next to them. With an almighty bang I rammed into an upside-down steel bike and two Ukrainians. "Izvinite Izvinite," I called. *Sorry, Sorry.* They were silent, staring. I righted my bike and moved on.

* * *

The border guard told me I had to cycle back to my point of entry into the Ukraine. I'd lost that damn exit card. You know, the one they told me not to lose. I'd lost it.

I sat and tried to digest what I'd been told. What to do? One guard came up to me and said baksheesh would help. He stated a lot of paperwork needed to be filled in and many guards would have to be paid to turn their backs. They might even have to give something to the Russians. Phone calls had to be made. This was a real mess.

Bartering to save my entire trip, I ended up handing over $50 to the border guard. It felt like a lot of money but he was going to have to grease palms, fill in all that paperwork and make calls. I was just hopeful they'd get it all done quickly so I could at least get into Russia before nightfall.

As the cash hit the guard's hand, he smiled at me and gestured with his arm and open hand '*Off you go, then*'. What about the calls, the paperwork, the greasing? This fresh-faced cyclist had been conned for the first time this trip. Lesson learnt. It wouldn't happen again.

On the Russian side of the border, after I had crossed a kilometre of no man's land, the sun had travelled from east to west, dipping below the horizon like a digestive biscuit dunked into a hot cup of tea. I was knee-deep in my kit again. The border guards went through all my bags, scrutinising the technicalities of each piece of equipment and talking together quietly. They would occasionally point at something and say, "LSD, speed, ecstasy, cocaine?" I would refute their accusations emotionally, then demonstrate precisely what it was for.

Warnings of people putting drugs in your kit are rife in these parts, so no matter how innocent I was, I was still scared to death. What if they put something in there and then accused me of smuggling? It would be so easy. Then they would pop me in jail and I might never see the light of day again. I was bricking it.

When the last piece of equipment had been examined, the captain turned to me and stated quite plainly, "You not drug dealer. We just look and see. Welcome to Russia." Well, as long as you're having fun, don't worry about me having pulmonary heart failure.

The continual diarrhoea, and my lack of hygiene resulting from the absence of any showering facilities en route, was starting to take its toll. I was getting spots where my legs met my buttocks because they were rubbing against the seat, my padded shorts feeling like they were stuffed with gravel, not foam. Popping my kit back in, I jumped on Shirley and winced. Every time I bumped the spots, they were agony. I knew it wasn't Shirley's fault that she was juddering along the uneven road, but I couldn't help shouting at her to be more careful. I realised we were over our dating period. We'd reached the next stage of our relationship. Shirley had aged, she'd got a bit grumpy, her chain whinged at every opportunity. It was as though we were married.

By the time my tent was up it was raining heavily, so I dashed out and showered in the downpour, running around in the nude with a foamy white Afro formed from my soap, while a few crows watched on and appeared unsettled by what this crazy Brit was doing. After a bottle of mineral water cleared the bits the rain couldn't reach, I felt ready to take on the best Russia could throw at me.

My introduction to Russia was fairly tame and mundane. Police cheered as I went by, farmers waved, dogs chased me. As I left the Ukraine, I was advised to buy something to protect myself against the dogs that got fiercer the further east you travelled. I visited a weapons shop.

It was like a scene from Pulp Fiction. I had to select my weapon of choice. Chainsaw? Too heavy. Baseball bat? Too awkward to carry. Samurai sword? Might chop at my legs. Gun? Man, I'd love one of those but I might well not get through the border crossing. Then I looked up and saw it. Shining. Beautiful. Oh yes! It was the high-pitched whistle. Watch out, bitches, I'm armed and dangerous.

As the first two dogs joined me, they barked, placing the dogs further down the route on notice so that they were waiting for me as I went past, ready to burst out into aggressive barking and snapping. Each house I went past, two more dogs came out to greet (or eat) me. By the time I'd gone about a hundred metres, I felt like the Pied Piper of Hamelin, but my followers were not rats or children but vicious dogs wanting to shred the flesh off my legs, and I wasn't playing my whistle.

"Why?" you might ask. Because I'd tucked it into my shirt to stop it swinging. As the dogs chased me, I couldn't take my hands off the handlebars long enough to get it out. I wouldn't make that mistake again.

* * *

The food I was managing to scavenge was passing through me

faster than a rat down a drainpipe. I hadn't kept much inside me for a week of continuous cycling. I was weak and miserable but I had no desire to rest for a day by the side of the road in my tent. I was becoming braver and more determined but I was still uncomfortable.

I managed to find a truckers' café with an outdoor shower full of excrement that I forced myself to use. Then a ginger trucker pestered me all night to buy him a beer and got quite aggressive when I refused to do so, so I slipped off to bed hoping he wouldn't be in my dorm.

To make matters even worse, the glands in my groin were swollen so that it felt like I had marbles in there. Surely this wasn't good. I seemed to be coming to pieces at the seams.

It was a single long road to Volgograd from the truckers' stop - a very narrow road with steep drops on either side. Far from escaping the industry of the Ukraine, I had joined a road to Industry Central. Massive trucks passed inches away from each other, sometimes dropping their loads all over the road. As a cyclist, I was dwarfed and irrelevant to proceedings. No one had any room to manoeuvre, so every other truck brushed me as it passed me and one in ten sent me careering into the gutter. Zoom, zoom, zoom, a truck flew past every second. They were nose-to-tail, no gaps at all.

At one point the road surface was particularly uneven and, as I was being driven off the road by a large truck, my back wheel slipped, sending my bike tumbling one way and me the other - bang into the middle of the road. It was as improbable as a lottery win that there would be a gap between the trucks. A row of wheels supporting a seven ton truck bore down on me, the driver pounding his horn. There was no way he could stop. I dived for the hard shoulder as he thundered past, whipping a thickness of smog up around my body. I sat down to pull myself together. I was shaking. My heart wasn't in it. I was reassessing the trip. I had wanted an adventure; I hadn't come here to die.

I came to a conclusion. Volgograd was ten miles in front of me. I had to get there, even if it was the last cycling I did. I'd already seen there was an airport. I'd made my point. Green travel is very difficult when everything around you is so filthy and rotten. I could fly from here to Southern India.

Rolling on, the smog thickened as I got closer to the city. A train carrying industrial material blocked my way. The dinging on the level crossing was the same as at home amid the green pastures of the South Downs. I'd waited many times at those level crossings back home sitting on my bike. I'd never yet been attacked by gypsies there though. As soon as I stopped here, dark skinned gypsies emerged from every hidey hole next to the road. They'd come to ask me for money and to try to pull things off my bike. Politely as I could, I held up my hand to say "No" while attempting to protect my prized possessions. When they started to grab my lucky lamb, I got really cross and told them to leave me alone.

Luckily the barriers were rising and I was able to pull away, dragging a few along with me for a while before they realized my kit was too well tied down. On the other side, children were playing in the road, blocking my path. I stopped to chat with them but they thrust a dead cat in my face. They were trying to sell it to me. I must have been looking hungry. With vomit rising in the back of my throat, I bust through the ring that was surrounding me and headed off with jeering kids following me as far as their legs would carry them.

Barring the episode under the venomous apple tree, it was the first time I'd felt threatened on the trip. I worried that it was going to be like this from now on. Smog, trucks, people trying to take your stuff ... A line from one of my favourite films went through my head, "I fucking hate pikies."

The heat was suffocating and, as twilight had arrived, I had become a buffet for mosquitoes. I just wanted out. I bought myself some comfort food.

Downhearted, downtrodden and downcast, I finally found a place to stay after searching the estates right into the city centre, suffering yet more interest from gypsies along the way. I lumped for a hotel that completely blew my budget. There just wasn't any other choice and, in the mood that had engulfed me, it didn't matter as my trip was coming to an end.

Sitting in the hotel, eating chocolate cereal and milk under the air conditioning unit, I asked myself one question. Why?

Chapter 12

It was six weeks since I had left my comfortable life in London town. Six weeks since I had seen friends and family. Six weeks since I'd seen the kids from school.

As I was fighting the weather, traffic, mosquitoes, saddle sores, lack of washing, sickness and thieves, they were all making their way to school, starting a new term with a new teacher. I'd heard a lot from the children in my first week but no students had written for a while now. I felt forgotten, a no-one.

Arriving at the hotel, I had thinking to do but, deep down, I'd already made my decision. I wrote lists, pros and cons. I asked questions: *Do you really want to do this? Is there anything to gain from continuing?* I'd proved I could cycle for a sustained period of time. I'd crossed Europe by bicycle. Not many people could say that. My green message had been heard by one and all.

The biggest factor that played over and over in my head was that I didn't want to die.

Volgograd (AKA Stalingrad) had witnessed so many deaths. The fiercest battle during WWII was fought here and two million people are thought to have died, the greatest number of casualties from any conflict in history. Prior to this it was also at the forefront of the Russian Civil War where the Red and White armies had done battle.

My fall onto the tarmac wasn't a near miss, it was a miracle. Any other time during the day I would have been crushed by steel. There was no need to add another death to Volgograd's statistics.

I had fought bravely; I could allow someone else to take up the mantle now. They could carry the torch. Now it was time for me to take on the next part of my trip, teaching at the school in Chembakolli and educating the children across the UK who would soon be learning about the village at school, and would be watching Mr Bent proudly sit with tribal Indians, living and sharing their lives. I'd book a flight tomorrow morning for as soon as possible.

Having made my decision, the calm that had been missing of late swept over me. Shower, porcelain and toilet roll had also added to a wonderful feeling that morning. I was bright; my eyes took up a shine again. One thing left. Book a ticket.

* * *

The internet café was full of students working and locals using the shared amenities. I sat quietly awaiting my turn. I logged on and accessed my emails to tell Mum and Dad that they could stop worrying and that I would be taking a flight the rest of the way.

There was something wrong. My email was showing over fifty unread emails, I'd checked them a few days before as I entered Russia. I clicked on 'Inbox' and waited as it loaded. The speed of the machines wasn't quite broadband and I had time whilst they loaded to log onto BA's website and start my search for flights.

Flicking back, I glanced up and down the email list. There were mails from Mum and some friends; there were also emails from Thalia, Jasper, Charlie B and Charlie J. Messages from Jody, Emma, Pixie, Jude, Olivia and Lolly saying they missed me, that school wasn't the same without me. That they were proud of me. Not one mention that I was embarrassing myself or that I had taken things too far. I had to control my emotions; I was still broken from the past few days.

Seeing the emails did more than make me feel happy and wanted. I was ready to take on the world again, literally.

I shut down the computer and marched straight back to the hotel, packed my things and stood looking in the mirror.

I was doing it for my class. 3B, I'm going all the way.

* * *

At lunch I sat and worked out stopping points on my map. I'd been pushing myself too hard. Let's make the days more realistic and stick to the plan. Why rush when you can chill?

In the back of my mind I was still asking myself the questions *'Does it just get worse from here? Will I get to India without being robbed?'* If Slumdog was anything to go by, all my kit would be stolen when I got to India and, if I were to lock the frame, everything else would be taken - wheels, seat, brakes, gears. But I guessed that if I made it to India, I'd have done blinkin' well. That should be aim number one.

There was still the trip through the Stans first. Nearly everyone I met told me I shouldn't go there. They are full of nomadic tribal peoples / gangsters / bandits / corrupt police and army and I wouldn't make it out alive.

Crossing the Volga River I still had a foul taste in my mouth, literally - from the smog in the air - and metaphorically. I was feeling very lonely even if the grey cloud had started to clear. But one step can make a lot of difference. Although this wasn't quite the border to Asia, I was leaving Europe as I knew it.

With each pedal rotation the scenery and my mood improved. Green replaced grey. The beautiful turquoise Bee-Eaters flew all around me catching the ample insect life sustained by the undergrowth and disturbed by Shirley and me. Spiders lined the lower scrubland and snakes slithered away from my ever-rotating wheels.

Stopping to watch a dung beetle roll a lump of poo about three times his size along the road as trucks rumbled by, I thought to myself 'Things could be worse'.

That night I walked around a rubbish dump looking for a place to set up camp upwind of the tip to avoid the smell. In an area where the flat plain goes on and on, it was my only chance of cover. On closer inspection, the piles of rubbish I was hoping to camp behind were tents like the ones in Slumdog. I moved on. It wasn't time to face this heart-jerking reality. Camped behind a line of thin, withered trees just holding onto their leaves before fall, I'd have just enough cover at the dead of night, but not much before then. I sat against a tree waiting for dusk before I put up my bright red tent.

Run-ins with the gypsies had dented my confidence around people. I was reserved, I held back. I hate to say it but anyone who didn't look quite like me was making me jumpy. As I was a blond-haired, ginger-bearded alien, that basically included everyone I met. People I would have normally reached out to unnerved me.

I stopped for the first time in Leninsk, thirty-five kilometres into my day, and people started to gather 'round me. My adrenaline was pumping. My senses were on full alert. I could even feel the droplet of sweat running down the concave of my spine. They drew closer in a rank. There was no way of busting past them. There were too many. They had darker skin than the Russians, as had the gypsies. Some people were laughing. Others stared expressionless. Then, all of a sudden, the people formed an orderly queue and each demanded to have their picture taken with me, shaking my hand vigorously and slapping me on the back, telling me I was crazy. Awesome!!

The people were from Kazakhstan and were working in the locals' fields. They didn't seem bad at all to me. My jaw ached from smiling and my hand was sore from being shaken so vigorously.

They thrust gifts into my hands. One lady gave me a tomato, a gentleman gave me a cucumber. As I was just about to start eating another women shouted "Stop!". She wouldn't have me eating them as they were and ran back to her house to bring me a little bag of salt.

With a lightness of heart I cruised on. 90% of the population were Central Asian in looks, with light brown skin, hooked noses, and high cheekbones. Their hair colour varied from the prevalent jet-black to blond, red and many shades of brown, and their eyes, normally hazel or green, shone under epicanthic folds - the skin which gives Asians the narrower almond-shaped eyes, developed to protect eyes from the cold.

They were obviously in Russia to do manual labour. Whole townships were sitting by the road on their buckets waiting for their lifts to arrive. As I passed them, I was greeted with silence but, once in their trucks of human livestock looking like they might burst at the seams, they waved and cheered as they overtook me. As they pulled into the side to grab more people, I would pass them again, waving like The Queen or pumping my fist in the air in celebration. The workers made fun of their driver, telling him he was too slow, only to pass me a few minutes later. This continued until they arrived at their destination. I was sad to lose their company.

This feeling of kinship and the knowledge that I would continue to meet nice people throughout my trip really lifted me from the rut I was in and renewed my excitement about the rest of my trip.

* * *

Writing my diary, I discovered that I was beginning to struggle to find English words. It'd been a long time since I'd had a free conversation with someone who could speak English fluently. Use it or lose it. Speaking English isn't like learning to ride a bike after all.

Riding along the riverfront in Astrakhan, trying to find somewhere to stay, I was surrounded by people enjoying the fun and sun at the estuary of the Volga River. It's like Brighton. Candy floss, archaic arcade machines and traditional funfair stalls.

Someone tapped me on the shoulder. "You look as though you've come a long way."

I was covered in mud. I'd taken a tumble earlier and had fallen into a muddy puddle. My bike and I were both coated from head to toe.

"I'm Mike."

Mike had spent time in America at the age of eighteen. On his first day in Michigan he was held at gunpoint and robbed of everything he'd taken with him and then had his face smashed in with the butt of a gun repeatedly. Rather than go home straightaway (I would have) he hung on strong, and began to meet people who righted all the wrongs, people who welcomed him into their embrace, their homes, their lives. He honestly believes he met angels on his trip.

In response he vowed to be a guardian angel of foreign people in his own country. At nineteen that's a fair burden for a man to carry.

He assured me that all the nice places to stay in this holiday resort town were hugely above my budget. He then took me to some dives that were still too expensive. This really is Holiday Central and the punters know it.

Mike suggested, "Why not stay at my house?" I jumped at the chance.

He lived in his parents' flat on the outside of town. The old Soviet high-rises grow out of every space in the city. The walls are one concrete block each and are slotted into supports to hold them up. The flats last for fifty years then have to be destroyed for safety reasons. Mike assured me they had at least a year left.

Outside each block was a small community. Everyone was sitting in the sun in the small gardens talking about the news. Kids played gleefully on the swings or kicked a ball against a wall. No one cared about the mud plastering my body.

Walking up the stairs, we were joined by a Barber Maestro and a few of his friends. I very much needed a haircut and the Barber Maestro was keen to hack away at the locks of the strange bog monster that had dragged itself into their city.

Looking spiffing and freshly showered, I was taken for a tour of the city. Astrakhan is Russia's southernmost outpost, crossed by the Great Silk Route. In history, the city attracted merchants from Khiva, Bukhara, Persia and India. There is St. Vladimir's Cathedral and it holds the headquarters of the Cossacks, the army of the Astrakhan Khanate when the city and surrounding areas belonged to one Khan (a Mongolian leader).

Throughout my trip I had seen groups of young people hanging out drinking beers socially, and felt jealous that I wasn't involved or invited. After our tour this all changed. I met about all of Mikkel's friends (which equals a lot) who could all speak English, and lime beers were passed round. As I tasted the first brew a classic Russian alcoholic walked past telling me to beware. It tasted great.

Just like in England when you're out on the tiles, we organised a kitty, except that everyone didn't throw in the same amount. In England we pop in £10 and then everyone drinks as fast as possible to get as much value as they can. In Astrakhan everyone puts in what they can afford and share the produce equally. It's an amazing sign of trust between friends.

Being told the drug man, who was a little crazy, was coming suddenly sobered me up. I didn't fancy facing a manic gun-toting drug dealer. When he arrived I almost laughed. He was a short, squat boy who made up for his lack of physical presence by being angry.

A resident artist had been one of the first people I'd met. She had pearlescent white skin but the eyes of a Tatar - with large pools of intoxicating green fluid – skin-tight jeans, a little, tight white t-shirt and the hair of a rock chick. I was forced to tear my eyes from her when her rocker boyfriend arrived with the crazy man. We headed off to a party and sadly left her behind. She called me back and said I had to come over the next day to pick up one of her paintings to take with me, but sadly we didn't manage to cross tracks again. I am definitely going back to pick it up one day.

Mikkel's father, an engineer, had spent six months working on oil rigs to be able to fund his family. Working hard he could afford a house outside of the city and a car to run his children around in. We were invited to dinner in his house in the country. Nursing our heads, Mikkel gave me a lift to meet his folks. He then headed back to pick up his mum and left me with his father. Not a big man by Russian standards, he still towered over me and his handshake dwarfed my own. He had red hair and a few days of ragged stubble on his chin, startlingly blue irises swimming in a spaghetti of red capillaries, and a red bulbous nose that is common amongst men in Russia.

Greeting me warmly, he proudly showed me round their house and the river that flowed through their garden with lotus flowers floating on their lily pad leaves. Astrakhan shares the lotus with India as its national emblem. We then went to the sauna, a must in all larger Russian homes. It was an old but solid-looking out-building. He told me how the big shots in Russian politics had used the sauna during the early 1900s. There was a slot for coins in the wall that was now obsolete but reminded visitors of the history.

He led me into the kitchen where he washed two shot glasses and filled them both to the brim, toasting free spirit and life. After four more he washed up the glasses and put the vodka way. He turned to me, smiled and put his finger to his lips, "Shhhh, don't tell my wife". DON'T TELL YOUR WIFE? I don't need to tell her anything. I'm struggling to stand up.

His dad was once proud to be Russian, telling people he met in his rigs how great it was. Since 1997, though, this feeling has dulled and now he has a bitter taste in his mouth about how his country is governed. Over dinner I watched a tear slowly roll down the big man's cheek as he told us how his country had changed.

I tried to lighten the mood by making jokes in Russian. As you can imagine, my jokes don't translate too well into Russian (they were never very good in English), so I learnt to say the word 'joke' to emphasise that was what I was attempting - *shutka*.

When I said it, all their faces dropped. They even looked wounded. I'd been starting the word with an 's' rather than a 'sh', so I had accidentally been calling his father a bitch rather than pointing out that I was telling a joke. No wonder I had received a few fierce looks. Even my jokes aren't that bad.

Chapter 13

For the second time on the trip I was looking down the barrel of a gun. This time I was more aware and already the fear and thrill of the experience was wearing thin. The gorilla-sized border guard had stopped me and was asking his partner to take a picture of us together on his phone. *Really guys, just ask - quit with the gun in face thing.* Looking at him as if he were a small child, his partner creased his brow, shook his head and said, "No".

The guard flushed pink realising what he was asking, straightened up, replaced his boy-like excitement with a stony-faced grimace and waved me through.

Mounting my bike, I heard the guards laughing behind me. I popped my head in and said, "Shutka?", and then jumped on the pedals. Grinning to myself over my raw wit, I tootled off down the road weaving in and out of the potholes and into Kazakhstan.

I'd left my new-found friends in Astrakhan and taken the short route to the border crossing. I was now in a country I knew absolutely nothing about, barring the education Sacha Baron Cohen's fictional character Borat had taught me – which I assumed was nothing.

* * *

As I entered the Karakum desert there was sand as far as the eye could see. This desert is in what's known as a depression. Formed where the Eurasian and Arabian plates meet, the land is below sea level. The high temperatures of the desert keep the depression from filling up. So, at times I was cycling below sea level.

It was dry, hot, barren, and deserted. The dust that mingled with the sand to blast my body day-in and day-out was blown on a powerful east-west airstream carrying pesticide residues that have been found in the blood of penguins in Antarctica. These winds certainly had plenty of momentum when they hit Shirley and me.

In Astrakhan I'd managed to put on a few pounds downing plenty of good food and drink. I'd been having a ball. I could hear the universe saying, "You've been having too much fun and beer, now do some work", as the gale-force winds hit me right in the face. I was cycling so slowly I almost fell off my bike. Five kilometres an hour. That's slower than walking pace. The first day past the border I

69

managed seventy kilometres in nine hours - that's not good. At lunch I sat in a rare spot of grass. The wind blew the sand sideways and encrusted everything I owned.

The second and third days were no better. The 'winds of hell' were playing a sound game against me. I was a marked man, unable to do anything, buffeted left and right. Barbed wire, tumbleweed, sand, it was all flying down the road. It was like an old Spectrum game - I had to dodge left or right to evade the obstacles coming my way.

Putting on my iPod I managed to drown out the monotony of the landscape. A random selection distracted me from my pain and suffering.

To make matters worse, everyone in Kazakhstan seemed to reserve the right to stop me whenever they wanted to take photos of me as though I were a performing monkey at the circus. A blacked out Jeep pulled alongside and drove at my steady ten kilometres per hour for a while. As the window unwound I was wondering whether this was the police, gangsters or drug pushers. It was the kind of Jeep you see in Hollywood films full of gun-wielding gangsters. I could see a shining black object in the hands of a passenger but it wasn't a gun, it was a camera. The other window wound down behind it as a whole football team of people hung out of the one window holding cameras, phones and video cameras. Always happy to take a rest, I took the opportunity to rehearse my improving Russian, pleased that I could freely talk about family and friends now.

I was also pulled over by a guy with a beer in one hand and his manhood in the other. He was peeing. He told me he'd seen me on TV the night before. There had been ten minutes of footage. With the photos everyone was forwarding to their friends and the TV coverage, I was beginning to get a Kazak following, but it also made me vulnerable to the evil of the world.

* * *

On the fourth day, I realised I'd only been playing the wind's reserve team. Beelzebub had had a broken metatarsal and the devil himself had been sitting out a two-match ban for eye-gouging in a pre-season friendly. Both were back in the team now.

Head down to make me more aerodynamic, legs pumping, eyes to the ground, it was not even possible to move forward. I was like

Rocky in 'Rocky IV' (the greatest film of all time) getting knocked around like a ragdoll in a washing machine.

I stopped for a bit but there was no shelter in the desert from this monstrous beast. The flying sand made it impossible to rest. It choked me, pummelled my skin and found its way into every crevice, chafing and rubbing. At midday I got mad at the wind and threw Shirley to the floor. As I sat down to sulk, swearing at invisible demons, 'Gonna Fly Now' came onto my iPod, Rocky's training song.

"Trying hard now, it's so hard now, trying hard now...........
Feeling strong now, moving on now, feeling strong now......"

I couldn't have written a better script. I wasn't only able to get back on the bike, but I felt as though I could have grabbed one of the lorry tyres littering the highway and dragged it along behind me with no hands. Shadow boxing, I dodged and weaved, ducked and dived the punches Beelzebub threw. I could hear him telling his coach, "He's not human. He is like a piece of iron," in his strong Soviet accent.

By the end of the day the strain was starting to show. I could see three roads. The coach inside my head said aim for the middle one.

* * *

That evening, after all the machismo of the day, I settled down in my tent to a bit of poetry and some light strumming of the ukulele.

My Fickle Friend

She wraps her arms around my shoulders,
Guiding me where I want to go.
Running her fingers up my spine,
Stroking them through my hair.
She whispers sweet nothings in my ear.

Why does she turn,
Throwing sand in my face,
Pulling at my hair,
Taking my clothes in her grasp,
Not letting me move on,
Whilst screaming in my ear?

The next day the desert started to look more like coral reef. Shrubs appeared that were thick and coarse; to avoid moisture loss in the abundant sun they have only small leaves. The mirages the sun created in front of me looked like the shimmering surface to a calm sea. The last thing you imagine seeing on a beautiful coral reef is camels. They were everywhere, their pert humps blown to sagging sacks by the force of the wind.

I stopped for food and met 'Happy', an eighteen-year-old Kazak who worked in her mum and dad's café. Four walls, some run-down plastic tables and chairs, sheep and lard were what constituted a café by this point. Holding her for a cuddle as I left, I realised my heart had been opened and her embrace filled me with the emotion associated with her name.

Atyrau is a port on the mouth of the Ural River on the banks of the Caspian Sea. Having found accommodation I needed to get some cash. At the *bankomat* (cash machine) there were hundreds of people all brandishing a number of credit cards. They were all trying to take out what small amounts of money they had in their accounts to feed their families. The young were helping the old read or understand the procedure for the 'hole in the wall.' It was obviously new to the area. An old man grabbed my arm and thrust me to the front where people parted allowing me to take out the cash I needed. "Spasiba." *Thank you.*

The room vibrated as I lay on my bed fully clothed. The beats from the disco below were in full swing causing the bare light bulb illuminating my room to do the same. A knock on the door disturbed my rest. Rina was on the other side. She said she'd come to practise her English, asking if I'd like a tour of the city.

Walking along the river we chatted about my trip and her dreams. Her mother was Polish and she hoped to return one day. Finances were, as ever, an issue.

Laughing and smiling she made jokes about the way I spoke and the way I dressed, my ginger facial hair and my ideas about the world. But then suddenly everything changed. Her demeanour flip-reversed. A tear welled in her eye. She said she had something to confess. She hadn't come to the hotel to practise her English. She hadn't come to show me round her beautiful city. She'd been asked to come by the manager. He'd requested her help as she was the only girl he knew who could speak English. Without knowing how well, he had phoned her to ask her to meet him at the hotel.

Her job was to warn me. On entering the hotel I'd shown the manager a map drawing my finger along the route I hoped to take through Uzbekistan and Kyrgyzstan, then onto India. She now told me that if I were to enter Uzbekistan I wouldn't return. The people there are little more than savages who would kill me to steal my shirt. The police would be no protection as the police were corrupt and would be looking to scam my money and belongings from me for themselves.

Chapter 14

Whirlwinds danced across the road in front of me, whipping my clothes around me and filling the air with sand and dust. When it cleared, I saw two buildings in front of me in equal disrepair. Signs indicated that one of the buildings was a mosque where you should get on your knees and pray to the west. The other was a toilet where getting on your knees would probably result in gastroenteritis, vomiting, diarrhoea and more time spent on your knees in front of the toilet bowl.

The toilet was simply a hole in the ground where waste was allowed to fall into a pit below. The temple was in rack and ruin and looked like it should only be used in case of an emergency, much like the neighbouring toilets.

Stopping beside the side of the road, I pulled out my stove. I was becoming a bit of a connoisseur of single stove cooking. My signature dish was noodle surprise – the surprise being that it was just noodles.

As I was unpacking, ready to rustle up some of that yumminess, a car pulled over and the driver asked if I was all right. This was followed by the obligatory mobile phone photo shoot. He handed me a half-drunk, flat bottle of Coke which tasted like pure heaven and washed the dust and sand from my throat. The sugar and caffeine instantly hit my veins and I could feel the high more than ever. I felt so grateful.

He said he was running low on petrol and that I'd probably see him later in the desert as I went past. I gave him a smile and whipped out my fuel bottle. It felt so great to be able to offer these people something in return for their kindness. Using the Coke bottle and his engineering genius, he poured the litre of petrol into his car, gave me a hug, and went on his way. Those that help get helped. What goes around comes around.

My noodles were even more surprising this time as they were uncooked. Since I'd given my petrol to a broken-down vehicle my stove was useless. I dropped the noodles into a pan of water and then lay my head down to rest as they soaked through. After picking the bits of fly and twig out of the water, I tucked into what tasted like edible chewing gum.

On the road a small snake weaved across the road avoiding my tyres. I stopped to take a closer look. Confronted by me, it rose up and began to thrust its fangs towards me. Cool! I got out my camera to try and get a decent picture of the aggressive little cutie to send back home.

* * *

Later I checked into a gostinitsa and café. Two men greeted me as I came in. They had a buffet of food spread over their table and several bottles of vodka. They beckoned me over and, as I sat down next to them, a tumbler was brought over and filled with vodka before I could refuse. They raised their glasses to me and, although vodka was the last thing I needed, I raised mine and poured the vodka down my throat, putting the glass down on the table with a resonating chink. Quicker than the speed of sound, even before the chink had reached my ear, the glass was full again. Other people from the café next door were joining us now. I was trying to see who was the manager, hoping to ask for some food and a bed as my third vodka was poured, then my fourth. As the fifth hit the back of my throat, I collapsed onto the soft cushions around me.

Two hours later I woke up with a very dry mouth and a heartbeat in my head. I was invited to eat with the couple who were still making headroads into their buffet and numerous vodka bottles. The chubby one was the owner and he commanded more food AND WATER – hurrah!

The conversation was flowing nicely. They'd run through the usual repertoire of questions. *Where are you from? What is your name? Where are you going? Solo? Do you have a wife?* I took my photos out of my wallet to show the onlookers a few pics of my family and friends. In doing so a condom fell out of my wallet (it'd been there for some time now and was barely recognisable) and in unison every one of the men (there were only men in the café) picked up their phones and started dialling their most desirable prostitute. In the end I managed to get my message across, even though the men were confused that any man might not want a prostitute. Another vodka seemed to deem me an all right bloke.

Asking for a banna, *shower,* I was given a bucket. I didn't want to clean the shower, I just wanted to clean me. Oh, this is the shower! When I was naked and covered in soap, one of the men, Ismim in the café, came in, handed me his mobile phone, and smiled. I said, "Hello". A sleepy voice responded. He'd dialled his brother's number in the UK and given the phone to me. "Speak!" he demanded. We

75

made simple chit chat for a minute, costing the friend a fortune, I bet. Ismim is an Uzbek. He told me there was more money in Kazakhstan. I looked around at our surroundings - a simple building made of mud bricks, two rooms, one for sleeping and eating, the other for cooking. These men when they sleep cover every inch of the floor, the mattresses are no more than a yoga mat, snoring fills the air. Mobile phones are used as music players repeating one song all through the night. The walls let in the lights and the fresh desert winds. The food is simple - sheep and, if you're really lucky, potatoes. What must Uzbekistan be like?

Leaving, I remembered my picture of the snake and asked them which snake it was. "Cobra" one man said whilst drawing his finger across his neck to demonstrate the capabilities of such a snake. A single bite ejects enough venom to kill twenty men or a full-grown elephant. That'll be the last time I take a picture of a snake at close quarters.

Chapter 15

The Kazak stage of the Dakar rally had ended in Zhanaozen, and the support crews, media, drivers and groupies were making their way to the final leg in Turkmenistan.

It was interesting to see the bright coloured lights and revving engines making a beeline out of the bloody desert through the desolate landscape. They didn't stop at any of the small roadside cafés. Hedging their bets with the cuisine and drinks supplied in the cities, they passed through.

In the distance I could see huge sandstorms and nervously made my way towards them. I had no idea what one did when one got caught in a terrible sandstorm. They have been known to strip the skin from someone's face in ten minutes, to ruin crops and to disorientate people so they walk into the desert, get lost and die of starvation.

Continuing on, I saw a pile of sand and dirt blocking the road. Road workers were blocking the road to allow the men to resurface it. With deep sand either side of the road, I now understood that it wasn't a storm I had seen, just the Dakar troops speeding through this deep sand.

As I stood wondering what to do, some of the younger workers came over to see me. They offered me sunflower seeds. In my gratitude I threw a handful in my mouth and crunched down. They were a bit crispy but I managed to get them down and smile (showing only small amounts of the seeds around my teeth). The workers looked at me with surprise and shook their heads before popping their own seeds into their mouths, turning them round their mouths before spitting out the shells and swallowing the fruit. Oops.

The boys wanted to have a go on Shirley. I asked them to treat her well and they took it in turns to ride her up and down the road. Their smiles said it all - massive white half moons embedded in their darkened skin. Their boots were covered in tar and I could see it slowly encrusting Shirley. I was worried about her mechanics but the boys were enjoying themselves; looking at her brakes and gears. Bikes in Asia have one gear and no brakes.

The pile of earth still obstructed my way. Cars had churned through the sand on either side. I took the same exit in the dunes and immediately slipped and slid to the ground, taking all the skin off my legs and arms. Luckily, a bush softened my fall. Unluckily, it was a thorn bush, leaving my body pierced, with leftover thorns waiting in my shirt to get me later.

I stopped for lunch and added five large Snickers to the luggage. Owing to the extra weight I thought it was probably best that I eat four of them within the hour. It was all for weight advantage. I'd also downed a pot of tea that must have been so strong I was shaking from the effects. I blamed it on that but it could have been my diet of sheep fat and bread. My nails had started to show signs of my malnutrition. The slightest knock cracked them in half. My waist was also a sure giveaway. My skin was pulled tight over my muscles and my body fat must have been well below ten percent, which left me little defence against bugs and viruses.

As I tried to sleep, I had to block out the TV from the other room. I don't watch much TV in England and throughout Europe had not even seen a TV set. People in Asia all have TVs and they play them as though they are proud of it, as if they want their neighbours to be able to hear them.

In the morning I questioned the owner. She didn't know the road I intended to take to Uzbekistan, which should have fired off some warnings in my head.

The road was horrific. Massive holes in the concrete road were joined by bits of wire sticking out at all angles. The wires once held the slabs together, but were now weapons for stabbing, tripping or impaling falling cyclists. I had to be careful.

Then it got worse.

The road basically disappeared and left sand, gravel and rocks. Walking some bits where the sand was too deep, I pulled muscles in my back, neck, arms and shoulders trying to keep the bike upright.

Part of the road was guarded by a huge cobra and this time I wasn't going anywhere near it. I tried to pass it on the left but it lunged at me with intent, so I tried to pass it on the right to the same end. Shirley came to my rescue, guarding me as I walked past the snake with her between me and the enemy.

Night fell and still I hadn't crossed the seventy kilometres I had hoped to do that day. I was utterly exhausted. A lot of pain later, I managed to get to the border and another 'hotel'. I swallowed a sob as I crossed the threshold and saw cold drinks and cooking utensils. I was so tired I couldn't feel the hunger and thirst. Rolling out my mat, I lay down and slept, waking shortly afterwards as the workers in the nearby mechanics came back and set up the table for their supper.

Looking for a bathroom, I saw the women out the back washing what I thought were sheets in a tub. Further inspection showed it to be a sheep's stomach. The rest of the carcass was hanging close by, bleeding all over the floor. I decided to try and help and poured the water into the intestine and other bits so they could be cleaned and used for sausages. The man had just ripped the sheep's jaw in half and the *babushka* (grandma) was hacking out the teeth with an axe. The teeth were flying at me, as were the sparks from the axe.

Surreal.

One of the sons, noticing my eagerness to help, brought something over for me to clean. I rinsed it in the water like the women had done and began squeezing it a little. Before I realised the others were shouting, "No". I'd squeezed a load of sheep shit into the cleaning water. He'd given me the anus to clean. The family couldn't look at me for the rest of the evening without laughing heartily. I was pleased to have entertained them so.

I wanted to know if they ate everything and, with some hand gestures and my almost pidgin Russian, I managed to ask whether they ate the brain. "Yes." I really wanted to ask about the sheep's more private parts but didn't want to ask the women *'Do you eat penis?'* due to possible sexual innuendos, and I was worried about asking the man as the men are generally very homophobic here and he had an axe in his hand.

Walking back to the café, I remembered I'd left my wallet out on the table with all the money I owned in it. Panic swept over me. There was probably more money than the workers earned in a year in the wallet and it was just sitting there in front of them. There was no way they could resist.

Walking in, I saw that the wallet had gone - my cards, my money, even my emergency phone numbers. What was I to do now?

I went over to my bed and lay down. The floor was lumpy and something jabbed into my back. I rolled the mat over to see what it was and there was my wallet with everything intact. They'd put it in my 'bed' to make sure I didn't lose it!

* * *

I sat up and smiled at the men as they began to question me. When people hear what I'm up to they can imagine the adventure, they see why I'm interested in the countries, why I might like riding a bike. The question everyone asks though is simple. Adin, one, solo? Why am I doing it alone? Where is your Jena, your wife? Your children? They simply cannot understand it, especially given the fact that I am thirty years old.

It's a good question and, each time, I give an answer that I don't believe: that I don't know people mad enough, that I like to be on my own.

Speaking with friends and colleagues before leaving, we discussed the lack of adventure in modern life. I think it has left a void in men's hearts all over the country. How do we prove ourselves? How do we show our loved ones how much we care, that we are prepared to die for them? Life is too easy.

I think wars and famine satisfied those urges in past generations. Working to keep your family alive, signing up for something you really believed in, that would make the people around you proud, putting your life on hold to better the lives of others.

I considered signing up for the army when I was working in the city selling my soul for money. I wanted to make a difference, make my mark on the world. Unfortunately I don't want to kill anyone, or get killed either, so I probably made the best decision not to.

It sounds obtuse to compare a long-distance cycle trip to war, to think of the uniformed men parading down the street on the way to the docks to stand up for what they thought was right, to protect the young and elderly. But I paraded through the streets to Dover in my uniform endorsed by the great Cotswold, and Bicycle, having friends and family cheer me off, knowing they were proud, worried, even envious. A step into the unknown that I knew was a step in the right direction. Of course war offers far more dangerous situations, but my trip has its fair share. My trench foot isn't so bad. My continuous marching is similar. My kit is more technical but equal in weight. Rationing is crucial every day in a desert. My talisman from school sits behind me on the bike. I write home as often as I can, trying to make it sound like one big adventure, when at times it is horribly dull, scary, lonely, depressing. The people you meet make it, or break it.

It's not war, but it is testing mentally, physically and emotionally. I know I'm making my loved ones proud and, with the money raised for ActionAid, I'm making a difference to the world. I can feel a change inside me. *Am I becoming a man? What me, 'Peter Pan'? Am I realising how fantastically lucky I am?* I always knew that. I can't tell if something is being ignited or extinguished. Either way it's a feeling like a big air pocket rising from the depths of the ocean getting bigger with each rotation.

All I can do is keep putting my feet in the direction that feels right with a smile on my face and a tingle in my heart.

Today was my last day in Kazakhstan. I'd made it to the front line. What awaited me when I got over the top no one knew. Only I could find out. I had to dig in now and hope for no surprise attacks.

Chapter 16

Heading out early for the border, I saw a basic stop sign for cars but thought I'd be OK to go on. I wandered aimlessly through the border, and could see the active Uzbekistani side, when two guards started running towards me with machine guns whilst another fired a shot into the air from the top of the low-lying buildings.

The border was closed.

"Are you crazy?" he shouted as he escorted me back to where the stop sign was.

Arriving earlier, I'd been surrounded by Uzbekistanis as a bus taking workers back home had emptied onto the streets. I've always loved being the centre of attention but this was intense. People stared at me hard; others pulled me this way and that, hoping to introduce me to their friends who could see me quite clearly already.

As the stop sign was raised I was allowed first into the barracks. Minutes later I was walking towards Uzbekistan. I could see the soldiers I'd been very much warned against. When would I meet the gangsters, thieves and vagabonds?

Before I was allowed to leave Russia, Mikkel had taken me to a gun shop. He said I needed something to ward off any Uzbeks who would kill me for my shirt. He encouraged me to buy a small handgun but I placated him by buying a can of mace. I'd thought I could perhaps use it on bears and wolves, if nothing else, if they got too friendly.

My first experience left me detained for two hours, filling in the entry forms and bowing my head respectfully at the well-armed men in desert camouflage combat gear. The paperwork didn't take more than five minutes.

"So why were you detained so long?" I hear you ask.

Each officer in the hut wanted to have his picture taken with me and Shirley. I was then ordered to retrieve my USB cable from the bottom of my bag and they ordered that I put the photos onto the team computer. They were the guys wielding the big guns - what else could I do? Then we had some group photos taken and again I was told to pop them on the big screen. Each soldier's posture looked identical; chest puffed out; head held high – these people were proud to be serving their country.

Tea was brought from an unseen source and then came a money changer, a lady with a bag full of Uzbekistan som. She offered me a rate and the officers bartered her up after she walked away indignantly twice. We struck a deal when the soldiers gave me the thumbs up behind her back.

Waving to my new friends, I cycled along the quiet road from the border post. The only traffic seemed to be tractors towing large carts packed full of Uzbek men squatting on their hind feet off to a farm, field, or workshop to do a day's hard manual labour. The first person to notice me would jump up and shout, swiftly followed by the rest of the human load. The cart would hover on the verge of toppling over until the driver of the tractor stopped under the demands of the workers.

Waving, they would demand I take a picture of them. These Uzbeks love their photography!

* * *

The dry, barren landscape was made worse by the unrelenting flies that'd tracked me, diving into the moist spots of my eyes and mouth whenever they got the chance. I couldn't blame them; it was darn hot out there and constant drinking made no difference to the dryness in my mouth.

I decided to do an experiment. I was riding at nineteen kilometres per hour and the flies were circling me. I wanted to see how fast these flies could fly. I upped it to twenty kilometres per hour then twenty-one, making my legs burn but the flies were gone. I was stuck with the dilemma of whether to kill my legs or suffer the flies. I decided to allow the flies the luxury of a drink from my tear ducts.

The other pests were the guards at the checkpoints which came thick and fast. They must have been bored to death sitting in the desert all day long and they bombarded me with questions, selecting a piece of kit (usually my glasses) that they took a particular fancy to, telling me I had to give it to them. "Prize, yes?"

At night there was absolutely no choice but to pop up the tent a few hundred metres from the side of the road and just hope that no passing cars saw you. There was no cover whatsoever. The flat plains went on as far as the eye could see. One evening I pitched my tent behind what I thought were some bushes – in the morning they had moved on along with all the other tumbleweed.

Without cover I would wake up at 7am soaked in my own sweat as the sun beat down upon my tent, turning it into a furnace. I'd pack up, get on the bike and cycle until lunch when I would cook some noodle surprise and then cycle on along a straight road that seemed to go on forever, before waiting till nightfall and pitching my tent behind the smallest of bushes to try and avoid the night travellers.

At night the heat was intense and would keep me awake, writhing in the dirt and sweat of the previous days. I wasn't helped by the fact that my mattress had another puncture. I'd used almost a whole pack of puncture repair kit on the mattress whilst having cycled for 4,000 miles without a single puncture to my bike.

It was my tenth day solid riding in the desert through Kazakhstan and Uzbekistan when I ran out of noodles with only a trickle of water in my bottles. The only food the desert offered up was the flies that pestered me day and night, and the occasional camel that had strayed from its flock and died. I was already looking gaunt from lack of nutrition. I had few fingernails left as they had all become brittle and had snapped from vitamin deprivation. Sheep and noodles surprise were not giving me the nutrition I needed.

I could feel my cheeks sucking against my skull. My eyes were sunken and dark. My suntanned skin was pulling taut across my muscles. My tongue was stuck to the top of my mouth. I was dizzy from dehydration and my speed had reduced to ten kilometres per hour, about the pace of a brisk walk.

As time went on I began to get really desperate. I was burning up. My body had stopped sweating; it had no liquid to spare. My cheeks were salt-encrusted.

I didn't see the point in stopping and waiting, I might have waited for days for someone to help me so I just kept plodding onwards. I knew there was a village ahead and if I kept rotating my scorched legs I hoped to get there eventually. Surely they'd be able to spare some water and food. Head down, I couldn't see in front of me, but I was travelling so slowly there was no risk of crashing into anyone. Suddenly two hands were resting on my handlebars. They brought me to a standstill without the slightest effort. "As-Salaam Alaykum". It was Ismim from the café in Kazakhstan, greeting me with the Muslim welcome, *Peace Unto You*. He thrust bread into my hands and held a bottle over my head and poured. I raised my face to the lip of the bottle and allowed the water to moisten my throat. I realised I hadn't swallowed in a while. I just had to let it trickle down my throat until the moving parts were oiled and I was able to gulp it down in huge quantities.

Giving me his mum's address and phone number in Xiva, he said I must visit her. With this he jumped back in his car and drove off in the direction of his work in Kazakhstan.

With the liquid and food I was able to get some speed up and I eventually came across a café perched on the side of the road. No cars were parked nearby and only the owner was in the bar. He was a huge guy, the biggest Asian I'd met. He introduced himself as 'Facker'.

I bought chai and three Snickers, bread, and some mutton. I would have stayed if it hadn't been for his behaviour towards his wife. He clicked his fingers whilst watching TV (Asian man's favourite pastime) and she would scurry in and put what he desired in front of him. How she knew what he wanted I had no idea. Was there a tone to the click? The man's attention meanwhile wouldn't leave the square box in front of him and the wife scurried out without the slightest recognition. I entertained myself by calling him Bolshoi Facker, 'Big Facker', for the rest of my stay.

Thanking the lady for such nice tea - '*blogadaria*' - I headed out. I only made a couple more miles before finding somewhere appropriate to pitch my tent. I'd managed to procure wet wipes at the café and my ritual of the three wipes began. One for my face and hands, one for my body and another for the parts in contact with the seat.

Sitting out watching the stars, I played my ukulele to the moon in the nude, allowing the air to pass over me, drying my sweat and washing my worries away.

* * *

At this point I'd cycled non-stop in the desert for fourteen days, and with no shower in five days. It was no wonder I was starting to slow down - I needed a rest. But a day's rest in the desert with just the flies for company? That didn't sound like any fun at all.

Once again I ran out of food and liquid and, driving into the middle of the road, I was able to stop a car to ask where the next shop or café was. They, in turn, flagged down a bus that was going in my direction and told me to get on it. "No, no, no. By bicycle," I stated lamely in my pidgin Russian.

The bus driver pointed to a number of crooked shacks about four hundred metres away and said there was a shop there. As I got closer, I could see simple homes set amongst cattle sheds. Uzbek people are nomadic by tradition and this was a temporary settlement that would remain until they were ready to travel on. It's a life that to

85

me is extremely appealing - always on the move, new faces, new pastures, a loving community you can rely on and care for. I guess I'm seeing past the poverty, the lack of education and the lack of hygiene.

I could not imagine a shop being here but, when I asked, they said, "Yes." They sent a boy to fetch the key. As they opened up a barn door behind me, I could see all my favourites: Snickers, Coke, and my very favourite of all, watermelon. I pulled out my penknife and chopped up the water melon whilst people sat around me and watched. I offered pieces to the children and women, who declined my offer. I didn't bother spitting out the seeds. I crushed the flesh with my tongue and swallowed. Every young female came to see the stranger and to sit at a distance and watch me with interest. It felt as though they were looking at me for a way out. Could I take them away from this life, could they cope with the ginger beard? They see the Western life as perfect - stability, water and money on tap. I guess they're seeing past the impersonal element, the way people stagnate, become miserable and forget how lucky they are.

Pulling away, I was joined by the boys of the village. As soon as they were out of sight and earshot of the adults, they asked for a taste of Coca-Cola. They sold it in the shop but rarely, if ever, tasted it due to the cost which for them was the price of three meals. I passed them a bottle and watched them share it between them. Boys of all sizes took their turn and no one took advantage. It was beautiful to see and when the bottle was finished, they threw it to the side of the road, with all the others, and set off ahead of me, racing the white man until they got bored, when they left me to my own thoughts again.

I was lost in my own head when I saw the top of a Land Rover approaching me. I waved as it went by. It pulled over and a Swiss couple jumped out. They were travelling back from China to Switzerland and were keen to hear the state of the roads ahead. I warned them of the stretch between Kazakhstan and Uzbekistan. They groaned, complaining of the sore bottoms they were getting from sitting in the car all that time. Laughing in unison they looked at me and said, "I guess yours must be worse," and we shared a sore-bottomed group hug.

It was amazing to be talking freely again to English speakers and sharing human contact. I had been missing affection, normally my staple diet, and realised that in the arms of these people I'd had only one hug since I had left home.

I asked if they wanted to share a camping spot but they were hoping to cover another few hundred miles before they camped. They said they were envious of my freedom and I said I was feeling the same about them - to be able to travel hundreds of miles in one day sounded fantastic to me - but they still said they'd have preferred to be on bikes.

This idea made me smile as I unwrapped another chocolate bar for my evening meal and sipped some more Coke.

In the night I could hear voices around my tent. People were passing by and discussing what might be inside. In a state halfway between waking and sleep I lay there unalarmed and allowed the voices to take me back to my dreams.

* * *

The next morning I was joined by a Russian travelling on a beaten-up old motorbike. We shared shutkas. Before he opened up the throttle and left me in a cloud of diesel, he told me the place I wanted to stay in Nukus was the Jepak Jolly, a hostel every visitor to Nukus stayed in.

As I got closer to Nukus, every state border guard, policeman and local bystander reminded me I had to stay in Jepak Jolly. Then a guard told me about the new bridge that takes you straight into town and probably saves you twenty kilometres. Passers-by whispered Jepak Jolly as I went past, people travelling in cars wound down their windows and said the same. It was becoming eerie, but I was excited. It felt like a conspiracy. The last person to tell me about it was a man on the arch of the large bridge into town. He grabbed me by the face and tried to kiss me.

Night fell as I crawled into Nukus and I stopped to devour as many samosas as I could buy with my change. I'd run out of money after only changing a small amount with the guards. A taxi driver led the way to the hostel where I rested Shirley against a post and entered the office. The light bulbs and glass looked a little strange after so much time in the desert. I could see two computers set up for travellers in the corner and heard European voices behind the thin wooden doors. The lady behind the desk smiled.

Bouncing off the walls and ceiling, I just couldn't believe my luck. They had showers, they had Western faces, I could hear English.

I asked if there was a room free.

She shook her head and said sorry, they were fully booked!

Chapter 17

I'd been five days sleeping in my tent without a shower. I'd cleaned a sheep's anus, cycled 1,500 kilometres, been blasted by sand, diesel fumes and tumble weed. I was dehydrated, and malnutritioned. I wasn't prepared for a knock-back. All the people had told me this was where I'd stay. It'd become an inevitability. Sitting down on a chair I winced as the paddling my bottom had taken during the off-road section hadn't quite healed.

My arms, hands, legs and back ached. Every muscle now gave in as my head hung low.

The lady, Nila, looked at me with sympathy and disappeared. I could hear her speaking quickly with the owner, saying "Angleški", *English* and "Velocipriate", *bicycle*. Returning, she led me into a courtyard and told me they had a storage shed that I might be able to squeeze into. It was not ideal but I followed nonetheless. In the courtyard stood the first yurt I'd seen.

A yurt is a portable, circular home made of a wood lattice and covered with felt made up of the wool of the owner's flocks of sheep. It's the traditional home of the nomads in the Steppes of Central Asia. The frame is held together with ribbons and rope and they look absolutely gorgeous. I'd seen these in pictures in National Geographic as a child and had dreamed that one day I would build my own and retire to the mountains and live happily ever after. It's so grand. Beautiful.

Yurts were brought to Uzbekistan by the Mongolian invasions in the early 12th century. Led by Genghis Khan, the Mongol warriors swept south-west, conquering and inflicting large-scale damage on the Khanates.

This particular one had hand-stitched pieces of canvas adorning the exterior and roof. The door was wooden and hand-carved, with well-designed dark black metallic handles. Mats made up of colourful woven wool hung either side of the door with tassels hanging to the side. *It must cost a bomb to stay here*, I thought.

Nila saw me looking at it with lust in my eyes. She pointed to it and said "OK?" I gave her two thumbs up and a big smile to show her how beautiful I thought their treasure was. She opened the door and allowed me to poke my head in. "OK?" It had some old TVs in there and a radiator but they couldn't hide the beauty of the inside of this yurt. Felt ribbons hung from the ceiling. Brightly-coloured ropes criss-crossed the walls, held together by red wooden lattice.

Nila wheeled Shirley inside. While I'd started talking to Shirley and almost developed feelings for her, I didn't think she was capable of reciprocating them, so I couldn't quite understand why she needed to see the inside too. Nila rested her against a felt wall. Shirley looked so comfortable, so happy.

As Nila returned to the cash register, I asked her where I would be sleeping, where the storage shed was. She looked at me quizzically. She re-entered the yurt and pointed at the bed. It took me a second to take in what she was suggesting. The yurt was my room. I almost screamed with joy - in fact, I might have done.

Unloading Shirley, I sang and danced, moving my performance over to the shower where I continued for well over the signpost-allocated time, as the cold water fell over my aching bones.

As I re-appeared, two French girls looked at me and grinned. They'd heard all the commotion and wanted to know why I was so happy. We were still out in the middle of the desert, surrounded by nothing; miles from anywhere. What was there to be happy about? Uzbekistan, a land-locked country that was once part of the Soviet Union, is home to one of the biggest man-made disasters in history. For decades its rivers were diverted to grow cotton on arid land, causing the Aral Sea, a large salt water lake, to lose more than half of its surface area in forty years. Tourists stop in Nukus on their way there, to crunch through the salt-encrusted land that used to be underwater and to inspect the fishing boats that had been stranded miles away from the current seashore.

When I started telling the girls about my trip, I couldn't stop. It was so nice to talk again. They couldn't get a word in edgeways. Only when I was taking long swigs of cold beer did they have a chance. They had come to Uzbekistan on holiday for two weeks. What an amazing choice of holiday. We continued talking into the night until one of them said they must go to bed. I was disappointed but definitely needed the rest. As I was getting into bed, one of the girls came into my yurt, giving me a goody bag they had been given with all sorts of treats in. They thought I needed it more than they did.

* * *

The next morning I met my first long distance touring cyclist, a fifty-year-old German, Peter. He'd been on the road for twenty years. His bike was more solder than steel, having been broken and fixed so many times. He told me of his journeys and I was in awe – he'd been everywhere and all by bicycle. Amazing.

He was leaving this very morning and I shared some stories about the roads he was taking back to Russia. He had neither tent nor stove and I was worried about him being on the road I'd taken which had little to no civilisation. What if the travellers had moved on? What if he didn't bump into friends along the way? But, then again, he must have known a whole lot more than me about survival.

As breakfast was served I found myself wondering why someone would travel by bicycle for no reason for an indefinite time. I had my destination I was heading for; I was raising money for the people I saw along the way. What was his motivation?

Peter was waving at the people in the kitchen trying to get their attention. I asked what was wrong and he said his eggs hadn't arrived. He seemed agitated. I said I was sure they'd be along soon and offered him some of my bread. He brushed this aside and yelled at the workers. I was a little embarrassed. They either didn't hear or had experienced this before, choosing to ignore him. Shouting "Where are my eggs?" at the top of his voice, he began cursing the lazy people of this country.

I made a note to myself that I wouldn't carry on cycling after I reached Chembakolli. I wanted to stay in a positive state of mind where everything around me was new, and setbacks were just part of the cultural experience. I didn't want it to become my life and to start unearthing all the frustrations associated with it.

* * *

I needed to change some money if I wanted to eat outside of the hostel. Access to foreign exchange was restricted, inflation was high, and people had very little trust in banks, so there was a very strong black market. Peter told me the best place to do a transaction was in the park square. He'd managed to get 1,950 to the dollar but someone like me could only hope for 1,800 at best.

The bank rate was 1,450, so I was more than happy to receive either of these rates.

Walking into the mêlée, I was greeted by four teenagers wearing baseball caps and jackets in the soaring heat. I was hoping to change $100, and they first offered me 1,500 per dollar. Smiling, I walked away and was swiftly offered 1,800. Turning, we both laughed and I made an offer of 2,000. They said they could do 1,950 and I thought of Peter suffering on the roads to the border and his prediction that I wouldn't get more than 1,800. We walked over to their car and they looked left and right before opening a boot absolutely stacked with cash. Surely this couldn't all be real? Pulling out four wrapped piles of notes made up of 1,000 bills (the biggest denomination), they took a number of notes from one stack and handed them to me. I was holding two inches of notes in my hands, just under two hundred notes. I handed over the $100 single bill and we shook hands. On the way back, I stopped at a shop to buy a drink. Pulling one note from my bag, I was almost surprised when the owner looked it over and accepted it. I bought some fruit too and again all was fine.

Leaving the fruit stand, I was joined by two boys who walked alongside me asking me questions about my trip. Hearing I was a teacher, they said I had to visit their school. Having recently graduated they also wanted to practise their English.

I got taken round a senior and junior school, meeting teachers and pupils, and taking a few pictures along the way. I was astonished at what I saw. There were four computer rooms, all the scientific equipment you could imagine, and three gyms. I was told that 97% of the population over fifteen could read and write. The Uzbeks associated this with the years of Soviet rule. "They [the Russians] brought education." In general the Uzbeks I'd met looked back with great fondness on those years.

When I got home, I shut myself in the yurt and couldn't help throwing one of the piles of notes in the air so that they rained down all around me. What a wonderful feeling! I took all sorts of pictures of me looking like a playboy gangster before reappearing in the hostel where two Aussie girls handed me a beer and we relaxed into conversation.

It turned out that one of the girls, Louise, was a famous opera singer in Sydney and she gave us a rendition of her favourite opera, Carmen. I couldn't believe the sound, and lots of locals peered over the wall to hear where this wonderful singing was coming from.

We were joined by Katya and Cedric. Within thirty seconds of Katya entering the room I knew that she was a teacher. I have no idea how, other than from the strength of her presence, her caring features and her articulation. Cedric had a smile Mick Jagger would be proud of. It formed half of his face, like the Cheshire Cat from 'Alice in Wonderland', and was virtually ever-present. It was no wonder really. Katya and Cedric had recently married and were celebrating their honeymoon by travelling the world overland. One of their presents was a dice game that, when mixed with beer, was a perfect way to spend a lazy afternoon.

* * *

Nukus hosts the second largest collection of Russian avant-garde art in the world (after the Hermitage in St. Petersburg). Kliment Red'ko, Lyubov Popova, Vera Mukhina, Ivan Koudriachov and Robert Falk, the gallery has them all. Although already recognised in Western Europe (especially in France), these artists had been banned in the Soviet Union during Stalin's rule and throughout the 1960s.

Despite the risk of being denounced as an 'enemy of the people', Igor Savitsky tracked down these painters and their heirs to collect, archive and display their works. With great courage, he managed to assemble thousands of Russian avant-garde and post avant-garde paintings, countering the Socialist Realism school, and shaking the foundations of that period of art history.

It was not until 1985, the year after he died, that Savitsky's extraordinary achievements and collections were truly acknowledged, and not until 1991, when Uzbekistan became independent, that Nukus, a remote, 'closed' city during the Soviet era, became accessible to the outside world, allowing fans to come and admire his work.

I took a tour with the two Australian girls. It was wonderful seeing the artwork depicting the caravans of Central Asia and the life I had witnessed on my bicycle.

* * *

A man sat watching me from across the courtyard. I was fixing the perpetual puncture to my roll mat outside my yurt with the help of a bucket of soapy liquid. He had long, flowing, dark hair and was devilishly handsome. His gaze made me feel awkward so I called out, asking him if he was OK.

He came over and spoke with me in perfect English. Yusup was a self-proclaimed VIP in the city and a group of them were going out. He asked me if I wanted to come along.

He said he had to pick up his car and left. Whilst he was away the Aussie girls said they thought he was a little suspect. My dad's words however still rang in my ears - "Make the most of every opportunity." I decided to give it a go.

On the way into town he showed me a Muslim crypt and graveyard. A story suspiciously similar to Romeo and Juliet meant people came from far and wide to visit the burial chamber under a porcelain blue dome, with golden spire and white tiled walls.

Then we met Yusup's friends, all dressed in suits with dark glasses. They took me out all over town to the best spots, teaching me so much about life in Uzbekistan.

He certainly gave the impression of being a VIP. When he walked into restaurants, people fought to grasp his hand. He didn't have to pay a thing for food. Everyone grovelled in a manner I had only seen in Hollywood films featuring Italian gangsters. I commented that they looked like gangsters when we all met up, and they laughed heartily without denying it.

Yusup had fought long and hard to keep his homeland on the map, helping charities and businesses alike to keep afloat during the hard times of the recent recession. His family depended on his business skills and his intellect made me feel like an amoeba. It was huge. Politics, history, languages, I felt like all his facts and figures had turned me into a new man.

He had once worked for AIDS projects until he had confronted one of the doctors he was advising. The evidence clearly showed the medicine they were prescribing to AIDS victims had absolutely no effect. The doctor agreed that this was true but explained that the money the pharmaceutical company was bringing to their projects meant they had to go along with it. This experience changed Yusup's perspective of the world and he got in with a different crowd.

Afterwards, the men retired to one of their flats where girls of the remunerated kind awaited them. Yusup asked me time and again to join them but it's not my bag. On the way home he said he'd give everything up to become a soldier. He wanted a Third World War so he could die for his country.

Chapter 18

When the people in Russia and Kazakhstan had told me it was all 'take, take, take' in Uzbekistan, I had assumed that they meant that my belongings and money would be stolen. So far my experiences had proved the contrary. They had done nothing but give since I'd arrived.

I was in Karakalpakstan – the area of the nomadic peoples. Nomads by definition have less interest in possessions than regular people. Perhaps my luck would change when I set off to the centre of Uzbekistan. To get there I tried a new form of cycling. I named it truck surfing. Looking behind you for a suitable ride (truck) you pedal like crazy when it approaches. As it passes, you pop up (veer into the middle of the road behind the truck). The truck forms a vacuum behind it as it moves forward, sucking your bike and luggage along with it. I wanted to try 'hanging five' and some 'gnarly' aerial moves, but I had no idea what any of that meant so I decided to leave them out. Wipeouts should be avoided at all costs. I am sure they suck in a 'one hundred foot reef break' sort of way.

My pace almost doubled when I caught one just right, but the best (read: slowest) trucks tended to have the dirtiest exhausts, occasionally vomiting diesel over you. I could feel the fumes in my mouth mixing with my saliva to form poison which, when swallowed, left me with a very sore throat.

Talking of gnarly; I had been getting bored waving at people so I decided to give a gnarly 'surf's up' hand signal (finger and thumb extended) to the bus drivers who all hooted their horns in response.

I could have done with a bit of help when three boys joined me. Determined to beat me up every hill, they thrashed themselves and me. They didn't speak English and were obviously on a long journey. I assumed they were visiting friends.

Helping them fix a puncture and sharing my food with the three of them won me their friendship and, although it wasn't stated in as many words, they invited me to join them at their friend's.

Weariness overcame all of us as the friend's house seemed to get further and further away. We spoke to a café owner and he pointed to an off-road pathway that led up to the mountains. Grudgingly I cycled behind them, too ashamed to turn down their invite.

Continuing, we took a turn to the right and great domes of grey stone hove into view, symbols of the Muslim religion. Passing under an archway proclaiming that this was Sultan Bobo, it dawned on me that this was where our cyclists were heading. It was the last day of Ramadan and I had been invited on a pilgrimage. I should have known better than to think people rode for social reasons. I was an offering to the gods, fate had thrown us together and the boys had assumed it was for a reason. I just hoped I wasn't to be sacrificed.

Sultan Bobo is the Mecca of Karakalpakstan. I had suspicions that I might be the first Westerner to visit this holiest of holy places. The architecture was wonderful and all around people lounged waiting for darkness to fall so they could pray and then resume life as normal.

I sat in a tea house with hundreds of pots of tea, and cups and saucers on every surface. It was the Mad Hatter's tea party with a difference. First we were brought bread and sweets. There seemed to be more flies than food. They buzzed around our heads, they covered the food we ate, they even pestered the food you brought to your mouth. I suspect if we hadn't consumed the bread it would have been writhing in maggots within a couple of days.

They then served us meat. I was offered a piece of chicken - a delicacy, the neck. I didn't really know what I was supposed to eat, it was just bone. Waiting until someone else picked up the other neck, I watched as he tore off the skin and sucked the bones. I tried to do the same, nibbling and pecking, but I don't think I did it right.

I played with a boy who wanted to ride my bike whilst the other boys went to pray. I took pictures of him and showed him them on my screen. He squealed with laughter when he saw himself on the bike, taking the camera to show all the adults in the vicinity.

We slept in the same room, waking to eat the bread left over from the previous night that had been marinated in fly the whole time. Slightly nauseous, I was ready to head off but the boys had different ideas.

We cycled in the opposite direction to the main road I was hoping to return to. We headed instead for the mausoleum where Sultan Bobo was supposed to be buried and walked around the building three times anti-clockwise touching the walls, before proceeding to pray.

Next on the agenda was a mountain climb. We all selected a rock at the bottom to take with us and climbed to the top where we placed it on top of a pile of rocks. Some were wrapped in pieces of material - prayer flags. I wondered why we didn't just select a rock at the top.

It would have made the climb much easier.

* * *

After saying my goodbyes to the boys, and being given a third eye on a bracelet to protect me on the rest of my trip, I headed out onto the main road. I was totally amazed when a coach driver gave me the gnarly sign before I even waved. It must have been catching on.

Cotton pickers were everywhere on the road, carrying massive bags full of cotton. It was harvest time and everyone had been put to work.

Entering an old café surrounded by workmen's caravans, I met Kola. He was a tall, slim man with a clear intelligence and dark brown eyes. He endeared himself to me almost immediately by telling me he loved his family. "It's a national custom in Uzbekistan." It was so refreshing after all the offerings of ladies of late. My heart melted.

He invited me to stay the night and to celebrate the fifty-sixth birthday of one of the workers. At fifty-six, Ramil had already outlived the life expectancy for an Uzbek male. It seemed as though he was doing his damndest to try and drink himself into a coffin during the night.

The most important and privileged workers had been invited to the dinner. Praying together before our food, we cupped our hands and, once over, touched our faces. The director was present and asked me to give a speech in Ramil's honour. First I sang 'Happy Birthday' and then toasted his health and family. Everything fell silent. People looked at my glass. I downed the vodka and everyone cheered and clapped, telling me it was a good speech. They so enjoyed watching me down vodka I ended up quite wobbly, obviously not as wobbly or pickled as the Uzbeks, but enough.

The following morning after taking breakfast in the canteen with hundreds of big, strapping Uzbeks, I was joined on my bike by a swallow. She took to diving in front of my Shirley like a dolphin at the bow of a boat. She would then disappear off to the right or left before joining me again at the bow.

* * *

The powers that be again decided I'd been having too much yin and threw me a curved yang. My stomach lurched and I had a split

96

second to get into the bushes, diving through the soft sand. I was wearing cycling bib shorts with straps that went over my shoulders. I had to remove my top and then pull these down before my guts exploded. It was horrible. Imagine having diarrhoea in bib shorts, surrounded by the deepest depths of sand that gets everywhere. Now times that by ten and you can imagine how miserable I was.

Even in my discomfort I couldn't help joking with the police I met as they waved me over and asked me for photos. I swapped my cycle helmet for their top hats before allowing them to snap away.

I had to find a place to stop, and preferably one with a half-decent toilet. I pulled into a café and the toilet had a soft, warming, material seat cover. It would have been awesome if it hadn't been covered in shit.

The owner of the bar, a forty-year-old man, made me a proposition as I tried to fill my now-empty belly. He offered me his wife for the night, showing me her assets in no uncertain terms. Obviously I said no and my distaste for the man began to simmer. I had no energy to do anything as the sickness had taken hold, and regular visits to the latrine were needed. I soon went off to sleep, on my own.

Whilst eating breakfast surrounded by local men and women, the same asshole who had offered me his wife sexually assaulted a girl working at the café. He pinned her to the floor with his weight, which was ample, and let his hands explore. People shook their heads and smiled. She was laughing but it was the laugh of a school child being bullied. I wanted to vomit in his face. Terrible.

The worst of it was that the performance was for my benefit, I am sure. Looking over at me, he smiled and I simply looked away. I hate myself for that. It still hurts almost a year on. But what right had I, a Westerner, to intervene in something that I had no idea about? Man is man here; women share the same privileges as the farm animals. It still haunts me and I know it's happening everywhere.

On your own travels, if you happen to come across Alex in a chai house just before the police station halfway between Nukus and Bukhara, and accidentally spill your boiling chai in a place no man wants to be burnt, then I owe you a drink.

Chapter 19

Bukhara, directly translated as *Beauty*, is an ancient and fairy-tale town, the land of magical lamps and eastern beauties. Ancient Great Silk Road caravans never passed this town by, the only oasis for miles. Nowadays Bukhara is famous not only for its superb historic monuments but for its lively trade. Every traveller finds something unique in this town.

Taking out my map that morning, I had tried to find a way to get out of Uzbekistan. Alex's actions had turned me off a country that I had loved before then. I knew it was silly, bad people exist everywhere. Without additional visas my route was fixed. Bukhara was my next destination.

Just outside of Bukhara, I stopped in a café where a woman bossed the men around, making them do the dirty work. A fat-tailed sheep lived in the garden. Sheep were specifically bred for the unique quality of the fat (called *allyah*) stored in the tail area. They have an ass like Beyoncé Knowles. The fat on the tail area is valuable and the sheep know it. As they walk, their booties shake. I just couldn't look at them with a straight face.

In Bukhara, markets line the streets and fill any open space, selling anything from dried fruit and nuts, to pixie shoes, to meat hung up in the midday heat covered in flies, to traditional musical instruments. The intricately sculptured Minaret Kalian towers over the city, the foundations of which are made with mortar plaster and camel's milk. It is nicknamed the 'Tower of Death' as condemned men were hurled to their doom from the top of it.

* * *

I wandered round the city, my sandalled feet slapping against the red earth that makes up the road system. I was exploring the markets for a teapot I could carry on my bike to make chai in whenever I met nice people. A man cycled past me with a traditional Uzbek cap on, selling naans as big as a table top. Unable to help myself, I bought one for less than forty pence.

Bread is sacred. It should never be thrown away. If people see it on the floor, they pick it up and find a use for it. I had a loaf of bread as big as a table and had to finish it. I had no-one to share it with. Trying to share it with the locals, I was given looks that perhaps I shouldn't be doing it. Many locals have harelips and are cross-eyed. I assumed this was down to the fact that the population of Bukhara is less than two hundred thousand and Muslim culture encourages inter-family marriage.

Holding a kilo of bread in one hand, I tried to change $50 on the black market. I was offered a good rate and beckoned into a darkened room where I met an elderly woman wrapped in many layers of material. Her skin was leathered and wrinkled from the sun; there was no way I could have even guessed how old she was. The lady disappeared for a moment and came back with two stacks of money, five inches thick. She wanted to exchange my single note for multiples of 200som notes. Can you imagine walking round with inches of notes in your pockets? It just didn't feel right so I apologised and left. However, many locals do pull out masses of notes when shopping in the markets.

The Chor Minor, which directly translates as *Four Minarets*, has four turrets with sky blue cupolas. In a labyrinth of winding streets, I bumped into Greg. He looked me up and down and said, "Cyclist?" in his strong Aussie accent. I looked confused as to how he knew. "You look friggin' skinny, you have stupid sock marks and are wearing sandals. It's obvious."

Greg was just the guy I needed to meet right now to make crass jokes about the way women were treated, the working conditions and the child labour. Although it is a serious matter, I'd been taking it too seriously. His jokes and laughter lightened my load. Everyone was experiencing the same and we could do nothing but set better examples.

We were sharing the same hostel, so we walked back together and, amongst the crowds of Germans and French people herded into and out of tour buses, I saw a flash of white, a smile, and a pair of eyes that calmed me at once. Katya and Cedric. They were in the hostel too.

At dinner the four of us sat at the low-lying tables, cross-legged and cramped. I looked around and saw other tourists in the same position, adjusting their butts and legs to make themselves comfortable. Sitting cross-legged isn't something we do in the UK after leaving junior school. On the surrounding tables with normal chairs and tables were all the Uzbek people who must have been wondering why we foreigners were still using this more archaic posture.

An Uzbek girl with bright green eyes caught my eye and I

wandered over to see if I could practise my language skills. She was with a family so I politely bowed, *As Salaam Alaikum*. They returned my greeting with smiles. *Wa Alaykum-as-Salaam*. I was offered food and enjoyed their company for a while. After eating, they asked if I was married. Checking out their new son-in-law, I thought. I pointed and smiled at the girl with the green eyes. "My wife?" I said in Russian. Some laughed but the table was empty within minutes and I was left sitting on my own. Cedric and Katya were laughing behind me in their own marital bliss. It's tough out here being a red-blooded male.

The next morning Cedric and Katya left with a Belgian couple who'd joined our table whilst I was off playing Casanova.

I went into town to visit the local Hamman. Hamman are famous all over Central Asia. Men and women go into separate houses, get naked, get steamed, and then get rubbed to remove dead skin. After washing, they are massaged in a manner that is out of this world. Cracked, squished and beaten to a pulp in a way I have never known. The hamman walked along my body - it was fantastic!

Afterwards a ginger and honey mix is rubbed onto your skin. It burns like acid. Giving me some in my hand, I look quizzically up at him. "Penis," he said. OK. Boiling ginger stem on my nob. Great. It took fifteen buckets of cold water to try and wash it off and it still burnt. But as soon as you are out of the hot rooms, you feel amazing, like you could cycle up mountains and through deserts.

This was quite fortunate. When I arrived back at the hostel, the owner ran up to me waving a credit card in my face. The Belgian couple had left their credit card. Could I take it to them? Travelling to Samarkand, two hundred kilometres away, they were leaving the following evening for China and they needed their card. I had thirty-six hours to get it there...

* * *

So it was with their card tucked in my back pocket I set off for Samarkand. On the outskirts of the city I saw a bank on my right - 'Agro Bank' - reminding me of the banks I'd had dealings with in the past. I lifted my camera to take a picture. Armed guards came out shouting, "No".

I told them there was no need to be so 'Agro', but my *shutka* went down like a lead balloon.

Cycling as far as I could in the little time remaining, I pulled into a shop in Karmana to ask where the nearest gostinitsa was. The old boy behind the counter had dark, wrinkled skin and only two teeth remaining - one in his upper palate, one in his lower. Gurning as he thought about his answer, an idea suddenly sprung into his mind. "You stay my house."

Before we could go home we sat outside his shop. A group of youths congregated around the two of us. My ukulele, camera and iPod combined to produce a beautiful cacophony of noise and lighting.

Arriving at his house, I was poured a small tea. The old man, Halim, put three sugar cubes as large as eight normal ones into my cup and I watched as they dissolved into the hot liquid. His granddaughter, Alexi, joined us. She spoke English excellently and so I was able to ask more questions about their family. They all lived in the same building. This was her granddad's section. She thought her granddad was a very nice man for allowing me to stay and that I looked silly, but enjoyed my iPod and walked around her house taking pictures of family members for me, together with one or two of her one and only toy – a dirty doll that had seen better days. Her name was Charlotte and she didn't like tea but liked to eat the sugar cubes raw. Together the three of us dined on more sugared chai and small boiled sweets.

As time wore on, Alexi was called to her bedroom and Halim and I set up our beds. The usual straw matting was rolled out. There was a bed in his room but it was used as a table for storing important bits and pieces. Halim also slept on a straw mat. Under the mattress was his bank. We did some black market exchanging and consummated the deal with another chai.

The boys I'd met the previous day were all waiting in the morning with their bikes at the shop. We set off together and the usual races ensued. The boys were on their way to the fields with scythes in their hands. The blades pointed dangerously towards their faces. A fall would have meant certain injury, so I slowed and let them continue without distraction.

Approaching Samarkand, I could see the smog like a force field over the city built in a perfect semicircle. Eyeing an empty café, I ordered chai and water. With my chai arrived a group of men from twenty-five to sixty years old who wanted to know everything about me.

I was becoming quite adept at answering the regular questions in Russian. *Where from? Where to? Where is your wife? How old are you? Do you have a wife? Where is your wife? What is your wife's name? How many children?* The questioning became more frantic with the men all wanting to know how a thirty-year-old man could not have a wife. It was completely unheard of. On top of that, a white man. *He obviously has money and this nice, soft skin.* It began again. *Where is your wife? How old? Wife?* In the end I just couldn't take it any more. I shouted, "Ya neit jena". *I no wife.*

With this sign of aggression the men moved away and talked amongst themselves.

As I readied myself to go, one of the group had a final question, "Do you have penis?"

Chapter 20

Passing through the bubble of smog, I entered the city. Prospering from its position on the trade route between China and the Mediterranean, Samarkand is one of the oldest inhabited cities in the world. What remained of the ancient dynasties was breath-taking.

I cycled past the huge Registan, the ancient city centre, a place of public executions where people gathered to hear royal proclamations heralded by blasts on enormous copper pipes called *dzharchis*. It comprises three *Madrasah*. The Muslim education institution, its archways and its intricate Arabic writing are quite awe-inspiring, not least because of the Registan's positioning between the old town and the newer upmarket cafés and hotels. Next, on my way to the hostel and my friends, I was longing to see the Guri Amir Mausoleum with its intricate mosaic artwork, tall minarets and blue tiled dome.

The first person I bumped into at the hostel was Greg. He was even more single than I was, and older too, and his sharp wit and gutter humour got me laughing immediately. Katya and Cedric heard the laughter and came running so that we were again able to share a hug. I passed the credit card over to the Belgian couple with due pomp and ceremony minutes before the taxi arrived to take them to the airport.

Katya was raring to tell me a story of their journey where they had been forced to make a prayer flag out of knicker elastic to avoid undue attention. It was so great to be around these people again with whom I had shared more time than with any others over the last three months.

Night time soon fell and I was reminded again that winter was coming fast and that I would be encountering snow in the high passes which lay ahead of me. Greg and I took our cameras for some night shots of the two buildings I'd seen on the way in. We managed to get some fabulous pictures before the police arrived. I quickly threw my camera into my bag as if we had just been walking. I feared they were going to delete our photos or, worse, confiscate our cameras. I let Greg's sharp tongue do the speaking and hung back sheepishly, listening to what they had to say. They asked where we were from, where our wives were, and how old we were before inviting us to climb one of the minarets in exchange for a big old hunk of baksheesh – bribery.

Leaving the police to their scams, we found the only hotel in town known to sell beer and spent their bribe on a few glasses. On the dance floor guys writhed with other guys and the girls sat in a separate room.

Sitting with the women, we were soon told to get up and move to the other room where the men gesticulated that we should dance with them, or have sex. It was difficult to tell the two apart. Having yet to recover from my incident in the restaurant, I couldn't handle the men touching me and forcefully dragging me to the dance floor, so Greg and I left, 'sexy dancing' all the way back to the hostel.

* * *

My camera was flashing.

I was at the Registan again. The sun was rising and the morning glow made the monument even more impressive than during my previous encounters. My camera however was trained on the people cleaning, polishing, wiping it. The people had equal if not more beauty than the monument. One or two pointed and laughed at my interest, encouraging their minder to come over with a broom and shoo me away.

The streets were coming to life. Scratch card sellers were offering people the chance to win small amounts of money. Then there were the usual chai sellers, mobile bakers and commuters.

Bibi Mosque was next on my itinerary. Since 1974 the whole mosque has been reconstructed after its collapse in an earthquake, but the bazaar at its foot has changed very little in 600 years. As I have already mentioned, I'd been searching for an appropriate teapot as a focus point for meetings with strangers in the streets and villages I was passing through on my bike. I wasn't looking for anything particularly aesthetic but I was very specific in my ideas of how the pot should make me feel. I'd been looking for weeks now in all the small bazaars. I'd searched Bukhara to no avail. But this market had it all. Passing a lady begging with a fist full of som, I saw the stall I was looking for and knew I'd found my pot. Between the rotting fly-covered flesh that was sold and made into our dinners in the evening and a hat shop selling a thousand varieties of the *Taqiyah*, the Muslim skull cap, there was a stall with a variety of kitchen implements - some brand-new modern kettles; other older lamps that were used in primitive houses for lighting. Behind all these was *my* teapot. It looked a little battered already but most things did in these stalls. *Skolko*? I asked how much it was. Amused, the owner held up a newer, more modern teapot. *Niet, shto*. No, this one. I said pointing at the original one.

2000 som – just over a dollar. I couldn't argue with that. As I handed over the cash, the shop owner emptied his used tea leaves onto the floor and handed me his pot. Little did he know how much I would treasure it.

Katya, Cedric and I shared a brew back at the hostel and were the first to sign the teapot with my permanent marker before heading off to Northern Central Asia. It was a tough goodbye – without the stimulus of the outside world and without my friends and family, Cedric and Katya had become both.

* * *

In the evening I met a German lady who talked about her spiritual journey. Although I kept telling myself it was all a load of poppycock, my breathing and heart rate upped when she talked about the centre of the spiritual world being in Tibet and India. Was I destined to find what my soul had been looking for?

* * *

The borders between the ex-Soviet republics are crazy. One road in the south of Uzbekistan winds in and out of three countries continuously over a stretch of a hundred miles. Surely there aren't border police at each point? An adjoining train line does exactly the same. My next leg led me to Tashkent, the capital of Uzbekistan. To get there, a direct route passed into Kazakhstan and then out again within a couple of miles. Another road wound round a little more but stayed in Uzbekistan.

Stopping for chai on the road that stayed within the border of Uzbekistan, I had a conversation with an English-speaking local. I told him that I still hadn't had a puncture and had no need for lights because I never cycled at night.

Alakazam...

A mile down the road a nail went through my tyre. It got dark while I found my puncture kit at the bottom of my bags after unloading everything – time for the mozzies to come out. I was being bitten to death. They were everywhere - in my ears, in my hair, in my clothing … it was horrible. Pumping up the tyre as quickly as possible so I could get on my way and leave these wetlands alone, I continued to pump away and **BANG!**, the other inner tube burst as well. I hadn't put it on right and the tyre had pinched it, so all the pressure went to one part. Again I had to unload my bags and again the mozzies bit hard. My biggest fear was malaria – although not endemic in Uzbekistan, there was still a risk of catching it.

I carried on with no lights, with locals driving carelessly down both sides of the street. The next chai house welcomed me in, fed me, showed me to a bed, and then the owner took me thirty minutes down the road to meet his wife and child. Once back, he brought out more food which I wolfed down whilst closely watching the progress of a big spider (a monster by UK standards, as big as my hand with legs like my fingers). The owner saw me freeze and calmly came over, smiled at me and stamped on it. I heard the squelch as its body exploded. Before he left, the owner made a point of making sure I knew I didn't have to pay for anything. I couldn't quite grasp his rationale. I was the only diner and he employed three members of staff at least to run the place. But there is no arguing with an Uzbek.

As I lay down to sleep with a curtain pulled round my bed, two women started talking, softly at first but then shouting and finally screaming like cats. Luckily someone else had the TV so loud that their screams were barely audible and I was able to sleep soundly.

The three hundred kilometre journey to Tashkent brought few surprises and I trundled into town ready for a rest in a decent hotel. For some reason hostels don't exist in Tashkent. I was looking forward to a treat.

Tashkent is the capital of Uzbekistan, a city that rivalled Baghdad in its prime. It is the oldest city in Central Asia and the most beautiful if you believe what its tourist board says. Either way I was looking forward to having a look round its numerous markets, monuments and tourist sites. Tashkent is also famous for a more sinister reason. The police here are notorious throughout Asia for fleecing the tourists.

Unfortunately, after visiting a number of hotels who wouldn't allow me to stay, it wasn't looking like I was going to be able to see these sights. In fact it was looking like I wasn't going to be seeing any more of Uzbekistan, let alone China and India.

Uzbekistan requires that you register with a hotel within three days of arriving in the country and then every day from then onwards. Cycling through the Kyzylkum Desert, I had been sleeping in my million star hotel - my tent - nearly every day since my arrival. When I arrived in the capital, the hotel owners said they would normally call the police at this point and that they would slap me with a $2,000 fine, my whole budget to get me to my final destination. Fortunately they took pity on me and Shirley, and told us to cycle onwards. As I walked out the door, the hotelier would pick up the phone with a serious look on his face. Was he speaking to the police?

My fourth hotel took my passport and gave me a key to a room. The relief was immense, I immediately relaxed and stepped into the shower to remove the usual grime. Then a knock came at the door. I answered it in a towel with soap suds still in my hair. "Mr Bent? Problem." Here we go again. But no...

The lack of papers was only the half of it. I'd also failed to notice that my visa was valid for ten days and I was on day nineteen in Uzbekistan. It was looking like I was going to be deported back to the UK.

I'd made it so far. I'd endured the wild dogs in Poland, the sand storms in Kazakhstan, the vodka drinking in Russia and the guns pointed at my head in the Ukraine. Surely I hadn't gone through this for nothing – to be thwarted by my lack of organization and my failure to do any research on the countries I'd be visiting. I needed to flee this city for the country, but the police almost certainly knew me by now and there was no way I was getting get out of Tashkent without paying out a king's ransom.

Chapter 21

I searched my brain in desperation. Was there anyone who might be able to help? Something triggered in my brain and I remembered the first day I'd set off to Dover with friends and family.

I remembered cycling with Derek, a guy from my cycle club, and his saying something about Uzbekistan. I grabbed my diary and searched through to that first day. There, stuck in between Day One and Day Two, was Derek's business card. On the other side in scrawled handwriting was: *Maksud – Tashkent*, and a phone number written below. He was the brother of a friend. Should I call him? What harm could a phone call do? Maybe he could help?

Maksud drove straight over. He spoke calmly but forcefully with the hotel owner. He knew a man who might be able to help. A member of the Russian Mafia. There was no time to lose.

Pulling into a darkened alleyway, we left the engine running. Twenty metres ahead, the door of a Tata Nano (a tiny old two-seater Russian vehicle) opened, and slowly our man unfolded himself from the car. He was well over six-and-a-half foot and almost the same wide. He opened the back door of our car and I felt the suspension sag under his weight as he sat down. As we drove away, the two men discussed the situation in Russian. Within a few minutes we pulled alongside a house that would have been big by English standards let alone Central Asian. Behind a tall fence the huge Russian - to whom I was never formally introduced - proceeded to unlock the door to the house. It took four different keys to deal with the deadbolts and, when he pulled it open, I could see that the door itself was two inches thick. Behind this door was another that required the same level of attention before it would open in its turn.

Inside, the house looked like a palace. Statues lined the walls and antiques were intermingled with high-tech gadgets and TVs. I was taken for a tour before the two people I assumed had been my saviours left, locking the doors behind them. I tried the front door, but no, I was locked into a Russian safe house.

Sitting in front of the TV watching Russian soaps and dubbed Hollywood movies, I waited. Two days later, Maksud returned and I was told to get my stuff, we were leaving.

I had to keep my head down as we drove through the police checks. When we hit the open highway, we pulled over and I extricated my bike from the boot, and my new friend waved to me as

I cycled into the mountains.

* * *

Waving goodbye to Maksud was like saying goodbye to a bodyguard. The rest was up to me now; he'd done everything he could.

I would pass through towns with my head down and stop to sleep in empty Chai Hanna where the owners were happy to let me lie across benches to earn a few extra bucks.

For three days I continued in this manner. There were police stops as usual, but it required little more than adding my passport number to a dog eared book and they were too interested in having their pictures taken, playing my ukulele and asking for presents to pay attention to the passport.

Trying to remain inconspicuous, I stopped to tighten up one of my panniers. I looked round as there was some serious Uzbek dance music resonating from the nearest house. I walked towards the music and, as I reached the house, two ladies jumped out from the front door, wrapped me in sheets of ribbons, and dragged me into the courtyard, leaving Shirley outside. Inside I danced with all the children and ate anything that was passed to me by the women waiting on their men.

After a few minutes, a boy came from nowhere looking particularly done up and riding a donkey. People stuffed notes into any of the boy's orifices they could get to. He looked absolutely scared to bits. I realised I'd arrived at a coming of age party and became afraid that they might drag me into the whole bizarre episode, but fortunately I was just seated in the elders' room (filled with the wisest and oldest men in the village) where the finest of foods were served. They could have put me in the regular men's room which was across the corridor.

The young boys weren't allowed in either but sat in doorways waiting and hoping for the year when they would be accepted to have reached manhood. They took scrap bits and sent for more food as soon as their Western guest showed any interest in any one type. One young boy had been staring at me for quite some time before he plucked up the courage to tap me on the knee and ask, "Wayne Rooney?" The eyes of the men lit up. How did these people in the middle of nowhere know Wayne Rooney, and what on earth was possessing the Uzbek man to think I was him? Yeah, I have white skin, yes I have a ginger beard, yes I have a round head and a barrel chest, yes I have small, sharp eyes ... oh shit ... I do look like him.

Highly privileged, I was shown the ladies' chambers. Again the the expression in the eyes changed. I was looked upon as an escape or as a money sack made of skin and bone. Mothers thrust their daughters towards me. I soon made a neat exit to find Shirley had made a friend too. The once-ridden donkey was nibbling at her handlebars. A strange pang of jealousy ran through me and I shooed the donkey off, wiping the saliva off Shirley to make her mine again.

* * *

Only the mountain passes lay between Uzbekistan and Kyrgyzstan now, between me and my safety. Cars were strewn along the way, victims of the steep passes and harsh climate. Some had crashed over cliffs leaving charcoaled remains, others had just been deserted.

Growing tired, I got more and more agitated at the attention I, Shirley and my belongings were getting. I was fed up of people saying I looked like Wayne Rooney. Before I reached the top of the highest pass I stopped in a restaurant where, as always, they allowed me to stay. The waiter wanted to ride my bike. I didn't see why he shouldn't. Unfortunately the weight was too much for him and Shirley dragged him to the floor, to the laughter of everyone around. He had taken my sunglasses for his ride (such a vital piece of equipment in these parts to protect from snow blindness) and in falling had broken one of the arms off and smashed the screen of my camcorder. The anger boiled up inside me, but what could I do, demand he take a three-year advance in his wages so he could pay for the damage?

However, he did make it up to me later, asking me to sign a 500som note, the second largest denomination. He stated he was going to frame it in his room that he shared with four siblings. Soon huge-bosomed women would be parting their shirts for me to sign their assets.

Climbing into the mountains, I was beginning to show my first signs of altitude sickness. I had a headache and was breathless even when I lay down. Sleep came quickly but so did my awakening. At 5:30 I was woken by a drum and bass beat pounding away. Looking up I saw the daughter of the owner praying. The pumping beat was surreal under the purposeful prayer.

As I was continuing towards the pass in the morning, a police car sounded its siren and pulled in alongside me. Shit! Looking at me sternly, the policeman started to speak. Drawing on all the energy in my body, I gave him my biggest smile as I greeted him. *As-Salaam-Alaykum*. He smiled back and through the window he took hold of my arm and made me hold on tightly to his wrist. He accelerated his car as he spoke to me in a kind and interested way. He was dragging me up the mountain. Just like in old Mega Drive games, I'd held down the fire button and blasted my way through with my finest of smiles. I was beginning to feel the faint glimmer of hope rising around me.

The descent to the border was a large hole held together by tiny bits of tarmac. I flew past cars as I swerved to remain on the road at sixty kilometres per hour, including one estate car whose chassis was dragging along the floor as it had been loaded with a whole house including sink and cupboards. They were clearly relocating.

Again stopping at a chai house I was offered a bucket to wash with. Humming after days without a shower and all the hill climbing, I set to scrubbing myself up as best I could. All the boys from the village were watching me standing in my boxers. I sensitively asked if I could clean what was inside my boxers but they gave a shocked, "No! People watching!" looking over their shoulders.

"I know," I thought. "You lot!!"

Slightly cleaner and more refreshed, I was invited to join a celebratory feast with twenty men from twenty to thirty years old. When I started to eat, I was told off for using my fork in the wrong hand. Being left-handed, it's natural for me to use my left hand but this is the hand used for cleaning one's bottom. I was then told off for pulling the spoon towards me rather than pushing away. I greeted any newcomers with the religious Muslim greeting "*As-Salaam-Alaykum*'" and everyone in the room burst out laughing. The guests continuously left the room and came back in again, encouraging me to repeat my statement. We were in the Benzin Bar – Petrol Bar. It seemed like an appropriate name for a bar in a country where I was sure they would drink benzene.

* * *

The next day it was time to face the border. It was a make or break moment for my whole trip.

It is hard to remain invisible when you are the only white guy in the queue, especially when all the locals were pushing me to the front, cheering and patting me on the back.

My hopes disappeared. This wasn't your usual Uzbek security check. Computers, printers, TVs and film equipment were conspicuously set up in a fashion that filled me with fear. The border guard welcomed me. *"As-Salaam-Alaykum"*. I took a breath and returned his greeting, *"Wa Alaykum-as-Salaam,"* as I handed him my passport. He flipped through the pages, typing my details into the computer. He looked at my passport then at the screen. Something wasn't adding up. Again he looked from one to the other. He turned to beckon over his supervisor. I had to do something. The game was up. There was only one thing for it. I stroked my beard and pointed at myself whilst enunciating as precisely and clearly as I could two words: "Wayne Rooney".

His eyes turned back to me. He looked me straight in the face. A pause ensued which gave me enough time to consider what I was going to say to mum when I called her from Heathrow Airport. The entire staff in army uniform had left their seats and were coming round to my side of the desk. SH*T. I put my hands up in the sign of surrender. They were upon me. They were smiling. They were holding their phones up to take pictures. My passport was thrust into my hand, freshly stamped and each and every guard wanted his picture taken with me before allowing me to cycle on my way.

Chapter 22

I made the short ride from the Dostuk border to Osh.

Osh is the second largest city in Kyrgyzstan, located in the Fergana Valley in the south of the country, and often referred to as the 'Capital of the South'. The city is at least 3,000 years old.

I followed the cryptic instructions to find the Osh Guesthouse. I was in a mood to celebrate. No fines, no deportation, my ego was still dealing with my likeness to Rooney, but I was sure a few beers would put an end to that too.

Before I'd carried Shirley across the threshold and dropped off my bags, I was asked to go out celebrating with French and Norwegians. I'd endeared myself to the Vikings by telling them my favourite words in Norwegian. "Rumpetroll", *tadpole*, and "du er djevelen", *you are the devil*.

We headed out for food first but, in true Central Asian style, vodka and lots of it accompanied the fine cuisine. The food had flavours, spices, substance, aroma and, most importantly, wasn't sheep fat.

Whilst we sat devouring plate after plate, and bottle after bottle, there was a scuffle in the club that was situated at the back of the restaurant. One man came out covered in blood. Then another. Another was wielding a rather large knife. We sat and stared, concerned for our own safety, as another guy with blood streaming from a head wound appeared holding a girl who'd been stabbed. No-one in the bar really paid them any attention.

If it had been in England, it would have either erupted into a mass brawl or people would have been killed in the crush to leave the restaurant. In the end a gargantuan man arrived to sort out disagreements. He didn't look like the kind of guy who was averse to a bit of blood, especially if it wasn't his own. He wore a tight vest encasing his voluminous muscles, and a scar down his left cheek running up into his hairline.

Just his presence was enough to calm everything down, and everyone left quietly without him having to even raise his voice. His face wore an expression of disappointment.

Everything returned to normal and so did we. I'm not really sure how we got there but quite a lot of vodka and beer later we were in a club dancing wildly to Asian Techno, throwing shapes that I thought were New Age Michael Jackson, but to anyone not completely inebriated probably looked more like old school epilepsy. Luckily there weren't any of that type in the club.

Slowly everyone left. It was just me and an Afro-French guy, Jean-Pierre, the only black guy I'd seen in Asia. A conversation I'd had in Uzbekistan about Central Asians having no respect for African people was completely forgotten as locals bought us drink after drink, dancing with us and laughing.

It was early morning and we thought we'd better leave. Neither of us was in any fit state to hail a cab, so one of the locals we'd been dancing with offered to share one with us to reduce costs. Not long after we left, he told the taxi to stop and we fell out of the cab looking for our hotel and giggling when we couldn't recognise it.

The guy we'd shared the taxi with asked us for money, politely. We'd forgotten to pay the cab. Ooopss. More giggles. JP gave the man more than double what a reasonable taxi should have cost but he wanted more. So he doubled what he'd given. "More". At this point the taxi was driving away. *Oh you want all of our money.* I was busy getting my wallet out but JP was saying "Non, fuck you" in his strong French accent.

The local kicked him in the balls and then punched him in the face, calling him racist names. I went to intervene but before I could even say, 'Come on that is quite enough', JP had fisted this guy more times than I could count in my inebriated state, had thrown him in the air, tied him in a knot and was pushing some pressure point on the man's shoulder that was causing him to whimper and beg for mercy.

He'd picked on the wrong guy. JP was a black belt in Ninjitsu.

An equally fast movement caught my eye to the right and JP was flailing on the floor having been kicked in his chest. I looked around and there was the big guy from the restaurant. Where did he come from? He was too big to hide behind the local housing.

The fight that ensued was nothing short of 'Rocky IV'. Speed and agility vs. strength and grit. My brain revisited the conversation I'd had in Uzbekistan, the knife fight in the restaurant. I told JP this wasn't England, that you can't do this here, before realising he was French. *You're not in France.* But no use, he was in fighting mood. He shoved me out of the way. With blood on the road, the big guy eventually had JP on the floor, pinned by his arms, and sitting on his chest. He kept punching into his face with fists like sledgehammers. I pulled at him and in my most fluent Russian to date got his attention. I tried to reason with him. I praised his machismo.

I heard cars arriving behind me and relaxed. People were here to help. I didn't take my eyes off the big guy just in case he started beating Jean-Pierre again.

As I heard footsteps running towards me, I looked to see who our saviour was, just in time to see a huge fist flying towards my face. I felt my lip tear as the fist made contact and then a whole storm of punches thundered into my body, pounding my liver, kidneys, face, and legs. I pulled myself free and realised our game was up. JP was being punched again. It dawned on me that JP was at risk of being killed.

Stumbling back, I saw a police car go by a few blocks away and ran for both of our lives. With my lungs burning, I managed to catch their attention and told them what was happening. They put me in a taxi and told the driver to take me to the tourist part of town. I only had an English £5 left after the robbery. The driver phoned his mate to see what it was worth.

Chapter 23

Waking up in the morning with a blood-stained face and sheets, I staggered into reception. My muscles were bruised, my joints ached, I felt like the walking dead. The owner pointed to a sign saying "DON'T STAY OUT AFTER 11pm especially if you have been drinking". Perhaps it would have been wiser to show me the sign when I first checked in.

Osh is a town that was central to the ancient trading routes, acting as a crossroads to the Silk Routes. It was prosperous and hence fought over constantly, and it has been wrapped in violence since the collapse of the Russian Empire. Initially, arguments with the Uzbeks over the closely located border led to bloodshed. As an ongoing issue, many Uzbeks live in Osh and ethnic violence simmers then erupts occasionally.

Sitting listening in the corner to our stories of the previous day was a guy skinnier than skinny. His name was Matt. He had just cycled the Pamir mountain range and was waiting to hear word that the Chinese border had reopened so he could continue to Kashkar, the end of his journey. The Chinese had closed their borders for two weeks due to it being sixty years since the founding of the People's Republic of China by Mao Zedong on 1 October 1949.

The Pamir was the next mountain range I would come across and I was already nervous about how Shirley and I would fare. Suffering heavy snow fall, closed roads and climbs that tested him to his very core, Matt surprisingly declared that the worst of all was the 'goat effect' - houses built out of goat's poo bricks entombing a fire fuelled by dried goat's poo briquettes that burnt like coal on a fire but gave off a less than pleasant aroma. On top of these fires would simmer a boiling pan filled with, you guessed it, goat. Goat soup was the staple diet of the Tajiks - half water, half oil, then a tiny bit of carrot, half a small potato and an unidentifiable lump of goat.

Matt complained of smelling like a goat, even straight out of the shower. His water on the bike tasted like goat and his toothpaste tasted like goat too. Goat had permeated every inch of his being.

I couldn't wait but before I could venture into these highlands, with their four-thousand-metre plateau, I had a town to explore.

* * *

Osh is known to have the most bustling bazaar in all of Asia. Inside the bazaar you can't stop moving. It was like a conveyor belt of people. Making your decision, you had to hand over the money before you were shunted onto the next stall. If you weren't quick enough, you'd grab some bananas and then hand the money over to the hat shop, leaving a very bitter banana man and a very happy hatter.

Venturing through the bazaars we were joined by Matt who laughed each time any of us made a purchase. He prided himself on the fact that he was barely carrying anything other than what was on his body. He had cycle shorts, two shirts and a pair of trousers - and that was it. Comparing it with my tent, stove, winter gear and sleeping bag, he was massively under-prepared. Without any kit he had to find civilization each night, and accommodating civilization at that. I was sad for him; I couldn't help thinking he was missing out on some adventures. His bike was a steel framed 1970s 16 speed, which looked quite stylish but, with aged tyres and rusting parts, I had no idea how he had made it so far.

As we bought nuts and sweets he asked me to pay for him because he only had a big note. I had travelled a bit after university and I knew from experience that you always come across a 'Big Note Guy' who will never pay for anything if he only has a Big Note. It's self-perpetuating, of course. If you never break a big note then you never have small notes, but I gave him the benefit of the doubt.

I told the others I'd meet them back at the hostel. I'd noticed a quiet area in the market where old men were playing backgammon. I was invited to take a seat and a hatter came over and put a big fur hat on my head for warmth. The winter was setting in fast which only made me want to get going and be over the bigger mountains sooner rather than later. Somehow I found myself on the winning side against the café owner. Admittedly, at about 117 years old (or thereabouts), he could barely lift the pieces or see the board. The hatter now took up his champion's mantle as the café owner went back to serving brews in thimble-sized white plastic cups. The two of us drew quite a crowd and the hatter and his supporters laughed as I made mistakes, not completely knowing the rules. Onlookers tried to find a taker for a bet; but no-one was backing the white guy. I eventually got the hang of it and, with the most amazing dice rolls, found myself in a tied position. The hatter was beginning to sweat and I began to laugh. The blacksmith made a bet with the man selling birds in tiny boxes, backing me. He received a look of annoyance from the hatter. Luck was in my favour and I managed to clear up without his having made any sort of dent. Not looking very happy, he shook my hand and took the hat off my head. It was time for me to leave. I offered to buy the hat at his asking price and this seemed to soften the blow. I discovered that wearing that hat meant I commanded more respect. People nodded as I went by. This was clearly the hat of winners.

The aggression in Osh was so clear. Youngsters wrestled in the street. No man made way for anyone. The fur hat gave me a presence and no one caused me any mischief as night fell on my way home.

(Shortly after I returned to England, a well-orchestrated, well-financed effort by armed groups to provoke conflict between Kyrgyz and Uzbeks caused 170 people to lose their lives and 250,000 Uzbeks to be displaced from their homes).

When I got back to the hostel, I encountered a bike outside encumbered with a huge amount of luggage - four large panniers, a stuff bag, a handlebar box and a rucksack. I couldn't imagine the pain of carrying all that up the mountain ranges. This guy made me look like a lightweight traveller. Sander had been travelling on his bike for nine months. He'd met a Turkish girl and had lived with her family for some time, and was now touring the world by bike, trying to leave his past of drugs, sex and rock and roll behind him for the simple, honest routine of a tour cyclist.

* * *

There is one quarter of the oxygen at 4,000 metres as there is at sea level, hence the body pumps more blood to the brain to compensate for this, causing headaches, nausea, exhaustion and shortness of breath. At anything over three thousand metres, High Altitude Cerebral Edema (HACE) can set in, which occurs when the excess blood causes the brain to swell. Symptoms of this are inhibited mental function, hallucinations, loss of muscle coordination, impaired speech and severe headaches. The result of this is that you could possibly end up in a coma.

Leaving Osh I had to climb to 4,000 metres, three times as high as the highest point in the UK, Ben Nevis. Cycling for one minute I would then stop and hang over my handlebars, sucking in as much air as possible in an attempt to get oxygen into my body. My head was pounding.

As I stopped by the side of the road, a lady said she would get me some soup to warm me. She came out with some grey liquid that was lukewarm and clearly made with unclean water. My brain couldn't think of an excuse fast enough as to why I shouldn't drink it, so I ended up having to down the lot. I knew this could only end up in a number of trips to the toilet but it made her happy seeing me eat and drink.

Wrapped up in all my winter gear, I plugged on doggedly with sweat running down the insides of my clothes and yet the cold was attacking my nose and eyes, my only exposed areas. I'd read about frostbite in Osh and, with my hands and feet numb, the same warning played over and over in my mind.

"If you have frostbite, you may not realize at first that anything is wrong because the affected area will be numb. With prompt medical attention, most people recover fully from frostbite. However, in the case of severe frostbite, permanent damage is possible, depending on how long and how deeply the tissue is frozen. In severe cases, blood flow to the area may stop and blood vessels, muscles, nerves, tendons and bones may be permanently affected. If the frozen tissue dies, the area may need to be amputated."

The Texas Mountaineer

I checked my hands regularly to make sure they weren't blackening.

Not far from the summit I could see a horse rider in the distance standing by the side of the road. I felt an uneasiness about this for some reason. Wearing a balaclava, he looked menacing, but my whole face was covered too from the cold. Struggling to hit walking speed he pulled out in front of me but I was able to dodge round him, only to be attacked by his whip. He was a bandit and wanted my belongings.

My good fortune continued as the first car I'd seen all morning pulled up alongside me. An arm through the window grabbed mine and the speed at which I was dragged away left the horseman in his tracks with a look of shock in his eyes.

It started to rain, washing the sweat from my face and feeling cleansing. Coming over the peak of the mountain, however, I saw that I faced a long descent. The wind, as I screamed along, penetrated every piece of my clothing. It went on and on and I got colder and colder. I was beginning to shake uncontrollably and I couldn't feel my hands or feet. I couldn't be sure about being able to use the brakes if I had to. If I hit a lump in the road it could throw me anywhere.

It was such a relief when I finally approached some buildings - I would have cheered if my lips hadn't been frosted shut – and to realise that one of them was my saviour, a tea house. Dripping muddy water over the floor and shaking uncontrollably, I rummaged through my gear for dry clothing and sat huddled over a cup of tea. The owner motioned with her hands to the side of her face that maybe I would like to sleep there. Oh my goodness, no more cycling. "Yes please."

I was taken to a metal circular building - a metal yurt. The room was full of budgies in cages that generated a small amount of heat for the room. There was also a table and chairs in there, but no bed. I was invited to eat with the family in their home. Warming up, I noticed the daughters were dressed in less than I would wear back in England on a cold day, let alone in the mountains. I popped back to my lodgings to find a family in there eating their supper. I felt sorry for them having to endure the smell of my kit but they seemed happy to have me there. The dad was the head of the local police and this, I was informed with a sweeping hand, was his family. I grabbed some of my warm gear - my down jacket, a jumper and woolly hats - and draped them round the shoulders of the daughters who looked awkward but appreciated the extra heat. After dinner, the daughters went into the kitchen where they had to prepare food for the guests. They were making *manti*, stuffed pasta. I asked if I could have a go at making it myself and, with a startled look, they said yes, giggling behind my back. I rolled and cut the pasta and then stuffed it with the meat before pinching the parcels shut. When I stopped, their younger brother, who'd sat the whole time watching them, asked if he could also help. It felt as if I might have closed the sex gap in this one household.

The father and elder brother came home from work and were also very cold. Luckily my collection of hats had only got bigger during my travels and I was able to give them fur hats to help them combat the cold that crept under the door of every house, taking the weakest with it as it left in the morning. Hypothermia can claim the old, the young or the sickly if the body is allowed to drop from its normal 98.6 degrees to 95 degrees.

Suddenly my stomach took a turn for the worse. The soup I had drunk earlier that day had decided to poison me and a brutal evacuation was imminent. Was this my punishment for being polite?

I had to make repeated trips to the toilet which was an outbuilding seventy metres from the house. Unfortunately it was pitch black and my torch was still in the building with the policeman, and I didn't want to interrupt them again. On the way out to the toilet, I fell into a roadside drain wearing sandals and my warmest woollen socks. Shit! (literally). These socks, which I'd brought to get me through the cold of the Himalayas, needed to be thrown away.

When it was time for bed, the mum cleared the table from the head of police and lay a blanket on top of it with another two blankets to wrap around me. This was my bed for the night. Luckily, with the hypothermia, bad guts and tough mountain climbing I couldn't have slept better in the Pea Princess' bed.

As I left the following day, the daughters gave me a colourful plastic bracelet and a keyring to attach to a phone which I hung on my mascot, my school sheep.

* * *

I pulled away into the mountains again and was greeted by laughing, smiling kids who threw stones at me. Jokingly I shouted out '*Moi Dumba*' in pain, whilst motioning that they'd scored a hit on my bottom which encouraged another hail of stones to fall on and around me. I'm not sure if the same kids released them but a pack of dogs chased me for another kilometre. They didn't scare me any more; they were just like everyone else, looking for something to do.

Looking for a chai house, I saw a large building that looked like it might be one, so I stopped. Arriving at the front door I realised it was a school. As I touched the door, two teachers ran over from opposite directions. They'd both been relaxing in their own homes, leaving the kids on their own.

Within thirty seconds I'd been pushed into a room of thirty children, all with their mouths hanging open at the sight of the Lycra-clad white guy with the ginger beard and sun-touched face. I read a story and made barking noises, smelling like the dog I was reading about.

As I went along, I introduced a number of other animals that I mimicked as best I could, and I imagined Lucy sitting in the class saying, "You're embarrassing yourself, Sir. You've gone too far," but the children's faces had lit up and some were laughing and smiling.

The school was made of two small rooms and a cupboard that was used as a staff room where I found myself drinking tea and eating biscuits with both teachers who had left their classes again.

On leaving the school, I waved to the children who pressed themselves against the class window. As I rode off I could hear a chorus of pig squeaks, mooing, and barking behind me at the school.

Chapter 24

The *Qur'an* is widely known to be the religious text of Islam. Muslims believe the *Qur'an* to be the verbal divine guidance and moral direction for mankind. It states that *Kafirs* (non-believers) will be subject to eternal torture, whereas believers will be able to trough in rivers of wine and enjoy unlimited sexual pleasures with supernatural houri virgins.

The Bible has its moments too. In 'Judges 21', God orders the murder of all the people of Jabesh-Gilead, except for the virgin girls who were taken to be forcibly raped and married.

In a chai house in the middle of nowhere surrounded by mountainous white peaks, I met three Muslims who seemed to believe they were already in the afterlife and were thus bathing in rivers of vodka in the absence of wine. As a non-believer, I was asked to join them while they tried to persuade me of the wisdom, perks and benefits of the Islamic faith, forcefully attempting to lubricate my enlightenment with ample quantities of vodka. However, with a stomach still doing loops and somersaults between regular explosions, I had to refrain, which elicited complaints that I wasn't being respectful towards them.

They then asked me if I wanted a prostitute and were again disappointed at my refusal (I think I can quite honestly say that the girls they were planning to call were not houri virgins). So they took me to their car instead to show me the gun they owned. Was this a more aggressive tactic to convert me?

Goodnight. *Spokoinoi nochi.* This was the final straw. I made my excuses and went to my room. For a change I had a lumpy mattress and a pillow stuffed with beans. I think I preferred the straw mats.

Whilst I lay there waiting for sleep, I couldn't help thinking about religion. I went over and over the events that led me to embarking on this trip. I was beginning to feel some belief, belief in the universe. When I was having trouble with my Russian visa, I bumped into someone who worked for the embassy on the underground in London. When I was questioning my ability, a stranger would speak of the positivity which enveloped me. If someone is trying to do something that can change the world for the better, then perhaps the world conspires to help them in the same way as a humane being would encourage something that makes us feel good and reject something that makes us feel bad. Is the universe a single being that evolves? Is this God?

* * *

Spokoinoi nochi rarely means goodnight in the Stans and here was no exception. I was fortunate enough to have these three men as my room companions.

A couple of hours after I'd left them, they stumbled in. One collapsed half-on, half-off his bed and started snoring. The louder of the three went next door with a prostitute (I know because their bed was next door to mine, only separated by a thin wooden wall). The third came to much the same conclusion but without the help of another. Good Muslims, huh? I'll have to re-read the Koran. I'm sure my Year 3 kids had a better understanding of its interpretation than these three.

The next morning, a turning over in my stomach was the only thing that could get me out of bed. It was freezing and I had three blankets and a duvet on top of me. I went to the outdoor loo. It's probably appropriate to warn you that all toilets are going to be outdoors from now on. Without the sanitary levels of the West, it just wouldn't be possible to have them indoors. This one was particularly ornate. Have you ever created sand castles by dribbling the sand between your fingers to form turrets and spires? This toilet had equally impressive compositions but they were all made out of poo, all round the sides of the hole in the floor, all over the piping systems. These people needed some intensive target practice.

On the road, the switchbacks started. Switchbacks occur when the mountain is too steep for the road and the road has to wind up it by going from side to side. Stopping to catch my breath, curse and shiver, I shimmied up the mountain. At 4,300 metres the air was so thin I was gasping for each breath. The snow was deep on either side of the road, my water bottle had frozen solid, I had frost on my gloves and needed my Buff to protect my face.

Disaster struck.

The rack holding my front panniers snapped and they fell off. I tried to fasten them back onto my bike with a spare bungee chord. My arms and hands shook uncontrollably. Each time I nearly had them fastened, a violent shiver would knock them back to the floor. I was getting colder and colder. Exhaustion sets in fast when you have no air to breathe and I was beginning to get the feeling that I wanted to curl up in a ball and sleep for what would have been eternity (the

124

first sign of hypothermia). Finally the chord pulled tight and the panniers were on, although my bike was out of balance with the right pannier pulling me towards the edge of the road and the steep run off.

It's hard to push yourself to raise your body heat on a descent and especially one where the road is covered with snow and ice, and I could see that for miles there was nothing but snow, ice and rock. Suddenly, in the middle of a rocky outcrop, I came across a metal shack where a family lived in a single room. It was here that I tasted my first goat soup. It was revolting but I gulped down the whole lot and asked for more. A fire kept this tin home like an oven.

I was assured by the owner that this was a café. The only thing confirming this fact was the gaudy food poster I'd seen in every café since my arrival in Asia. The fruits were so bright they hurt your eyes and, more often than not, there were mistakes to be found where a computer had been used to edit the picture.

Abandoning the warmth, I continued my descent until the white Pamir mountain range came into view in the distance and I reached Saritash.

* * *

A crossroad for travellers, businessmen and traders, you'd think Saritash would be a hive of activity with vendors fighting for business, with bright signs, smart buildings and an array of over-enthusiastic people wanting to take your money off you.

None of that could be seen. It was deathly quiet. Not a soul moved.

My first job was to find somewhere where I could operate on Shirley. One of the rails on her seat had snapped as well. Searching high and low, I eventually found a mechanic working from his own home who would help me. He looked Shirley over and told me to come and pick her up tomorrow. It was a strange feeling. We'd been together non-stop for the entire journey and I was loath to leave her overnight. But I was just being silly; she'd be safe there.

As I wandered past later in the day, I popped in to see how she was doing. She was being screwed, banged, nailed and poked with a red hot iron. I had to turn away.

As I ambled through this desolate village, I met Daniel who had passed me on the other side of the mountain. He made faces at the pain I was experiencing that day, but then invited me into his home to meet his family and share some dinner.

As I saw when I approached it, Saritash is a village overlooked by the towering Pamir mountains. Thousands of people come here each year to travel the length of the Pamir highway. At the place where I was staying alone, there were seven bicycles all belonging to people who wanted to cycle to China and who had no desire to stay in Saritash. Why weren't people making the most of the tourists' dollars? For me it was great. The locals were accustomed to seeing tourists but there were no other tourists around so I simply relaxed and waited for Shirley to be ready and to hear word from the travellers passing in the other direction that the Chinese border had been reopened.

Rumour had it that it had been closed indefinitely while the Chinese government dealt with uprisings and protests over the communist occupation and suppression of Tibet and Xinjiang province.

The season was coming to an end. It wouldn't be long before all the roads were closed due to snowfall. I was just hoping they'd hold out till I got through.

I went to the only café (read: a house that served food to tourists) that remained in business. As soon as I opened the door, the warmth hit me. Beckoned inside, I was shown a small room with a low table. Straw mats were rolled out for me to sit on. This room, like all others I'd seen so far in Saritash, had a primitive and extremely dangerous heating system made from a length of wire wrapped round a section of concrete sewage piping, with each end of the wire being poked into the plug socket. The wires glowed red and radiated heat, but if you were to touch it you would be toast.

A delicious serving of goat, bread and tea was brought out. I was more than happy with this, but there was one snag: the wrinkled woman serving me the food couldn't break the flat bread in two. I offered to help, but she was determined. She scuttled back to the kitchen and came out with a bread knife. Sawing at the bread, she was making very little impact on it. Saying, "OK, OK," I took the knife from her but couldn't break the stale bread either, however hard I tried. I resorted to attempting to dip it into my chai to soften it, but the circular bread was too big. So, with all my might, I hit it on the corner of the table, breaking it in two and reducing it to a decent size to dip into the chai to soften it and make it swallowable.

Afterwards, spending as little time in the cold night air as possible, I dashed back to my hostel room where there was a heater which made an ominous humming noise when it was on, and which was therefore too dangerous to sleep with. Unfortunately it was also too cold to sleep without it, so I was left with the choice of not sleeping for fear of being burnt alive or electrocuted, or of not sleeping for the cold.

For two days my routine was the same: rest, break bread, eat, drink chai (with soggy bread at the bottom), rest and repeat.

Matt arrived on the third day. He'd heard the Chinese were considering opening their border in a few days and thought he might as well be one of the first through. He suggested I go with him. I deliberated for a bit before deciding I might as well as it had to be safer with two people, even if one of you is very skinny and totally unprepared, so we started making plans to get to China.

Putting our differences aside, and picking up Shirley who wasn't looking too happy after spending two days in a shed, we set off along the plains that led to the Pamirs, well-stocked with food and drink. The land was as flat as a pancake until it hit the mountains where it rocketed into the air with jagged, snow-covered precision.

We passed the time singing, making jokes and taking pictures of each other (it's one of the setbacks of the lone cyclist that you never get pictures of yourself). We then ascended into the Pamir range and my newly-welded pannier fell off again. Matt happened to be a bit of an amateur engineer and managed to fix it back on pretty sturdily. The going was steady and the ratios on Matt's bike weren't really up to these sorts of hills, so I told him to grab the lock that hung off my rear panniers and I towed him up the hills.

Higher and higher we rose, crossing the snow line. The snow would gather round our brakes and gears, making the going tough. Every so often there would be ice beneath the snow and Matt and I would hit it side-by-side and end up falling and sliding like synchronized divers. Lying on the floor laughing our heads off, we'd get back up and carry on only for the same thing to happen again. What else could we do? If we weren't laughing we'd have been crying.

A bit later it was my first opportunity to use my teapot. Matt's rear derailleur had snapped, meaning he couldn't change gears any more. He soon had his bike in bits working out how to fix the problem, tinkering with this and that. Chipping away at the ice and snow that had gathered on his bike, he had to remove his gloves which, in these surroundings, was terrible. Matt had laughed when he first saw my teapot hanging off my bike but he was happy to share the brew now. His hands were shaking but he was able to summon the concentration he needed to make his bike ridable again. My romantic idea of sharing my tea with locals hadn't come true, but it still felt great to be sharing it with Matt. I think we'd bonded in adversity, struggling together to get to the top of the mountains, to pass the impassable by bicycle. All that was left was the easy bit - getting down. Or so we thought.

* * *

The roads down were treacherous. Cliff faces lined the sides and the road was made of gravel at best, rocks and potholes at worst. Ice and snow congregated in shaded areas. Our brakes were beginning to wear through and the bumping and jumping were testing our bikes to the max.

As we flew down a totally unmade road, fortune was again against us. My other front pannier rack snapped and the pannier fell off. This time it got stuck in my front wheel, breaking spokes and stopping the bike in its tracks. As you can imagine, going from 30 mph to 0 mph within a very short space of time catapulted me over the handlebars; landing me at the boots of a police officer who demanded, "Passport," before my bike had quite finished somersaulting before landing on me.

As Matt checked into the checkpoint, I ran off to the surrounding houses and found an old woman who was willing to have us stay the night. She'd made a massive pot of meat and potatoes for her and her husband and we were invited to have some. The potatoes were amazing. I could feel the nutrition flowing through my veins, but the meat was pretty damn tough. I couldn't chew through it, so I had to suck the meat dry and then leave it discreetly on the side of my plate. The house was pitch black and you couldn't see what you were eating which was probably just as well.

We'd ditched our damaged bicycles outside, unsure as to whether Shirley could be fixed. My wheel had bent with the impact and wouldn't turn. My front panniers were both unable to be fixed to the bike. I was wondering whether I was going to need to hitch a lift to the nearest town which was probably Kashkar, hundreds of kilometres away and in a separate country, whose borders we were informed over lunch were still well and truly closed.

We decided to ignore all this till the morning.

An array of delicious boiled sweets was laid on the table and we were encouraged to finish them off, which we very kindly did.

When I awoke the next morning, I could hear the sound of metal on metal combining with a donkey braying and Kyrgyz talking loudly. I peeked outside and there was Shirley laid out in front of Matt with a crowd of locals around him, many of whom were still sitting on the donkeys they took to work. Shirley, although not looking her best, was resembling a bike again. Matt had managed to round off the wheel and attach my panniers to the rear.

I couldn't believe it. How lucky was I to have been picked up by Matt on his way through?!

* * *

We weren't far from the border but we underestimated how long it would take to get there. Matt was still riding a single-speed bike which made the hills near enough impossible. My knees were beginning to give way after we had worked together to get through the mountainous scenery so far, climbing through valleys with beautiful rock formations on either side of us, with blue skies above us and towering mountains all around.

Starving hungry, we found ourselves in a massive queue of trucks trying to get through to China. As we passed them, Jon, an Israeli, travelling on a bus full to the brim with Kyrgyz, beckoned us over to give us some bread and honey. The taste was supreme. We stopped to brew a tea to share with him.

We made our way to the front of the queue, winding in and out of trucks whose drivers had turned off their engines and placed stones behind their wheels as handbrakes, and were now congregating under their trucks to avoid the sun.

The gates were still closed.

Chapter 25

China had closed its borders for fourteen days owing to the National Day celebrations. I reached them the first day they re-opened, arriving at 2pm. The Chinese authorities had decided to close them again for lunch.

At 4pm the guards finally marched up to the border post from their barracks. Their shoes were polished to perfection, their khaki green uniforms were pressed, and they were clean-shaven and wearing flat army caps. The rhythm of their marching was so perfect it was almost hypnotic. As they arrived at the gate, expectant truck-drivers started their engines, passengers scrambled back into their trucks, and we hopped onto our bikes ready for the race to the front of the passport queue. The gates did not open. Instead, the soldiers pulled out dusters and mops and started mopping, sweeping and polishing everything in sight. You could already see your reflection in the brass knobs and could eat your dinner off the sparkling paving stones. Eventually, a man, who'd been standing on a pedestal, started waving his flags in a manner that said the border was fit for use and things were ready to proceed.

The gates swung open and a scrummage erupted, generating a dust ball that exploded over the guards as the trucks whizzed down, leaking gasoline onto the pristine road surface, dirty fingerprints tarnishing everything they touched, as people tried to leverage themselves into prime position.

Eight different officials checked our passports. We proved we didn't have any fruit, the swine 'flu or a map of Taiwan showing it as an independent state (the Chinese still consider it part of their empire). I was stamped, saluted and ejected from the gleaming immigration centre into the single filthiest village either of us had ever seen or smelt – Irkeshtam.

Donkeys and dogs rummaged amongst rubbish piled high on the streets. Nuzzling through newspapers, beer bottles and cardboard packaging, they sought out the severely rotting flesh of fruit and vegetables thrown away by the street sellers who sat amongst the filth on stools waiting for customers to whom, on all accounts, they sold rotting fruit and vegetables. A layer of dirt sat on the road mixing with the water coming down from the mountains, and splashing against buildings and passers-by as trucks accelerated to leave. Fast food restaurants served noodles and rice from large cooking pots outside their premises. The only thing fast about this food was how quickly you'd be running to the toilet after eating it.

The cafés must at one point have thought it would be a good idea to buy in pool tables and leave them on the street to attract custom. Unfortunately, with the disregard that the people of this town paid to its upkeep, the tables must have been left out in the rain time and time again until they resembled the Pamir mountain range rather than the flat Taklamakan desert that we hoped would to take us to Kashkar, the capital of the Xinjiang province.

The largest province of China, Xinjiang covers 1.6 million square kilometres. Only 4.3% of its land is fit for human habitation. We may have just left Moscow's sphere of influence and entered Beijing's, but, border or not, this wasn't really China yet. Throughout history, the Chinese have maintained a decidedly intermittent hold over Xinjiang province as it has also convincingly been claimed by the native Turkic Uyghur people - closely related to the Kyrgyz, Kazakhs, and other Central Asian types back over the Tien Shan mountains - who have lived on this land for two thousand five hundred years.

Irkeshtam did have one thing in its favour, though - packaged foods. From the shop we could buy crisps and chocolate, nuts and an array of Chinese snacks which, although they bore no resemblance to European food, were decidedly tasty after eating goat and bread three times a day.

A law in China prevents foreigners from staying in anything except special state-sanctioned hotels, so logistics dictated that this dump of a town was ours for the night. Our hotel room may have been officially approved by the CCP (The Chinese Communist Party), but it certainly hadn't ever been cleaned. Outside the hotel was an old chest of drawers hanging together by a few wooden fibres. Matt opened the drawer and dropped in his old derailleur. Inside, the hotel was no better. There were human-shaped sweat-marks on the sheets, dirty handprints had been dragged across the walls, and piles of old food and empty bottles sat in the corners. It wasn't quite what I was expecting from my first night in China.

As he walked in, Matt was clearly deliberating something with his panniers in his hands. "I can't decide whether it's more disgusting to put the panniers on the floor or on the bed," he stated simply.

Walking around town in the evening, we looked for somewhere to eat that wasn't going to give us first degree gastroenteritis. When a restaurant's endearing feature is a lack of rats outside the front entrance, you know you are sinking to new levels.

Without an ounce of Mandarin between us, and with our phrase book written in Chinese English, there was only one way to decide what we should eat. Grabbing the waitress' arm, I led her into the kitchen. After the steam cleared from my glasses, I could see chicken's feet everywhere - no chickens, just their feet. I pointed to them and crossed my arms to say, "NO!!" In other pots I found noodles and something resembling vegetables. I gave them the thumbs up and held up two fingers. She smiled broadly and offered me the peace sign back. Leaving the kitchen, I pointed to the feet again and reiterated that I wanted nothing to do with them.

We sat and hoped.

* * *

Having seen the public toilet - which doubled as our hotel toilet - on our way to the 'restaurant', I'd looked up at the sky, to the God of bowel movements, and prayed. My intentions were very clear. There could be no confusing them; no bowel movements tonight please. The toilets were based on a modern, open plan design, eight holes side by side dropping down a bank that ran along the side of the road. Six of the toilets allowed for a degree of privacy with a wrought iron fence between them and passers-by. The smell emanating from the toilets monopolised our attention and, once we were hooked, we couldn't avoid letting our eyes explore the piles of excrement lying on the floor.

Sitting in the restaurant, I felt a twinge but ignored it, hoping, against all odds, that it was a fart in the making waiting for an opportune moment to depart my body. As we left the restaurant, I felt another one and my stomach swiftly sent a message up to my cerebellum to say, "Get to a toilet. Fast."

Unfortunately, by this time it was dark and tiptoeing round deposits from other caring guests would have been like playing Russian roulette, so I had to choose one of the two toilets under the glaring street lamps in full view of the passing public in this godforsaken town. Pulling down my shorts, I was forced to reveal my porcelain white bottom to the creatures of the sewage. Ten seconds later a man ran in and stopped right in front of me to assess why I was there. One would have thought it quite obvious. He quickly pirouetted and skipped his way to the other end of the barn with aplomb. As I got back to the job at hand, a delegation of people came from left to right, chatting to each other and stopping to laugh

132

at the white man sitting in the toilets, grimacing.

I kept on all my clothes that night, including my hat, to keep out not only the cold but also the slime and sweat on my bed sheets that looked like it might dissolve a body if it were lain upon in the raw form.

It was around 250 kilometres east and two kilometres south to Kashkar, the next city on our route. We were hoping that it would all be downhill from here and, indeed, traditional logic would suggest that the best route down from a pass such as this would be to pick a river valley and follow it to the plains. One of the lessons of this trip, however, was that the passes were rarely what they seemed, let alone what I was expecting. In this case the Chinese had inexplicably decided to build the descent from this particular pass across the valleys, so we dropped down into each one, only to climb out the other side and into the next.

The valleys were beautiful. The sides of the road were still green but the mountains on either side were made of red rock that folded as it emerged bare from the earth, leaving ripples running across it and peaks and troughs in-between. On the up, Matt held on as I twiddled up in the granny gear, and on the way down we raced whooping like children. On the occasional flats we chorused Take That, Chris de Burgh, S Club 7 and other trendy songs. Luckily there was no-one else to hear us, so we escaped without anyone knowing our taste in music.

Then Matt taught me my greatest lesson. I was struggling up a steep hill, but knowing Matt was faring far worse made me carry on. Then I heard his singing 'Life Is A Roller Coaster', a Ronan Keating special. He seemed to be enjoying himself. I heard an engine too, and was fearful to turn around and find myself under the wheels of a passing truck. His singing got louder and louder. He was catching me up and preparing to overtake me. My legs were screaming as I tried to stay ahead of him. He flew past at about twice my speed. I stopped dumbfounded, out of breath, and pissed off. Where had all this energy come from? How had a man who'd never really cycled gone past me when I was supposed to be a decent rider? Then I noticed it. He wasn't even peddling. He only had one arm on the handlebars. The other was stretched out in front of him. He'd waited for a lorry to come, had grabbed hold of part of the bumper and was allowing himself to be dragged to the top. I couldn't believe it. Cheeky bugger. But a brave cheeky bugger. Surely that was death-defying to be on these roads and riding one-handed at twice the rational speed. Matt informed me this was called 'skitching'. I had to give it a go.

Waiting at the bottom of the next hill, we could see the dust from an approaching truck. Psyching myself up, I could feel my pulse quicken and my legs becoming taut, ready for the sprint. The truck got within ten metres and I set off up the hill as fast as I could. My legs were burning, my lungs felt full of glass and, whoosh, it went by. I had no chance. Collapsing over the handlebars, sucking breath in, I heard Matt laughing in exactly the spot he'd been in before the truck had appeared. He hadn't moved.

"You don't try and catch hold of the Chinese trucks, just the old Kyrgyzstan trucks!"

I swore under my breath. "You could have told me that before."

Again a truck was coming, this one a lot slower than the one before. Again I accelerated and this time I was racing alongside it. As it trundled by, I let go of my handlebars, balancing with one hand. The bike was jumping left and right as it hit the stones that littered the road. My heart was racing. *Almost there, you can do it* and, bam, I had hold of the back of the truck and was disappearing up the hill at a tremendous pace. I felt like E.T. flying across the moonlit sky. On the other side of the truck was Matt. He'd confidently and swiftly grabbed the right-hand side. It was an amazing feeling. A bond formed between us for that split second. We laughed, we joked, there was no complaining, no pain. We were flying.

Chapter 26

That evening we put up my tent in a mine after being turned away from all the hotels in town by the owners who clearly wanted our much-needed custom but kept a keen eye on the military who were always close at hand. It was as illegal to camp, and probably more so, in an industrial area like a mine. It was a stone mine and quiet enough. Assuming all the workers had gone home, I felt we were safe to proceed. Matt didn't like it but it was my tent. And my stove. And my food. He had no choice.

After burnt noodles, apples and oranges we squeezed in and fell to a blissful sleep.

We were woken by the crashing of machinery - the late shift had arrived. The diggers arrived first. Lorries then came to carry away the stone and finally the foreman arrived. We immediately turned off our torches and sat and watched, or I should say Matt sat and watched. I lay in the tent scared out of my wits. Matt gave a running commentary on what was happening. The digger was smashing the living daylights out of the rocks. It was filling the first lorry. The first lorry was half full. The first lorry was full. The second lorry was full. They were leaving. They were leaving. Yes. Almost gone. Oh shit... The foreman was turning this way. He'd got his lights on our tent. He was driving this way.

Matt stood up in just his tight Lycra shorts, revealing the true extent of his malnutrition. I was cursing under my breath. As Matt walked forwards, I popped my head out to see how things were developing. Matt explained with hand signals that we just wanted to sleep and that we would go in the morning. The foreman released a tirade of Mandarin, then gave us the thumbs-up and smiled. Bloody brilliant, Matt!

Kashkar is an oasis in the middle of the Taklamakan Desert. It was a central focus of the political intrigues of the late nineteenth and early twentieth centuries between Britain and Russia known as The Great Game - two great empires tormenting themselves over each other's penetration into Central Asia.

Eric Shipton was a famed mountaineer of these times. He lived in Kashkar in the 1940s and was a source of much information for the British military who were concerned with the comings and goings of Russian spies in the area, buying Khanates' support with lavish goods from the Russian Empire.

The first sign for us that the enduring sands might be coming to an end was that motor cars replaced the donkeys and carts. Earlier some children had burst into tears upon seeing my face. I was assured by their father that they hadn't seen a white man before - it wasn't my unfortunate looks that were causing their distress. Now children ran alongside us waving and cheering.

We knew we were close, but it was still difficult to see the city. The dust that now rose from Kashkar's old city no longer came from the sands of the Taklamakan Desert but from the debris of centuries-old houses being demolished in a residents' resettlement project. This historic urban heartland of Uyghur society was once given its character by the lively trade in the bazaars, the vibrant alleyway communities, and the cool refuge of shaded courtyards. Today its defining feature is the gap-toothed and pockmarked landscape of flattened houses razed by Chinese bulldozers.

When Shipton came here as British Consul-General in 1940, he described the city as being surrounded by massive fifty-foot high walls but now the old ramparts can be seen in very few places where a small section of wall has been preserved. He noted that the narrow streets were lined with people on donkeys, but these have now been replaced by wide boulevards lined with cars and buses.

The Chinese authorities declared in early 2009 that 65,000 homes in Kashkar's old city - an area that encompasses nearly eight square kilometres - were unfit for habitation due to poor drainage and concerns over potential collapse in the event of an earthquake. Only one square kilometre remains of the city where 'The Kite Runner' was filmed. A significant number of Uyghurs have been relocated to new apartment blocks eight kilometres from Kashkar's centre, and find their new residences conveniently fitted with the accessories of modern surveillance such as CCTV cameras.

The demolition of Kashkar's old city is a great loss to world heritage and a serious threat to the survival of what is most distinctive and precious about Uyghur material culture, architecture, and human community. What makes the process all the more sinister is that it is being accompanied by a relentless diluting of Uyghurs in their own homeland as the Chinese are encouraged politically and through monetary incentives to move into the area.

We dived into the dust on our bikes, weaving in between the old and the new. A ten ton truck hooted its horn as we overtook a cart being pulled by a donkey. Tuk-tuk drivers pulled alongside to get a better look at us touring cyclists. Businessmen in the back discussed politics. Children played in the street, oblivious to the thundering buses that passed them by. Convoys of army vehicles carrying soldiers approached. Every soldier was standing to attention. Each one looked us over, not because we looked funny, but trying to see if we were breaking the law.

Amongst the expensive, featureless hotels the Chinese were offering up as Western accommodation was a little hostel tucked into the old town. It was squashed in between a butchers serving meat heated by the midday sun and a stall selling woodwork crafts. Squeezing through the gate, I was greeted by Hai, a Chinese worker enticed to come to Kashkar by incentives. Wrapping my arms around him, I received a cold push. The Chinese aren't famed for their affection and this served as confirmation in my eyes.

Rumours of a variety of food and drinks in Kashkar enticed us out of the hostel. We walked down the road eating fruit and walnuts bonded with honey. We named this delight 'Uyghur Gold' due to the fact that we paid such an extortionate amount for it but also due to its sensational taste.

We bought a bag of chicken's feet and heads and wandered around the arcades. Nibbling on the crest of a cockerel or biting the toenails of a foot, we shot bullets at balloons and hit sadistic-looking fluffy moles with hammers.

Life went on around us. No-one seemed interested in the white faces that drifted down the street eyeing up the weird and wonderful sights that were on offer in the streets of Kashkar. Street vendors plied their trade and we bought it all - hats, mobile phones, dried fruit, swords, and nuts and bolts to repair our cycles. China was selling everything you could imagine and more.

A large statue of Chairman Mao watched over us from up on high. More army vehicles passed, first in one direction and then in another. I was dying to take a picture of them, but my new camera would have been crushed in an iron fist if I had done so.

Trying to use our basic Mandarin to ask for things, we endeared ourselves to vendors. Mandarin is a tonal language, so one word can mean several different things according to the tone with which it is enunciated. For example, the word *Ma* can mean mother, donkey, hemp or scold depending on how you say it. It would make dating a Chinese girl very difficult. Pointing at her mother and saying donkey wouldn't go down well at all, I shouldn't think.

* * *

We got up early the next day and I headed off to the live animal market using two buses and following the road signs. Fortunately for me, the local authorities have signs in English as well as Mandarin. Uyghur has been removed not only from signs but also from the school syllabus, replaced by Chinese, thus diluting the Uyghur culture further.

The English signs have all been written by the Chinese with what looks to be no collaboration with any native English speaker, hence what follows is known across the world as Chinglish and is guaranteed to keep a smile on your face all day. Signs adorning all streets and corners proclaim "Don't press the glass to get hurt" on breakable glass, "Cash Recycling Machine" on a cash machine, "Slip and fall down carefully" when you need to be careful not to slip.

In Kashkar, two time systems operate. The official Beijing time – which is enforced by the government and is thus the time used by big business - and local time which is only communicated between locals. It's amazing that the whole of China should have the same official time zone. It would be like the whole of Europe or America being on the same time zone.

My Chinese had not served me very well and I arrived in local time, not Beijing time. I was there before any of the animals. Fortunately, this gave me the opportunity to have an insight into how some of the animals arrived. A car pulled up. A group of five men, all sharing the same cross-eyed gaze, got out of the car. They limped to the back of the car, pulled open the boot, and began a discussion in the same manner a group of English gentlemen might discuss a crossword. Looking over their shoulders I saw what they were puzzling about. Inside the boot was a fully grown cow. It had its legs tied and it took the five men about ten minutes to extract the cow.

Wandering around, I saw huge goats, plenty of sheep with fat bottoms, bulls dragging owners around, and the occasional camel. Men grasped the udders, ears and legs of the animals. They forced them to open their mouths and they lifted their tails before bartering for a decent price.

It didn't seem as though the purchasers gave any thought to how they would get the animals home. As I hitched a lift on an empty cart heading back to the city after a good day's business for the driver, a scooter overtook me with two live sheep strapped to it, thrashing their legs and muzzles.

* * *

Back at the hostel, I found a few figures I recognised sitting in a circle chatting: Katya and Cedric, Jonathon (the Israeli who had given Matt and me honey in Kyrgyzstan), Matt, and an English girl, Ali. Ali was heading into Pakistan where she'd taught English the previous year. She was nervous about the change in political stability but was adamant she would see her friends.

We all set off to the night market. A cauldron on a makeshift fire bubbled away giving off a steam that glowed green under the fluorescent lights that lit up the old square. Men gathered round, cupping their brownish bowls in their hands and eating the soft substance that was being served. At one point the mist cleared and I was able to see into the cauldron. Eyes that seemed attached to skulls bobbed like apples on Guy Fawkes Night. Jumping back in shock, I bumped into a man wearing a skull cap and with what looked like an eye between his fingers. Pointing at the broth, I made monkey impressions, trying to ask if they were monkey heads. The crowd grew interested in my gesticulations and gathered round. The man shook his head, laughing. He released a "Baaaaaaa" as he popped the eye into his mouth, crushing down on it. As the eye burst, juice gushed out of the man's mouth, spraying into my face. I wanted to vomit.

Noting my interest, the vendor pulled out one of the skulls and offered it to me. It was a gift. The Westerners among us backed up fast. No-one wanted what was being offered. A prod in my back pushed me into the centre. Matt had volunteered me, and the skull was thrust into my hands. My legs went weak as I sank into one of the chairs, dropping the skull on the table in front of me. An axe head whooshed through the air. I rocked back on the chair to avoid the swing which took the top of the skull clean off. A white mass of neurons and synapses was revealed. Chopsticks were thrust into my hand. I couldn't get the picture of the cute sheep I'd seen and stroked at the market earlier out of my head.

Using the sticks to prise a piece free, they cut through the soft, white flesh quite easily. The once-bustling street, the music, the chatter seemed to have stopped. All eyes were on me or, more to the point, on the little piece of brain on the end of the two sticks I was holding tentatively in my left hand. I brought it towards my mouth, opened it and dropped it onto my extended tongue. I had no idea what to expect as my tongue drew it into my mouth like a factory conveyor belt. As I bit down, the life around me started again. No-one cheered, no-one gasped, it was business as usual. The last thing I expected was Philadelphia. It tasted like soft, smooth, cream cheese. I finished off the brain, leaving an empty skull, and I popped one of the eyes into my mouth for pudding. It tasted like old chewing gum, the kind you found under your seat in the classroom as kids.

As we strolled home through the old town, we saw a number of police storm an Uyghur house with the people protesting outside receiving the raw end of police batons as the price of their interference.

Throughout Kashkar, if Uyghurs voice discontent at their treatment, they are branded as at least ungrateful and as, at worst, separatists or terrorists, and treated accordingly. The Chinese used September the Eleventh as an excuse to round up all the leaders in Uyghur Muslim society and execute them.

There has been fleeting international interest from the media on the trials and tribulations of the Uyghur community under the Chinese government, but this media attention is always short-lived. Many put this down to the fact that the Uyghur people are Muslims rather than Buddhists, like the Tibetans, whose treatment provokes continuing international outcry.

I had hoped to pass through Tibet to Nepal, and then India, but with riots all over Xinjiang and the anniversary of the fifty-year occupation of Tibet, no tourists were being given alien permits allowing them to travel freely. I considered my options. Should I take a trip to Pakistan, a highly unstable country in the grip of terrorism, should I try to make my way across Tibet chased by the military, or should I fly to straight to India?

Chapter 27

As Shirley and I pulled out of the hostel, Hai called me back. As he opened his arms wide, I realised he wanted a hug. Wonderful.

Matt was leaving for a flight to Vietnam where he intended to build a boat and learn to sail. Katya and Cedric had hired bikes from the market and were joining me until lunch time. They said they needed some exercise and wanted to see me safe. They were worried about me going to Pakistan. Sharing a breakfast of *lagma*, then seeing them suffering on their bikes just so that we could spend a little extra time together, was amazing. Their legs soon got tired. Cedric held onto my bike, Katya held onto Cedric's, and we managed a few more miles together. Eventually they had to say bye and head back. They knew they would be aching in the morning but still they smiled and joked as we had a group hug and went our separate ways.

Making my way towards Karakul Lake, a popular tourist destination famed for its unreal scenery and the clarity of its reflective water - mirroring the mountains that remain snow-covered all year round - I took a road that felt as though it led to nowhere.

As I rode around a river, I heard a call. "Hello, hello, over here!" Two people were waving from a spit leading to the water's edge.

A German couple with family, kids and mortgage had retired, sold their house and were touring the world by bicycle off the profits. Hans sported a full-blown white beard and an ageing body warmer that had probably seen every continent on the planet. Eva was still incredibly youthful after three kids and a taxing career. She moved like someone in her twenties, jumping up to get more ingredients, or bowls or plates to serve with. They'd popped their tent right next to the river and had built a fire. I pitched up next to them. We talked about our experiences and plans for the future whilst cooking our dinner. They had somehow managed to rustle up a three course lunch. I, having picked up some pasta in Kashkar, ate pasta surprise. At around 11 o'clock we saw torch lights up on the hill meandering down to where we were. Was it the Chinese police? We were in serious trouble if it was. The people came closer, seating themselves near the fire in silence. Using arm movements, they communicated that we should cover up the fire when we slept. They were simply farmers scared of forest fires.

The following morning, as we ate breakfast, Hans switched on the World Service on his long wave radio. It was the first contact I'd had with the world outside of China since arriving there. From Xinjiang province the Chinese had banned Internet and phone calls outside of the country. I'd asked Katja to call my mum as they were leaving that night for Beijing where phone and internet rights still existed, just to let her know I was safe and well and on my way to Pakistan.

Breakfast meant more pasta for me, and porridge with fruit, honey and nuts for Hans and Eva. It was a beautiful day. The sound of the river was the bass, the wind in the trees the treble. The sun shone brightly and the air was crisp with the incoming winter. Wrapped up warm, we all suddenly stopped. The presenter was stating that war had broken out in Pakistan. The Pakistani army was launching an offensive against the Taliban in the northern areas that I would be visiting. The initial thought that crossed my mind was that my mum would be receiving a call just about now from Katya saying I was heading to Pakistan at the same time that the newspapers and TV were showing the bloody consequences of war in the area.

With the radio blaring I couldn't think straight. The gun fire. The explosions. I decided to get on my bike and head off so I could retreat into my own world and work out what to do. I was not allowed into Tibet - now Pakistan too? Surely I'd be turned round at the border if things were too hairy.

That night I hoped to reach Karakul and sleep in one of the yurts that occupy its shore, lie next to a warm fire and eat cooked food. The lake is at four thousand metres again, so it was a steep ascent all the way. Every few pedal strokes I needed to stop and regain my breath. The altitude was starving me of oxygen and I couldn't function very well without it.

The days were getting short now and, before I knew it, the sun was dropping to the horizon. I knew that Karakul Lake wasn't far ahead so I kept on. The reflections off the snow were keeping the darkness away as the sun dropped behind the mountains and, with this, the temperature plummeted. It was literally freezing. An hour later I was wondering whether I had somehow missed the lake. Were my distances correct? I couldn't risk it. Soon the road and I would turn to ice. Darkness was now complete. Nestled behind a wooden stable, I put up the tent and tried to boil water for tea and noodles. The lack of oxygen in the air meant the flame was very weak and I ended up soaking the noodles in lukewarm water and ditching the idea of tea altogether. I had managed to get the water from a pump in a local village, confident that in these surroundings there would be nothing to pollute it.

Tucked up in my down sleeping bag, I fell fast asleep whilst all around me turned white. I awoke to a frozen sleeping bag and my tent frozen both inside and out. Thanks again, Cotswold - I was super warm!

The silence made me feel like I was inside one of those glass Christmas balls you get which contain beautiful winter scenery and which you shake to generate artificial snowfall. Everything was totally silent. When I touched the top of the tent, the frost flaked and fell, hovering on my heat thermals before landing beside me. It was like the ball had been shaken to create a blizzard inside.

* * *

Once the tent and my belongings had defrosted, I packed up and got on my way. I cycled for approximately five hundred metres before rounding a bend. The sight that greeted me was absolutely stunning, a wide-open, flat expanse framed by white-tipped mountains and, as its main feature, Karakul Lake. I'd given up last night about three minutes too early. The lake was breathtaking. I walked through a *paifang* (the typical Chinese archway made of two ornately colourful pillars supporting a roof-type structure) as I pulled off the road and approached the water's edge. In the distance I could see yurts with smoke rising from their chimneys.

Even this short cycle had allowed the bite of the mountain air to take hold of me and I decided to try to find a yurt serving some food and warming chai. A light-skinned man wearing the typical Uyghur hat greeted me and motioned for me to sit down by the fire. My wet gloves were taken from me and set out to dry. The smell in the yurt was intense. Yak dung had been used to insulate the house and yet more was dried and used as fuel for the fire. This, along with the distinctive taste of yak milk, was enough. The tea was salted as well. Wow – taste sensation of the bad variety, although it served well enough to soften the dry bread I was served for breakfast. Four other tourists had shared this yurt last night but had headed off early to Pakistan, so other people were making their way there too. Did they know about the war?

Concrete yurts also lined the side of the road. I guess the traditional felt and wooden yurts wouldn't handle the extreme weather at this altitude. The landscape changed as the altitude dropped. I found myself in a desert of silver sand. It gave off a glimmer like fairy dust, the sand dunes looking like velvet in the shimmering sun.

I was pulled over by the Chinese police. I was worried about the photos I'd taken holding a hamburger with a large statue of Chairman Mao in the background so that it looked like he was holding it. They told me to get my camera out but only so that they could pose for pictures with the fabulous landscape in the background. I asked them if there was anywhere I could eat and they pointed to a village just off the main road where there was a celebration going on. I passed a lady in traditional formal dress comprising a red skull cap with silver coins hanging over her eyes and a red sari with silver lace wrapped around her head and body. Nervously three men sat next to each other on a bench outside, scowling at me as I walked past in my Lycra and smelly gear.

In the home I was greeted by two people whom I assumed were the mother and father of the girl in red. A table was laid with all sorts of delicious goodies. They asked me a variety of questions about my life in England and my trip. Nodding and smiling, I stuffed my face with whatever I could get my hands on. The parents then turned their attention one by one to the other men waiting outside.

I suddenly realised that the parents were looking for a suitor for their daughter. I was the first to be interviewed. No wonder the other guys looked a bit cheesed off as I walked past.

As I left, the father said something along the lines of, 'Don't call us, we'll call you', so all you ladies are still in luck. I haven't been married off yet.

Arriving in Tashkurgan, the Chinese border town, I met Ali from the Old City Guesthouse in Kashkar. Travelling with Matt, a gem hunter, they'd left Kashkar that morning and were heading to Pakistan tomorrow. Ali was as sick as a dog, having to run into the street to vomit every few minutes, but somehow she remained in good spirits.

At the Chinese border no one ventures past the border post by foot or cycle or motorbike. All are placed in extortionately priced buses that take you to the Pakistani border. Unhappy at having to take any part of the trip by anything other than bicycle, I had to come to terms with it. It wasn't very far and I guessed I'd be able to forget about it.

The next morning we were woken at 6pm by loud announcements in Chinese over the tannoy system. An Aussie, who was sleeping when we arrived and again when we got back at night, announced it was the Chinese call for exercise which made us all giggle in our tired state.

I met the bus driver who was destined to take me to the Pakistani border. He told me to cycle to the border post and meet him there. Leaving my gear with Matt who would be riding the bus from the hostel, I cycled to the edge of town. No one stopped me so I carried on, looking for a big Chinese border. I regretted not asking the bus driver how far the border was.

Continuing, I stopped a car and asked, "Border control?" I was met with perplexed shrugs of the shoulders. "Passport?" As I mentioned the word, a realisation hit me. Matt had my passport. What if I'd taken a wrong turning and he was on his way to Pakistan? Shit! The driver smiled in recognition of the word and held up ten fingers eight times - eighty yards, eighty kilometres? I carried on and asked again. They replied this time, "Tashkurgan". Had I cycled past the border? I'd cycled about fifteen kilometres since the edge of the town. Turning, the men nodded in agreement and pointed back the way I'd come.

I pedalled like crazy, I was shouting at myself, at the surroundings, at the Chinese authorities. I swore over and over. When I arrived back at the edge of town it was a hive of activity. Matt and Ali were in no man's land between the two countries like me - in a wire mesh pen. So was the bus, my belongings and my passport. Skirting the barrier that now lay across the road, I motioned for Matt to come to the fence and give me my handlebar bag. As he handed it over, a soldier ran at us with his gun aimed and his finger on the trigger. Were we smuggling? I pulled out my passport in the nick of time and he made me give the bag back to Matt. The bus driver was shouting at me to hurry up, completely frantic. I made my way through customs, accepting all the excess charges that the border guards seized the opportunity to apply.

The bus driver scowled as I came through as though my delay had cost him dearly. The entire luggage from his bus was on the floor as the Chinese guards rifled through it to ensure no smuggling was taking place. Two hours later we were still there. The bus driver had been placated with the large stock of sweets I'd hoarded just in case I encountered trouble in Pakistan. The soldiers still looked at each other each time Matt and I spoke, and I was far from relaxed.

Eventually the luggage was loaded back on. I was told to wait with Shirley and, in the end, the bus was too full for me to take. I had to wait for another as Matt and Ali waved at me and passed over the horizon. I got a Pakistani bus which I shared with a fat Pakistani who was all smiles and laughter and who sat next to the driver talking incessantly at him. The only other passenger was a man with a turban wrapped around his head and a beard that hung down to his waist. He had dark eyes and simply stared at me...

Chapter 28

As the bus filled with exhaust fumes and the cold crept through every crack and crevice, my two companions were talking of the war. I heard talk of bombs, the Taliban and the U.S. When I asked them what they were talking about, they said, "Business."

Taking me to one side, the fat man said it wasn't safe in the tribal areas on the road from Gilgit to Islamabad. The tribal people, he motioned with his head towards our other passenger, didn't understand the idea of cycling for fun. I would be taking a massive risk to cycle this route. The road was rough and the people were equally rough to match.

In this mountainous area of Pakistan, there had been constant fighting for ten years. That August, Baitullah Mehsud, the leader of the Taliban in Pakistan, had been killed in a drone attack. That October, the Taliban, to show they were still a united fighting force, had started a string of attacks in cities across Pakistan. The Pakistani Army retaliated with a large-scale offensive soon afterwards, taking towns from the Taliban but also some of those under Islamic Uzbek fighters' control.

Undecided as to whether I would cross the border, I was still slowly being taken towards it by my Pakistani bus, imagining bullets and bombs whistling through the air from all sides, extremist fundamentalists looking to make examples of any Western infidels they discovered in their country.

The bus passed under a paifang archway and entered Pakistan.

* * *

As I stepped off the bus, the first thing I noticed was the lack of road. Which way should I go to get to Pakistan? The Chinese border guard pointed in a southerly direction where I could make out a rough track of stones and boulders which looked like a dry riverbed. That was my road?

This pass was the second highest I'd seen in my life at 5,000 metres – five kilometres - above sea level. It was dwarfed by the surrounding peaks, grey monsters sprouting all around me with snow-white hats covering their peaks. It must have been very cold up there. My panniers were almost empty; I was wearing every piece of clothing I owned. If there had been people to see me, they would have recognised the Michelin Man cycling on a little bicycle that he seemed to consume in all his layers. Little storms of steam bellowed from my nostrils like a cross dragon as I took short breaths.

Luckily the slope was so steep there was absolutely no need to pedal. As I sat on the seat, zombified by the altitude and its consequences on my body, I discovered that, as I got lower, my pulse lessened, my oxygen levels rose, the carbon dioxide poisoning in my blood dissipated, and my sensors came back into action. As I whooped, with my legs out like a kid, the sheep looking on no doubt couldn't believe their eyes. I wasn't sure if I could believe mine. Swerving around one corner, I came across a large, bony sheep with long, arching horns. Later I was told that they are a very rare breed and that you have to be lucky to see one. Americans come each year to Pakistan to hunt these sheep, paying $5,000 for one shot at them. If they miss, that's it; game over. If they score a hit, the sheep can earn them ten times the fee when they take it back to America. The sheep are so rare the government only issues twenty permits a year but the locals are known to poach them owing to the huge price they can raise on the black market. These fees are nothing compared with the $25,000 people pay for one shot at the Marco Polo sheep, a beautiful white beast with huge, twisted horns. They earn up to $200,000 for their trophy back in the US. The lamb chops had better be good.

Clouds began to envelop the mountains and run down the valleys like locusts, consuming everything they came across. My visibility was starting to drop. Rounding a corner, I crashed into the back of a bus. There was a hold up. The best thing about bikes is that you can squeeze through little gaps and I was soon at the front. The locals travelling by bus were huddled together, wrapped in their woollen blankets that became the distinguishing feature of the Northern Pakistanis. Sharing food and cigarettes, they chatted without a care in the world. The fact that they may be delayed for hours wasn't an issue. I remembered people on the M1 during my last visit to my grandparents. A lorry had shed its load and there were tailbacks all the way up the road in both directions. People were hooting their horns, swearing under their breath, brandishing their fists and pulling out their hair with the stress of the delay.

I was told there'd been a rock fall but this was clearly not true. The road had been blocked by someone or something. There was a neat pile of rocks and soil blocking the road. This could be an ambush. Didn't anyone understand? We were potentially seconds away from having our lives extinguished. The Taliban were coming. As I stood shouting at those who would listen to me, I turned to catch two people lifting my bike over the rubble. I ran back. Thieves! They stopped, rested the bike on the other side of the rock pile and walked towards me with smiles. "You can go."

Once on the other side, I realised why the road had been blocked. The Chinese, who were remaking the road, were turning this single-lane track into a multi-lane highway to traffic their goods to the sub-continent to be sold. They had big yellow diggers up in the mountains throwing stones onto the road.

I had to keep moving to keep out of the cold. Tentatively I set off. Again it was like I'd been transported into my old ZX Spectrum computer. I had to get across the ledge whilst there were no stones being thrown. I got my timing wrong and a rock as big as a TV set flew down the rock face and ripped my pannier clean off my bike, carrying it halfway down the mountain side. Pulling the bike to safety, I had to re-live the treacherous route on foot to grab my pannier and get back.

Further down the road I was stopped by border guards asking to see my passport and subsequently refusing to let me pass.

"You have to be on a vehicle."

"I am on a vehicle."

I was taken into their hut where nine to ten men sat around a log fire, each one carrying some form of firearm. Unlike the Chinese, these men lay their guns on the side (precariously close to the fire at points) without a care in the world. I was getting a picture of the Pakistani people who seemed to be so laid back they were horizontal.

I kept asking to leave, only to receive the same response. *Solo? Too dangerous.*

They fed me an aubergine curry with naan which tasted delicious after the desert and mountain food. They also gave me salted tea which wasn't growing on me despite my efforts to acquire the taste, but I forced it down anyway.

When I asked to go to the loo, I was pointed outside. Anywhere. I was reduced to squatting outside the police station to do my business and to using rocks as best I could to cover it up afterwards. It felt a little unreal.

Whilst sitting there, I considered my escape plan. Those buses could be up there all night. I wasn't waiting. Shirley was propped up outside on the down slope of the gate. She was chomping at the bit, ready to rock and roll again. So was I.

On my way back I went to my bike and pretended to get something from my bag. In a split second I was on it and pumping my legs like crazy. I waited for gun shots and shouts but, to be honest, I don't think they even noticed.

* * *

Dark closed in and those drops into the ravines became more and more treacherous. At the last minute I would swerve to avoid hundred metre drops. I passed people with nothing more than a shawl to keep them warm on the mountainside, waving as I went by. They were as surprised to see me as I was to see them.

A vehicle revved its engine behind me. Its lights lit up the road so I didn't let it pass. The driver didn't seem to mind one bit that I was hogging the middle of the road. Finally I arrived at the Pakistani border post, forty kilometres from China.

The vehicle behind me contained Matt and Ali. It was the bus from Tashkurgan. The Pakistani travellers congratulated me and shook me by the hand as we three Westerners were taken into a separate room.

The laid-back nature of the Pakistani Guard was again confirmed when they couldn't find the key for the cupboard where the visas were stored. Telling us to come back in the morning, they let us wander into Pakistan without visas to find some lodgings for the night.

We waved to the other bus companions as they drove away – little did we know that within twenty-four hours the driver would be dead and the bus would be a burning wreck on the road side.

Chapter 29

Ali was now a vision of health, bouncing around practising her Urdu, but it seemed she'd passed the relay baton onto Matt who sat on the loo, bucket in hands, as he exploded from both ends. I wondered when it would be my turn.

When you step out into Sost in the light of day, you are greeted by a whole new world of market stalls set up under a radiant blue sky on the side of road in front of snow-peaked mountains, filled with goods from China, Afghanistan, Pakistan and India. It was like walking around Diagon Alley in Harry Potter. There were foods that looked like creatures from the deep, brightly-coloured Chinese packaging containing who knows what, gems and handmade crafts. It was beautiful; so colourful.

This beauty was only surpassed by the trucks that waited for their loads at the border. The Chinese articulated trucks pass their goods to simple Pakistani trucks which are inferior to their Chinese counterparts on every level except one - their external design. They are completely decorated from bumper to bumper using paint, plastic, wood, jangling chains, shiny objects, metal, fairy lights, windmills, glass and mirrors, the more elaborate and vibrant the better.

The custom started in the 1920s when bus drivers decorated their buses to get more custom and the truck drivers followed suit. Now it is a regular day-to-day occurrence to see a truck looking like a Harrods Christmas tree trundling along at five kilometres per hour carrying ten tons of potatoes, or brick, or wood.

Walking through the markets and gawking at the trucks, you can't help but be distracted by the guns. They are everywhere. Soldiers have them, security staff have them, street vendors have them. I felt compelled to greet each stranger carrying a weapon of mass destruction with a firm hand-shake. I wasn't sure whether my smiles were reflecting their faces or theirs mine. It was a chicken or egg question.

One soldier, standing on an elevated area surveying the road below, was dressed for warmth in a fluffy pastel blue dressing gown with white clouds floating over it. He gave me a massive smile and posed for several pictures with his AK47 under his arm.

"It's two hundred kilometres of the worst road ever imaginable. The Chinese are blasting big holes in it. Landfalls are smashing it to pieces. There are climbs that take a day to do. There are perhaps twenty kilometres of tarmac. It's frozen in places. Other parts are sand. The rest is boulders, rocks and stones." The people were warning me against the next leg of my journey. They thought it wasn't doable.

The whole atmosphere in Sost played on the strings of my heart. The friendliness I experienced was something else. It was a Sunday; there were no banks open and we couldn't get any money. A man I'd met at the police station on my way down said he could help us. We went for tea, the catalyst for all good transactions. The tea was accompanied by chicken curry, then more tea and biscuits. Eventually he pulled out $100 worth of rupees and put them in my hand. As I handed him the dollars, he looked insulted. He refused to take them. He was trying to give us 10,000 rupees, about a month's wages in Pakistan, for nothing because we'd shared tea with him. I couldn't have that and forced the money into his jacket pocket. Later I was told to ask three times and then, if they continue to be adamant, it is a true offer.

An hour later I was hunched over, wearing prison shackles, with my hands chained, being led around the passport control area like a pet monkey by a border guard.

* * *

We had arrived to pick up our passports an hour before and the guards still hadn't found the keys, so we waited and drank tea and ate biscuits. As time dragged, I joked that we were prisoners. The guards, to relieve their boredom, started treating me like a prisoner. The shackles were brought out, photos were taken, people slapped me on the back and everyone laughed. If I had been a real prisoner, then things would have been very different indeed.

Eventually a guard walked in brandishing the key, looking very proud of himself. Visas were stuck in passports using Pritt Stick, and goodbyes were said to Ali and Matt. We were all heading towards Gilgit, our next destination, but they would have the comfort of a jeep; I was cycling. What a luxurious way to travel in Pakistan.

The road out of Sost was one of the worst on the trip but the scenery blew my brains out. Is this the most beautiful place on earth?

A turquoise river cut around the monstrous mountains. Glaciers worked their way down, filling it with melt water. Small villages were

152

positioned along it, linked by the road. The people went about their daily duties and stopped to wave as I went by. Old ladies laughed, beautifully wrinkled, their worn, dark skin reflecting and radiating sunlight with bright, sharp eyes and shining white teeth. Young children ran alongside me until their legs gave up. School boys gave me the thumbs up and the girls giggled, then asked my name. Each and everyone possessed the most wonderfully welcoming energies. Their smiles and waves passed a little bit of light onto me and within ten miles of setting off from Sost I had to stop. I couldn't see straight. The ravishing beauty of this country filled my eyes with tears.

I'd grown up feeling like I was an alien, the jigsaw piece that couldn't fit in no matter who I was, where I went, what I wore. I was surrounded by friends but I'm sure they had no idea of who I was or what I was. Suddenly I felt like I was slotting into place. I was where I was meant to be.

Something was pulling me forwards along the right path, not only towards Chembakolli but towards my entire future. I could feel a calming of the soul, a releasing of tension from years of being out in the social wilderness.

A bus of Taiwanese tourists drove past and stopped. Twenty people came out brandishing cameras that looked bigger than my bike, and others leant out of the window. The view was stunning; I couldn't blame them. But then the cameras were turned on me. Flash bulbs blinded me and the clickety-clicking sounded like a train line. It was lovely to have some contact with the Taiwanese who the Chinese had alleged I favoured.

One hundred metres further on, the view opened up. The valley parted as the river widened and gave me a perfect view of Cathedral Rock, the most photographed mountain in Northern Pakistan. As I sat on my saddle taking in the surroundings, young girls came out to watch me. Farmers stopped as they came from their fields, their herds of goats down from the freezing mountains, enjoying the freedom to stop and graze. An older woman hobbled closer using a staff to prop up her aged body. The people of Hunsa are the most longevous in the world, often living till over a hundred years old. This is thanks partially to a natural diet, clean air and a lack of stress but the gene pool must play its part. She was clearly at the upper end of the scale. Moving towards her, I could see a fire in her eyes which was wonderful to see in such an old lady. She came within a metre of me and smiled. I smiled back. Then, with the grace of a Bruce Lee or a Jackie Chan, she swung her staff above her head, stabilising herself with her legs, and whacked me on the back of my bare legs. Laughter echoed round the mountainside. My legs stung but, as the old lady smiled, I had to laugh too. Another barrage of hits rained down upon me and something similar to a Benny Hill sketch ensued. The old lady chased me round and round, occasionally landing her mark with the stick. By this point people were rolling on the floor. I asked one of the school girls what I had done wrong and she said it was my shorts. Showing your legs is not appropriate.

This was Hussaini village. I liked their style.

Once the lady thought she'd taught me a lesson, she hobbled off into the village nearby using her staff for support. A group of professional photographers who were creating a portfolio of Northern Pakistan took some pictures of me and invited me to have dinner with them at a local hotel in Gulmit.

Meanwhile, Matt and Ali were thundering down the road to Gilgit. The bus leaped and jumped left and right as they crawled along at a pace of about ten kilometres per hour. Matt was squeezed in between five Pakistani men, all of whom had managed to fall asleep instantly as this roller coaster began. On the front rows, the women, including Ali, sat comfortably with free seats next to them. Unless you are a brother or cousin, no man can sit next to a woman on a bus. Matt was quite jealous as one head slipped onto his lap and the other rested on his shoulder.

Gulmit is in the Upper Hunsa Valley and used to be a very popular tourist destination, a hustling, bustling village surrounded by mountains, peaks and glaciers for climbers, hikers, and walkers to play on, attempting ascents of the various peaks around. Now rows upon rows of hotels lie there empty. Still people smiled at me as I came by.

The people of Northern Pakistan are Ismaili. It's a branch of Islam that separated from Shiah during a crisis that spread through the Muslim community. Ismailis choose to focus on the mystical path and nature of Allah, with the Imām of the time representing the manifestation of truth and reality.

Unfortunately for the Ismailis, the most recent heir to the throne, Prince Aly Khan, became an international playboy, socialite and racehorse owner, not to mention Rita Hayworth's third husband. This wasn't the kind of behaviour which was acceptable to people rooted in the laws of the Koran, so he was skipped and ignored, the Ismaili people preferring his son, Prince Karim Aga Khan

Today the Ismaili Pakistanis were celebrating the day Prince Karim Aga Khan, their spiritual leader, came to visit Hunsa. They lit fires up in the mountains and set fire to tyres that they rolled down the hillsides. Before dinner the son of the owner of my hotel, Zahir, took me to see the fires.

In the pitch dark that envelops Pakistan at night we made our way up the mountainside with only a mobile phone screen to light the way. Losing our path in the dark, we followed the distant fires which guided us up the mountain. We dragged ourselves through thorn bushes and over piles of loose rocks, up cliffs and along ledges. Finally we could see the people around the fires. A number of teenage boys were keeping them going all night. The fires were made of old tyres and the smoke was putrid if you got the wrong side of them. Having climbed up to the highest fire with the children following behind us, we sat watching the firelight dance over the surrounding cliffs. Suddenly there was a shout from one of the boys and Zahir grabbed me and pulled me down behind a small boulder. A handful of rocks crashed past over our heads, bouncing off the boulder that was our protection. We'd scared some goats up above who'd caused a rock slide.

It was a scary story to retell over dinner while we ate curry and chapatti with our fingers. I didn't realise then that this fall would be emulated in a few weeks' time when a massive landslide would wipe out Gulmit's neighbouring village, Atta Abad, killing twenty people.

As my dinner was once again being paid for by the locals, Zahir ran in to tell us that the bus Ali and Matt had travelled on from China to Pakistan had been blown up by rebels in Chitral.

Chitral was on my route from Gilgit to Islamabad.

The Taliban had stopped the bus, shot the driver in the face, asked politely that everyone leave the bus, then blown it up after stealing belongings and money. It was a harsh warning of the treacherous route that lay before me. Zahir and the photographers re-emphasised the dangers. In stark contrast to those I'd received earlier in my trip about Uzbekistan, these warnings were backed up by the knowledge that someone I had plied with sweets days earlier had made his last journey as a bus driver and had started out on his journey to Allah.

I was worried about Matt and Ali. I knew they had left the bus but I couldn't help wondering whether either of them had decided to bypass Gilgit to head straight for Islamabad. I wrote them an emotional email asking them if they were safe.

What a first day in Pakistan, the most naturally beautiful people and country I've ever seen. I felt as though I was in love, yet at the same time incredulous at what people can do to each other in such a country. I dreamed of machine gun fire and bombs, tears and family.

* * *

Zahir insisted I stay for at least another day. Fearful of what lay beyond this beautiful village, I swiftly agreed. Hearing I was a teacher he wanted to show me his old school, a government-funded school with a playground that looks over the mountains. Inspiration indeed. The heights you can reach towards. Unfortunately, most of the children take on jobs in the cities, leaving this town with an imbalance in age groups.

The children are taught outside as often as possible. However, when the winter kicks in, they have to huddle into the small classrooms for months on end. When I entered the classrooms I noticed there weren't any teachers, so I asked the children where their teacher was. "Away," was the answer, but the children worked with determination knowing that only an education can change the lives of their families.

I met Zahir's cousin whose family lived miles away from a school. She boarded with Zahir's family doing odd jobs around the small house they chose to live in rather than the big hotel.

Later we went for a walk with Zahir's old teacher and role model, Rahim. We strolled through the countryside, walked on glaciers that are constantly moving - creating new holes and chasms big enough to swallow a body without trace – and we crossed the rushing glacial rivers on rope bridges that swayed terrifyingly with each step. Children ran past me as I moved one hand and foot at a time, gripping so tightly that my knuckles were white. The children laughed and shouted encouragement. We ended up in Hussaini.

Down by the river, women washed themselves and cleaned clothes. Zahir asked if we could come down. They replied. I asked what they said. Zahir told me they'd told us to, "Piss off." We hung around like school boys hoping to elicit a further verbal assault from these ladies, young and old.

Apparently a boy came to spy on the girls washing down here once and they grabbed him, stripped him of his clothes, tied him up and left him down there. I love these guys.

* * *

I was taken to a tea house below the glacier with a view of the mountains where Rahim told me stories of the fairies that live in the hills.

It is believed that fairies take away their children and offer them a bowl of milk and a bowl of blood to drink. The children who drink the blood are allowed to return home, but the others have to stay with the fairies.

Another story concerned a woman known to have good relations with fairies. When guests arrived unannounced, they would find her cooking their favourite meal, even though the vegetables were out of season. They firmly believed that she was given food by the fairies.

Belief in fairies runs deep in Pakistan and, as there are so many woes, many believe that only a cruel person would attempt to debunk these myths.

I smiled and laughed at the right moments and eventually asked,

157

"Do people really believe in fairies?"

The teacher replied that he did. His grandma had once fought a fairy who was determined to take him from his parents' house with the result that she was left physically scarred for life.

We didn't fancy the long walk back to the hotel, so we tried to hitch a lift. Unfortunately, most of the vehicles were ram-packed with animals, vegetables and minerals. Eventually we managed to persuade one radiantly decorated truck to stop. It was carrying potatoes, so we all had to squeeze in the cab with the two other occupants. Each of these trucks has a driver and a boy apprentice who, I was led to believe, doesn't pay for his tutoring but is supposed to offer himself up to the driver for sexual purposes. This seemed like quite a presumption but in a society where sex with a woman before marriage, or infidelity, results in the death penalty, I guess anything is possible.

* * *

I was invited to spend the night at one of the local homes which comprised of one room about the size of my bedroom at home. In the centre was the stove which kept the house warm and was used for cooking up master meals. A chimney rose to the top of the hut, keeping most of the smoke out of the building. In winter, having the chimney open lets in too much cold so they shut it off and suffer the smoke which stains the wood and, I suspect, their lungs equally. Mats are laid out in the evening near the fire and then packed away in the morning when the area is converted into a lounge with a TV. A small section is reserved for eating. There are no chairs or tables, and very few pots and pans. Just the essentials. People are used to sitting cross-legged and, unlike us Westerners, they can do it for hours without the cramps and numbness that assailed me halfway through the meal.

Being invited into a home in Pakistan is something not many people experience because of the social restrictions. If something were to happen to the guest, it would bring shame on the entire village and hence people tend to choose not to get involved.

The meal started very politely with us sitting cross-legged as we discussed work and studies while our meal was cooked in front of us on a wood stove. We were eating traditional Hunsa food. Bread cooked on a wood-burning stove was broken into a pan containing cheese, butter and milk, and served. It didn't look too good but the taste was fantastic. The pudding was made of honey and apricots. It was all served on the floor in front of us where we sat eating with our hands.

After dinner people started to relax. First Sonia (my host) sang, then I sang some Chris de Burgh and we all sang the Beatles. Sonia's mum danced and sang but only after the dad had been sent to the bazaar to pick something up. He knew full well what was going on but couldn't be seen to be encouraging this freedom in his wife. It was quite beautiful seeing him leave the house. After he returned, the finale to the evening was him teaching me to dance Pakistani style. Everyone was in hysterics, not because I was rubbish - I'm a groover - but because of the surrealism of the situation. Two cultures, poles apart, enjoying a night of dance and education together.

Before I slept, I logged on wondering about the fate of my friends. Matt had replied to my email. "Everything is closed in Gilgit after secular violence between Sunnies and Shias resulted in a grenade being thrown into a shop and then retaliation of machine gun fire into a full bus. But Ali and I are safe. We're staying at the Madina Guest House awaiting your arrival."

Perfect.

Chapter 30

Who would have thought I'd experience life in prison in Pakistan?

Saying goodbye to Zahir and my friends in Gulmit, I wondered to myself what else this wonderful country had to show me. It didn't take long to find out.

Dropping below 2,000 metres through the Nagar Valley, the air gets thicker and the soil more fertile. The panorama was awash with reds, gold, greens, yellows and oranges. The colours of the trees in autumn were phenomenal.

Roadworks on the KKH seem to be as common as the beautiful peaks. Two different labour forces were at work: the Chinese with their high-tech equipment moving tons of rocks using dynamite to widen the path, and the Pakistani workers who were using pickaxes and chisels to hack away at the rocks and shape them for the walls that were being built to protect the roads in notorious landslide territory. As an alien concept to the Pakistani workers, there were female Chinese operating some of the big machinery.

I was invited by a Pakistani road builder for tea in a tent that the workers live in whilst they're not on the road. Bahaar, a good-looking student who was working for $5 a day to fund his own education, apologised for not having something better to offer than the chapattis and curry that I was gratefully gulping down. Inside the tent it was absolutely freezing, Bahaar wrapped a blanket round me. It was still the middle of the day with the sun beating down. What must it be like at night? Sleeping on wooden makeshift beds, fully-clothed with just your shawl and a blanket, I just couldn't imagine getting warm enough.

Bahaar wanted to question me on politics. Election fever was striking in the northern areas. It was the first time the government had allowed the people of Northern Pakistan to vote in an election, and people were very excited about it. Groups of men gathered in the streets talking on every corner, outside every shop. Flags and banners adorned every village.

Seeing a group of old men playing draughts about fifty metres from a lively political broadcast, I couldn't resist sitting down and challenging them to a game. Within ten minutes the political broadcast was all but over. All the people who had attended it were now grouped around the draughts board. I'd been well and truly beaten in three games and the crowd enjoyed poking fun at my incompetence.

When I arrived in Aliabad, the elections had got a bit out of hand. A mass of men marched up and down the road in trucks or by foot in front of a huge police and artillery presence. The police motioned for me to come with them. We walked into the police station and Shirley and I were given our own room. The door was shut and the key turned in the door. We were prisoners. After I had sweated it out for ten minutes, the chief came in bearing gifts of tea and biscuits, explaining that they thought it was too dangerous outside for me and that I'd be safer being locked away until the riot stopped outside.

* * *

When it was considered safe for me to leave – much to my relief – I rode on to Gulmet, a village overlooked by the towering giant of Rakaposhi with its 7,788 metre peak. From the road it rises 5,800m in just eleven kilometres and is the 27th highest peak in the world. There was one guest house at its foot. I knocked on the door and enquired about accommodation, to be told that only their expensive rooms were available. My heart sank; my money was running out fast. Were they just playing me because I was a tourist? I asked hesitantly how much they were asking for, with damage limitation to my budget firmly on my mind. With a pained look on his face that said, '*I don't make up the prices, I just work here*', he replied "400 rupees", which roughly works out at around £3. For a further seventy pence I was treated to the sweetest milky tea, dhal and two roti – an unleavened flatbread made from atta flour.

Lying in bed I tried to construct a life for myself out here. Here in the north the people seemed much more open, more giving, more accepting than I'd expected of a devout Muslim country, and they needed tourism to return as soon as possible. Was there something I could do, perhaps organising cycling trips for tourists wanting a back-to-basics experience or a marathon up the KKH? Could I help fund one of the orphanages or schools? I wanted to give something back to these kind, honest people.

The next day I strove to get to Gilgit. The road was in a terrible condition. I could feel the organs in my body getting entangled as I hit bump after bump. Dust encrusted my face. Pulling my sun glasses off, I looked like a panda, my blue eyes shining out of a black face. I passed buffalo with blue eyes and assumed they were blind, but was reassured that they could see perfectly well – they were just

161

like me. They had the same genetic mutation affecting the OCA2 gene in our chromosomes that gives people blue eyes.

* * *

I never knew seeing grown men beat the hell out of each other with mallets could be so much fun. Occasionally they would hit a ball up and down a pitch. I was at a 'No Rules' polo game. A game originating in Persia (Iran), it dates back to 5,000BC and was developed as a training game for cavalry units. To the warlike tribesmen, who played it with as many as a hundred to a side, it was a miniature battle. A team sport played on horseback, the objective is to score goals against an opposing team by driving a small white plastic or wooden ball into the opposing team's goal using a long-handled mallet.

I wandered through Gilgit town feeling so proud of myself for having got so far. It was perfect timing; the national 'No Rules' polo match final was taking place that evening.

Habib, the manager of the hostel, wanted everyone there so he had an excuse to lock up the hostel and see it himself.

In a stadium overlooked by the mountains, the Northern Scouts, the local team, were playing Chitrali. The Scouts took an early lead and the crowd went absolutely mental. Sitting in the first class area, we had protective mesh to stop the mallets and balls smashing into us. On the other side of the field, the stand came right down to the pitch and had no protection so, when the ball headed their way, the spectators had to scramble up the stand to avoid being smashed with mallets.

The disadvantage of being in the higher society bit was that there were lots of people with guns. The man behind me kept jabbing his machine gun in my back. I would have turned round and told him to piss off if I hadn't been scared half to death that it might accidentally go off. The action on the pitch, though, soon took my mind off it and I was leaping around and whooping with the best of them.

Despite blood dripping off their knuckles and down their legs, the players kept going. It seemed dangerous, but not as dangerous as the job done by a single member of each team. The stick man's job was to run onto the pitch when any player had broken his mallet over some poor unsuspecting player on the other side. The match ended with Chitrali just pinching it in the last minute.

In celebration, the winning team did a traditional dance as the crowd whooped and cheered at their exploits. A door to the first class area was opened and an overly-excited Westerner was thrown ungraciously out there too, Habib being the ring leader who orchestrated my demise. The dancing stopped and the crowd went silent. I stood still, star-struck for a moment. I was expected to perform. The pressure was on. I thought of the guns. I started self-consciously to mimic the dance I'd just seen, swinging my hips and waving my arms, and the crowd let out its biggest roar of the day. The players came and danced around me, smiling and laughing. One gentleman even handed me his broken stick with blood all over it 'n' all.

* * *

My dancing talents, or lack of them, had made me infamous around Gilgit. People were even more generous with tea than ever, and I was invited to play volleyball for the Muslim League. The Muslim League was the party that had orchestrated a free independent Muslim State of Pakistan in 1956 and helped eject the Brits from India as it was handed back from our occupation. It felt ironic really that I was now helping them win a game of volleyball. All good for international relations.

They were playing the Muttahida Quami Movement (MQM) and it seemed the fate of the election hung on this game. As a member of ML, I first had to learn their chants. Rasha rasha sher rasha, *Come, Come, Lion Come*. If I'd had time it would have been good to have learnt how to play volleyball too. MQM took advantage of ML's weakest link and each and every ball was smashed at me. I threw myself all over the place, and once or twice even made contact with the ball, getting whacked on the nose in the process. Fewer hands from the ML were extended after the game, but I'd found a new fan club - the MQM.

The Madina Guest House is the only place to go when you are in Gilgit. All travellers seem to congregate there and many find it hard to leave. People travelling in Pakistan all seem to have a story, or issues, which makes the Madina a lively spot to be if you fancy a discussion on politics, religion, or simply travel adventures.

Matt was slowly collecting a room full of gems, so much so that he had to upgrade his room because hiding them under the bed wasn't working any more. He had one piece of aquamarine that was as big as my thigh and worth $100,000 in the U.S.

Pete was an Aussie who wanted to be the photojournalist of the year, travelling round all the hot spots in the world taking photos that he hoped would launch his career.

Isabel was working for the government in Rawalpindi, Islamabad's sister city. She spoke Urdu and had been living in Pakistan for a year. She was currently pregnant by a Pashtun (a Pakistani warrior) and seeing whether she could have an abortion in Pakistan. Seeing as abortions, sex before marriage, sex with an infidel and sex with a white lady were all punishable by death, I suspected that she would struggle on that one.

Nat and Simon had just returned from the Chinese border. They were trying to walk back to Switzerland with their donkey, affectionately called Bert. The Chinese had rejected their application to take the donkey across their borders.

Enjoying the town, I saw a man with the long beard, sunglasses, and the looks and confident swagger I associated with the Taliban. I lifted my camera to take a picture of him for the people back home when a passing salesman hit my hands down hard and said "No photo. Taliban." People involved with the Taliban walk around unopposed in these areas. The power they wield is immense in such humble towns.

The U.S. funded the Taliban when they were fighting the Russians in 1979 - the year of my birth - hoping to weaken the Russians at a time when the Cold War was particularly heated. The money and arms they pumped into the regime are still being used against the U.S. army today. The U.S. interfered with the Iran / Iraq War funding the little known Saddam Hussein in his battle with another arch-enemy of the U.S. Again the tables turned and the weapons started to be pointed at their providers.

* * *

The stones I'd seen in Matt's collection would one day be sitting on the finger of a Western woman as her prospective husband kneels in front of her with the words, "Will you marry me?" still ringing in her ears. A girl from England, Sue, was sitting by her husband-to-be. I was the only member of her family in the room. I'd only met her once before.

She had come to Pakistan to teach at a school for girls, and I'd been introduced to her as a fellow teacher. The girls live in a hostel throughout the year where they aren't allowed visitors and they aren't

164

allowed to leave the school. They are, however, against historic Muslim principles, gaining an education that could change their lives in the future, and change the lives of every girl born in Pakistan. In the course of her teaching stint, Sue had met a Pakistani man, Muhammad, or Munti as she affectionately called him.

"I came to Pakistan as one step on a long backpacking trip. It was winter so I planned to come to Gilgit for just two or three days. Everyone said I was mad to come at all, but three other backpackers I met in Lahore were brave enough to join me. On our second day here, we met Munti and his cousin, Kamran. Munti wanted to learn English and so Kamran encouraged him to just say hello to the boys in our group. The next day we went on a trip together and got on fantastically. I stayed in Gilgit, and Pakistan, longer than I had planned as we got to know each other. After three months I continued on to India but not before securing my visa to return. Three months in India was a long time away from Munti and I rushed back to Gilgit to see him. Here I lived in a girls' hostel and taught English while we made some life decisions and I got to know his family, friends, town and a very different culture to my own."

Sue's family weren't prepared to travel out to Pakistan and, in their absence and as the only white man invited to the wedding, I was proclaimed her brother and asked to be her chief witness.

In preparation, Habib lent me his best *Shalwa Kamis* and I thought it was only fitting that I should arrive in a Pakistani-styled mode of transport. I headed down to the shop where the Pakistani trucks get made to look beautiful and showed them the vehicle I wanted to have pampered, painted and polished. They finished the job moments before the wedding and I went to pick her up. Nervously I pulled off the sheet hiding my ride from me. She looked beautiful. Shirley stood there shining like a star.

I rode in convoy with the bride's car to the wedding celebrations at her friend's house (it would normally have taken place at her family's house but that was obviously in England). Celebrations in Pakistan tend to revolve around a buffet full of food at which one stuffs oneself silly. The bride was nervous and couldn't touch a thing. However, when we went onto to the groom's house afterwards, he was in an even worse state. It's at the groom's house (their future home) that the main ceremony, *Shia nikah*, takes place. The wedding had been in full swing for two days already whilst the assembled horde of relatives observed certain traditional ceremonies.

Sitting in a circle we were each given a Pakistani sweet dripping in sweet oil. The Qazi recited verses from the Koran.

A man on the groom's side kept close to me the whole time, watching my every move, albeit casually. We made some very small talk but I could tell he had something else he wanted to say. After some deliberating he asked me, "Are you all spies?" He was questioning whether all the white people in Pakistan were here to spy for the British or U.S. military. I thought it was hilarious but he expected a straight answer.

That evening we left the wedding couple to have some privacy in a house filled with the groom's relatives. Matt met me on the way out. He said I needed fattening before I headed off. Joining him at his new hotel, I found him knee-deep in boxes packing up to go home – he had probably a ton of crystal to ship for starters. The miners that day had gifted him some of the finest hash from Afghanistan. He asked me if I wanted a smoke and I had to refuse. Smoking and riding bikes up mountains don't readily go hand in hand.

So he suggested I eat some. I tried a nibble, waiting nervously for the consequences. My friends at school had smoked weed but I'd never had a desire to partake. It tended to make them talk about politics whilst playing computer games – neither of those being my favourite pastime. Nothing seemed to happen. We headed out to the finest restaurant in town where another buffet was laid out, my second of the day - eat all you can. The food was sumptuous and I devoured one plate after another. In all I gobbled five plates of food and then had polished off two plates stacked with deserts. Looking at Matt I realised we hadn't spoken in an hour. We locked eyes and I realised we were stoned out of our brains. We collapsed in giggles. As the effects wore off, so the ominous awareness of how full my stomach was grew, and my giggling suddenly stopped. It felt like my stomach wall was about to rupture. I had to lie down. The ex-President had just entered the bar with a host of men carrying guns, and I wasn't sure they'd appreciate me lying on the floor groaning. We had to get home. Struggling to walk whilst supporting my over-inflated belly with both hands, I bumped into Matt's gem dealer whom I found a little creepy. He fell into step beside me and tried to persuade me to buy his gems, immediately giving me an amazing ruby worth $200 as a sweetener.

Back at the hostel, I tried to sleep it off. Paranoia set in and I was concerned I wasn't breathing. When CO_2 builds up in your lungs, messages are sent to the brain to say, 'breathe'. At this moment my body was so numb from the hash I couldn't feel the message. I was afraid that if I slept I wouldn't wake up. Kevin, an Irishman, was in the dorm room. I woke him up to ask him if he'd speak to me outside where I urgently explained the situation and my fear of dying in my sleep.

He calmly confirmed that I was definitely breathing and suggested maybe I should make myself sick. Fingers down my throat, I vomited all over the hostel's flower beds. Other travellers who'd heard our conversation were laughing their heads off but remained in their warm beds, leaving the joy of dealing with me to Kevin.

The next morning I decided it was time to leave Gilgit. My experiences had been so wide: I'd met so many people, been to a wedding, decked Shirley out and danced at the final of the Polo Championships. I would have one last day there to say goodbye to Habib and my friends at the hostel. I therefore organized a Pakistan vs. the Rest of the World game of cricket out in the street.

The Pakistani team was made up of friends of Habib and workers at the hostel, all of whom seemed to know how to hold the bat. The Rest of the World team was made up of Aussies and Brits who one would have thought would know about this great game but, unfortunately, had a penchant for holding the bat baseball-fashion and bowling like children.

All over Pakistan men and boys were playing cricket in the streets, the ball being wrapped in tape to stop it flying too far. The drainage in the street was a bit of a difficult one. If it landed in there, the nearest fielder had to dip his hand in to get it back. Sarah, an Aussie girl and our best player, was pulling it out of the gutter when she screamed and ran back to the hostel. On closer inspection there was a dead cat in the gutter and the ball had landed on it. Slowly interest waned and people wandered back into the hostel. Two musicians, Darius and Oshan, had arrived. Both half-Iranian, half-English, they'd brought violins, guitars and mandolins with them. With me on ukulele, we had a massive jam session until we felt peckish.

Ali had returned from her travels deep into the Pakistani countryside delivering presents and, accompanied by Matt, we went to our local for the famous chicken Kurai with naan bread. On one end of my naan was a big piece of mould which must have fallen from somewhere as the bread was fresh out of the oven. Tearing it off, I left it on the side of my plate, not wanting to make a fuss, while I polished off my curry. The fresh meat and sauce were so delicious that when I spotted I'd left a bit of bread behind, I used it to mop up.

Swallowing it down I realised that it was the piece with the mould on it. Oh dear.

* * *

Oh dear indeed. I awoke at 1am that night with my stomach turning over and over like a tumble dryer. I ran to the toilet and that's where I remained until dawn. Even when my stomach was empty, I still found more liquid to expel every hour. I had food poisoning of the Asian variety.

The next three days and nights blurred into a delirious haze. I would wake with either Matt or Ali by my side, asking if I was OK and whether they could help. I could barely walk to the toilet by the end. Every ounce of my energy was gone. Sander, whom I'd met in Osh, joined my aid party. Having seen me in Osh, he said I looked like death and insisted I go to hospital. I refused, not knowing how I could manage a cab ride without a toilet nearby.

Sander was keen to get the next leg of his journey over. He too had been warned about the dangers of the next stretch of road. I was keen to do the route with a friend rather than alone. As soon I was able to sit on a bike, without a cork, I suggested that we go the next day. He agreed.

* * *

Two days later we were still at the Madina. The hostel had locked its doors and it wasn't a plot to get us to spend more money there. We were woken by gun shots. The results were out in the election. A pact had been made between the Shiite and the Sunni Muslim factions that people would vote with their hearts and not with their religion. As the results were announced, each accused the other of voting according to their religious beliefs and all hell broke loose. Tracers whizzed through the air at night, shooting could be heard, fires were lit in the streets and shops all closed their doors for forty-eight hours.

Habib assured us the gunfire was in celebration but I couldn't help feeling that some of them screamed with malice.

Chapter 31

Ignoring all warnings, we headed south of Gilgit towards Islamabad.

Studying a map over breakfast we hoped it would take us five days. Habib had said as we set off that he thought we might be OK but, "Please don't travel at night."

We hadn't taken sufficiently into account the fact that the road was horrendous. It was littered with huge boulders and large sections were covered in landslides, or had themselves slid down into the river. We had to edge around corners and jump over rocks whilst at the same time avoiding any other vehicles. Time wore on and owing to the steep sides of the road we hadn't found a camping spot. As it got dark Habib's final warning started to echo in my ears. I kept my eyes out for tracers flashing through the sky, or bandits.

Five men stood in the road blocking our passage.

As we pulled to a standstill, they asked who we were and where we were going. I replied saying I was cycling to India to raise money for children. A smile emerged and widened and I knew we weren't in trouble. We were grasped by the arm and marched into their makeshift hut. Guns again littered every surface. Positioned out here to protect the Chinese workers against Taliban attack, the Pakistani police kept their eyes peeled for any strange travellers. The Taliban viewed the Chinese as infidels and had been known to attack the workers building the new KKH.

China is perhaps the most reliable friend of Pakistan. Despite some unfriendly acts by the Pakistani secret agencies supporting 'jihad' in parts of China and forging too close alliances with America, China has continued to be friendly with Pakistan, helping it in various mega-projects.

When India developed nuclear weapons, the rest of the world claimed they were giving India nuclear technology for civilian energy production and peaceful purposes. When India detonated its bomb in 1974, they said it was a peaceful nuclear device. What on earth is peaceful about a bomb that can destroy a city? To add to these crazy ideas they called it the Smiling Buddha. The symbol of peace across the new world, the Buddha now had his name associated with a nuclear bomb.

The test generated great concern in Pakistan, which feared that it would be at the mercy of its long-time arch-rival and quickly responded by pursuing its own nuclear weapons program with financial and educational help from China who, after numerous wars with India over the past decades, had a vested interest.

The police welcomed us into their camp, feeding and watering us, and telling us all about life in the area. As normal, the conversation turned to women and matter-of-factly the policemen told us that their wives were not allowed to leave the home. One man in town had four wives and twenty-five children. At less than five foot, he had climbed all of Pakistan's highest peaks – or at least that's what he told the ladies. They went on to ask us about our relations and wanted graphic details of our love lives. When we said we were free to have relations before marriage, they were amazed. If someone were to do the same thing there, both parties would be publicly executed.

"Do you have to pay for these relations?"

The next question made me giggle. "Do you get shot for being an atheist?"

The Chinese returned from their work smiling and joking, and passed us by without a glance. Perhaps it was not uncommon to have cyclists in this area, or perhaps they were exhausted after fourteen to sixteen hours heavy labour.

With food in our bellies, both Sander and I started to droop after the arduous day we'd had. Our escorts showed us to an external tent and kicked out the guards who were currently sleeping there to allow us some privacy. Sander's sleeping bag had got wet when he was in the mountains and now smelt like rotting flesh. Laughing at our luck we launched ourselves towards our dreams.

When I woke the following morning, I was accosted as I staggered out into the morning sunshine, handed an AK47 and told to fire it into the air. The officer then handed me his revolver to shoot as well. I, like most, have a small fascination with guns, built around Hollywood movies and war coverage. Whether it's the power, the excitement or the loathing, they can't be ignored. Surprisingly, firing one isn't exciting at all. Guns were common here and having it in my own hands was neither exciting nor scary.

I got much more excited taking shots with my camera of all the policemen balancing on one motorbike. As we left they told us of news that during the election four people were killed in a polling station in Chillas, our next destination.

As we cycled down the road we saw that the Chinese were everywhere, working feverishly on the road like worker ants. They never stopped, nor did they acknowledge us, unlike the Pakistanis who all downed tools and cheered whilst trying to get us to stop for tea.

Sander was not looking good. Over the past days he had been getting sicker and sicker. He was just managing to keep his pedals moving. I pushed onto the next village to get us some food to try to give him some strength.

The next village was Jalipur, a bustling market town like any other, except for one major difference. There were absolutely no women. When I asked someone about this, they corroborated the policemen's story of the previous night that they literally weren't allowed to leave their homes. It's like lawful house arrest. You marry into prison life.

Waiting for two dhal to be served, I got to people watch for a while. It's my favourite pastime even when I'm in London. Nothing beats watching the quirky characteristics of people going about their normal lives. A group of children were dragging a dead dog around the street for fun. A small homeless boy, dressed in rags that were barely holding together over his scrawny body, was throwing stones at an older gentleman. The boy could not have been older than five or six, and the man was edging up on his personal century. As the lentil broth was served, I noticed that the old man was now throwing stones at the boy. The boys who had been playing with the dog now noticed the child and a chase ensued. When they caught the boy, they presented him to the old man who hit him. He was then passed around to anyone else who wanted to give him a whack. Surely people should have been helping this boy, not making things worse. One of the older boys tore a branch off a tree and gave it to his dad to bestow a few lashings.

Sander couldn't have come sooner as far as I was concerned and, as soon as he had wolfed down the dhal, I was badgering him for us to get away from this place. It was giving me the creeps. It was clear to me that the lack of women was destroying this place. Where was the compassion, the care?

Just as we were about to leave, an albino boy was thrust in front of us. His skin was white and so was his hair. His eyes were a very pale blue. He was obviously used to abuse and bowed his head, preparing himself for a Western onslaught. They said he was the same as us, and laughed.

There are far more albinos in Asia than in the UK. Some villages are up to 5% albino. These children face severe problems in society with the result that they end up with a poor education and weak social skills. The physical side is the extreme photosensitivity of their skin. It could be worse, I guess. In Africa they are hunted for medicinal purposes. Parents who care have to hide them away to stop the slaughter. To try and set an example, I grasped his hand and shook it, as I would a member of the royal family, and bowed my head slightly to try to show him some respect. *As-Salaam Alaykum.* The abuse stopped, but I suspect only for a few moments.

We made it to Chilas, our last stop before it was head down to get the hell out of this here territory. The next two hundred kilometres were real tribal and bandit country.

It was just south of Chilas that Matt and Ali's previous bus had been hijacked, leaving the driver with a bullet hole in his forehead, all the passengers deprived of their belongings, and the bus smouldering in pieces on the road.

As we pulled into our hotel, someone came up to us and said to Sander, "I like your clothes". He was wearing the traditional *Chalwa Kames* - a shirt that hangs to your knees - and a massively baggy pair of pants whose waistband you wrap around yourself numerous times. Turning to me in my Lycra shorts, he said aggressively, "I don't like yours." I decided pretty swiftly it was now time to put on some trousers and to try to blend in as best I could.

Leaving Sander to get better in Chilas, I set off for this much-dreaded section of the Swat Valley on my own. Tribal mountain villages were scattered along my route and a police convoy was required for this part. The police followed close behind me, making me feel like a cross between a hardened criminal and the President of the U.S., which during the Bush administration was very much the same thing.

I called into a café momentarily to discover that its floor was covered with excretion.

The Swat Valley was only a few miles away now. There was no time like the present to get through it. Hopefully.

The Swat Valley with its high mountains, green meadows and clear lakes, is a place of great natural beauty and used to be popular with tourists, being nicknamed, 'the Switzerland of Pakistan'. However, tourists have been replaced with Taliban soldiers, and the Pakistanis who had reaped money from their international guests have been replaced by soldiers. Swat had been home to some of the fiercest fighting between the Taliban and the Pakistani Army.

A tailback of cars indicated where it began. At the head of the tail was an assortment of police vehicles. Again fears of ambush, robbery and killings filled my mind. No-one in the queue seemed stressed, so I continued on, inching past the stationary trucks and vans. Shirley slipped and I watched stones falling hundreds of feet to the valley floor. Gathered around the front vehicle were thirty or more people. The van was jacked up on two boulders and people were squabbling about how to change the wheel. Another ten people were cooking by the side of the road to feed all who were involved in this much-debated operation. It was a true display of teamwork and ingenuity.

The wheel was fixed and the spare secured to the roof. Assuming that the people had come from the tailback of other cars, I was surprised when all but two got back into the van that should have seated only twelve people. Contorted bodies could be seen through the windows but still I could see smiles on the faces of those who hadn't already fallen asleep. The police waved me on.

Chapter 32

Mansehra was my next stop and I fell into bed as soon as I arrived. Gunfire sounded in the distance. Tiredness took over and sleep enveloped me.

A loud bang woke me in the morning. I was up and out of that place like a rocket. I didn't want to hear, see, or smell another bullet. The next one could have my name on.

Outside the town an older gentleman told me to wait. I sat and waited for the notorious teas to arrive. They didn't come and neither did the gentleman. Looking at my watch and stretching out, I relaxed, giving him a few more minutes. Another minute later and a tapping on my shoulder brought me back to the real world. The old man had a Browning *Chalwa Kameez* in his hand. It was his own one. It was a gift for me and he wanted me to put it on right now.

I soon came across civilisation. The single-lane track became a four-laned dual carriageway and at times six lines of traffic filled the road. The outside lane in each direction – which is usually the cycle lane – was being used for traffic coming the opposite way. The habitual dome of smog showed on the horizon. It got bigger and closer, and I soon plunged headlong into it. The mountains disappeared as did the cars in front. Dust and diesel coated me inside and out. Still, when people looked up they nodded in recognition of my traditional dress before getting back to work.

Isabel, Nat and Simone were in town. Nat and Simone were the Swiss couple who had wanted to cross China with a donkey that had been refused entry – it didn't have a passport.

Islamabad is the capital of Pakistan. The name translates as the Home of Islam. Bombs laid by extremists were exploding regularly in Islamabad now, targeting the infidels.

Celebrating having survived the Taliban and the bandits, we all headed for the diplomatic enclave and the French embassy. This place is full of diplomats who don't venture past the walls and barbed wire for their whole stay. They walk around as though they are travellers of the 1800s, dividing and conquering. But in addition to these frauds there was also beer. None of us had touched a drop for the weeks or months we'd been in the country, and we were so excited we were even able to pretend we were interested in the diplomats for a few moments. Being back in this Western civilization was fun for a night, but the stimulus of our surroundings was nothing compared with the streets of the old town of Islamabad.

Despite the horrendous traffic and smog, Islamabad - or *Pindi* (*Rawalpindi*) – is quite beautiful and colourful in its own special way. Flocks of eagles swoop left and right, whilst *pan* is spat, colouring whatever it hits red. Cars hoot, goats casually graze on the piles of rubbish in the street, tuk-tuks swerve round the traffic, calls for prayer are drowned out by breakbeat Indian tunes emanating from the shops, sumptuous material is used to cover the women, and the men chatter around burning rubbish to keep warm. Drinking in the sweet fruits of the juice shop, I listened to the world go crazy around me.

The smog on the journey to Islamabad was still having its effects on my body. I was coughing heavily, with black bogies crystallising in my nose to form sharp shards.

Karrar Haidri, one of the photographers from Gulmit, left a message at the hotel saying I would be picked up in the morning to meet some of his friends. He told me to bring my bike along. Just what I needed - a cycle ride in the bustling streets.

Arriving at a sports complex nearby, I was greeted by the flashing of camera bulbs and the scrutiny of video cameras. Microphones were thrust into my face. Karrar had organized a surprise press conference during which I had to relive every moment of my trip as I cycled in circles and waved to the cameras.

That morning the hotel had pointed out that my visa had expired and that I had to move out today. Karrar gave me a lift back to the hotel with my bike hanging out of the back of his boot. My clothes were all on the landing. The manager said I had to leave.

Typically, the TV was turned up so loud as the background noise to the hotel that I couldn't think of a reason why they should let me stay. Karrar was gesticulating towards the TV, but I ignored him, wondering what to do. If only they'd turn the sound down.

Before I knew it the reception was empty and everyone was in the other room watching and listening. What had happened? I was able to see over everyone's heads, being the tallest person in the hotel by far at only 5"9.

On the TV was a face I recognised, slightly hairier than I'd seen it before and a bit wind-swept. But it was clear to see. My face was blown up to about a foot in size on the TV. Beautiful Urdu-scripted subtitles adorned the bottom. It was the interview I had done that morning. The interview finished, so someone switched channels. Another news programme was showing the same interview. Flicking through the national channels I saw myself time and time again telling the same story, talking of the money raised back home for the charity in the sub-continent.

The manager's attitude suddenly changed. He gave the receptionist a clip around the ear and told him to return my clothes and equipment to my room. Touching my hands and bowing slightly, and advising me to avoid the police, he helped Karrar up the stairs with my bike.

Karrar stepped into my room and almost vomited. I hadn't really considered it in a critical way but it was indeed pretty gross. The walls were coated with dirty finger marks, the floor was covered with dust. Unidentifiable stains had never been cleaned, smoke had stained the roof, mould hid in every corner, holes punctuated the walls, the stench of sewage penetrated every fibre of our bodies, the curtains were torn netting, and the door was held shut by a single nail. At less than two quid a night in a capital city, I couldn't complain.

* * *

From then on I was on TV constantly across all channels. People in the street pointed or laughed at me but, to be honest, that wasn't too different to how it had been the whole way. Friends throughout Pakistan sent emails to say they'd seen me. However, nice as it was, time was ticking away and time dictated that I should leave Islamabad.

A knocking on my wall woke me in the night. It was from Isabel's room. Getting up, I pushed her door which swung inwards. Isabel had taken a cocktail of prescription drugs which she'd been told acted as a do it yourself abortion kit. She had decided that there was no way she was going to have the baby and consign herself to a life in a kitchen with nothing to do but clean and cook. The man she was involved with was a Pashtun and many of his tribe were mixed up with the Taliban. The consequences of being exposed as having had sex with an infidel would be swift.

She was in extreme pain. I sat down next to her and held her hand as she convulsed in agony. I didn't know what to do. Telling someone might put her in grave danger, but not doing so might do the same. She calmed down after a time and was able to sit upright. She pulled out some white powder, rolled it into a spliff and lit it. I asked her what it was. Heroin. Man, it was definitely time to leave.

* * *

Before I could do so, however, I had a favour to do for a friend. Abdul, with his most childlike enchanting giggle, was the one and only Pakistani hippy I'd met. He was in his prime during the 60s which he'd spent mostly travelling Europe, smoking and meeting ladies. Owning a guesthouse in Gilgit now, he smoked with tourists and generally did his best to keep everyone amused. He'd been invited to Spain by one of his old friends and needed a visa. Since Pakistanis were forbidden from entering the diplomatic enclave, it was pretty difficult for any local to get a visa for another country. I had promised him earlier in the week, when he'd told me all about Pakistan's and his own vibrant history, that I would act as a go-between and take the passport in for him. I felt extremely nervous walking past all the armed guards with a Pakistani passport in my pocket, I can tell you. Arriving at the Spanish embassy, I sat waiting for someone to see me. When finally they did so, I soon found out that they were far from pleased that I had brought a Pakistani passport inside their embassy, and the situation got rather heated as I argued Abdul's case. Despite this, I managed to persuade them to at least consider him for a visa, at which point they checked over his passport and began laughing. His passport had expired in 1967. They apologised but there was nothing they could do for him under those circumstances anyway. I couldn't argue that one. So Abdul was left to fight his own corner as I boarded a bicycle, destination Lahore.

Chapter 33

I was able to see first-hand the extent of slum housing in Islamabad as I left the city. Plastic sheeting, branches and anything else the owners could get their hands on made up a whole village where people squatted, cooking on fires. Without the poverty it would look like a colourful modern art exhibition.

The same smog-ridden air that was filling my lungs was also filling handmade kites. Made from plastic bags and sticks, they were flown by the children in ragged, if any, clothes.

I thoroughly enjoyed returning to being the unknown guy on a bike again and waved cheerily at people who either returned the gesture or simply stared open-mouthed as I cycled past.

I was repeatedly advised to avoid crowded areas or going out at night, however, within three hours of checking into a hostel two floors above a busy road and market stall in Lahore, I found myself surrounded by thousands of people in a passionate mood in the pitch black.

I had been invited to a gypsy festival and I felt I couldn't turn down the opportunity. I was told it was only one hour away, so why not? Three hours of driving later and still on a bus, I was squeezed between eight people on three seats. Geoff, Aron, Nisa and Aban - our hostel owner - were a few rows back. We had our legs and knees intertwined and, if the bus had hit the brakes suddenly, it would have been goodbye to Dan's future children and hello to agonising pain. Luckily the bus' brakes didn't work. Instead it just swerved left and right around any obstacles.

One of the Pakistani boys in front of me had his phone out and was encouraging me to look at it. Whilst the bus bounced down the road it was as if my eye sockets were on a spin cycle and I couldn't make anything out. When we came to a standstill, I saw that the boy was showing me Western pornography in which a powerfully-built white guy was standing proud, with a girl on her knees in front of him. Pointing to the guy, I asked if it was him, to raucous laughter from his friends. One of the friends didn't laugh. He was gazing at me with a faraway look in his eyes, his hand rested on my leg. There wasn't much room to put it anywhere else. "You are so beautiful," he said as he squeezed my cheek between his thumb and forefinger. "Can I kiss you?"

This brought about no laughter from his friends. They wanted to know how I would respond and were looking quizzically at me. I had been warned that local men on the sub-continent might take a liking to blond men, but I hadn't realised they would be so open about it. Isabel had told me that many of the tribal boys practised sex with each other before they were married. Simply calling it 'practising', both parties would be highly offended if it were to be suggested that they were engaging in anything that might be considered homosexual.

Back looking at the phone, the first boy said "I used to like English girls. ..." He paused for effect, "... until I found out they like to have sex with horses." Someone had sent him some disgusting animal films. He assumed if one English girl would do that, so must all the rest. This is life in Pakistan. No-one stands out or goes against the grain.

As we took photographs during the festival, we were swamped by male Pakistanis as interested in us as we were in them. The attention got so frenetic that it started to feel like a rugby maul. We were quickly whisked to the ladies' chamber where we were served dhal with rice. There were no chapatti. With the chapatti bread it had been easy eating with our hands, pinching the bread between thumb and forefinger to make a scoop. Without the bread, it was impossible to grasp the sauce or the rice. We couldn't put our whole hands in our mouths, so we got it as far as our lips, opened our fingers and spilt it down our fronts. I resorted to holding it above my head and dropping some into my mouth like birds feeding their newly-born. The local women thought this was very funny. The most fundamental of tasks, eating with your hands, had to be retaught. It was only some weeks later in India that I actually managed it without dropping it all over myself and anyone else unfortunate enough to be within a couple of metres of me.

When we'd been ushered to the ladies' enclave, we realised we'd lost Geoff. As I sat there feeling very sorry for myself and embarrassed about my eating techniques, he was out taking cool pictures. Gutted.

As festival fever erupted, the band was still nowhere in sight. It was decided it would be safer to move us to a home in the village for tea and biscuits as our security had been compromised. Biscuits! Couldn't complain about that.

On the way to the local house, Aban returned from looking for Geoff having concluded he wasn't there. Offering to go back to the festival, I found myself in an atmosphere that could be cut with a knife. Gypsies from all over the area were here, and each tribe viewed itself as superior to the next. There was now a heavy police presence so, of course, lots of dark metal was reflecting in the lights around. I could feel the aggression and saw a fight broken up by tough-looking tribal men.

We duly scampered back to the house, assuming Geoff had somehow decided to go home. Worrying about this, we were told to form a line like school children before being dragged back to the festival. The music had arrived and, with it, a serene calm. Walking hand in hand like the Brazilian football team, we stepped over people crammed into the small tented arena until we were right at the front, just ahead of the spiritual leaders and organisers. We were VIPs.

The singing and drumming started to make my hair stand on end. My body convulsed with the energy and passion of the music. I could see how it plays a massive part in the religion. By the end of the first song, grown men were weeping and the organisers were dropping 5R notes all over the spiritual leaders and the band members. Some fell by my feet. Nisa looked at me and mouthed, "Not for you."

Nisa, a Turkish girl with gorgeous golden skin and dark pools for eyes, and with enough energy to power an Indian city – with none of the usual power cuts - was travelling with Aron, her Estonian boyfriend, a man who maintained the most caring and happy nature even when projectile vomiting. They had travelled overland from Turkey to Pakistan and were planning to get to Mongolia. They had brought bikes with them, enjoying the freedom to cycle or to take a bus, depending on dangers, distances and desire.

The night progressed and I was asked to stand. A wedge of 5 rupee notes was forced into my hand. I dropped them over the spiritualists and band before copying my Pakistani neighbour who threw a handful into the air, allowing them to fall like snowflakes all around me.

The music got better and better, hypnotic in its expression.

* * *

We were relieved to find Geoff tucked up in bed on our return. He'd actually got lost on the way from the bus to the festival. How he'd managed that I have no idea as it was only a stone's throw away.

During the process of Pakistan becoming independent, Lahore was made capital of the Punjab State in the new country of Pakistan. Almost immediately, large-scale riots broke out among Muslims,

Sikhs and Hindus, causing many deaths as well as damage to historic monuments. Punjab is the only state in the world that straddles two borders. Half is in India, half in Pakistan.

With its cultural and religious history, it is inevitable that music of many genres should centre around Lahore.

The next night we went to a Sufi night. The music wasn't a touch on the previous night, but it still left us energised and humming a tune. The dancing was out of this world. The Sufis are religious icons who relax until they become the music. Their most prominent feature is the wobbling of the head. Starting slowly and increasing in speed, their features blur making them look featureless, or at times as though they have faces on either side of their heads. Looking away as the tempo increased further, it looked like their heads were going to fall off. The music went on to have a real 'drum and bass' feel, and the Sufis spun in circles faster and faster, beyond the limits of humankind.

One person in the whole crowd was asked to get up and dance with them. Who? That's right. Me. Spinning onto centre stage, I tried the head wobbling. Relaxing my neck and keeping my shoulders still, I gave it everything I'd got until I felt as though I was going to vomit. I had a headache for one hour afterwards. The pressure they put on the brain can only be compared with repetitive road accident whiplash or going twelve rounds with Mike Tyson. Is it any wonder some of them were losing their hair in chunks and seemed a little brain-damaged?

The next morning it was time to brave the border guards with my expired visa. Nisa and Aron joined me on their bikes after I'd done a little DIY on them. Their wheels were almost flat, their handlebars were loose, and their seats very low. How they'd got this far I had no idea. It showed wonderful perseverance.

Their tyres were worn so thin they suffered repeated punctures. I was happy to lend a hand. Also struggling with food poisoning, Aron had to stop and vomit every few minutes.

This all somewhat delayed us and, by the time we'd made the thirty kilometres to the border, it was closed. Happily we put up their small two man tent in no man's land and all squeezed into it until Aron needed to vomit and we had a bit more space.

We surreptitiously packed up the tent whilst being serenaded by a drummer from the local housing. I took a deep breath. This was the last country on my itinerary - India. I stepped into the border post with trepidation.

Chapter 34

The Pakistan / India border is a very fragile one, running almost three thousand kilometres. Both countries claim Kashmir as their own, killings are common, fighting is continuous and both refer to the other as 'The Enemy'.

There is only one official border crossing and it proved to be my most dangerous yet. It has very strict hours of opening and on our first night we had to camp beneath the watchful eyes of the Pakistani border guards.

The guards themselves are far taller than any other Pakistani men, whom I normally tower above. Possessing the size and physique of NBA basketball players, plastered with medals of honour they have no doubt earned fighting the Indians, their long fingers play with their weapons which hang caressing their legs in the perfect position for a grab-and-fire.

You can imagine the tension I felt approaching this border. Adrenaline ran through my veins, my muscles were taut, my eyes watched every move and my ears listened out continuously for a trigger being cocked ... the feelings I experience watching horror films, as I wait for the blood to flow, when I hide behind a cushion, hair on end, and wish for it all to be over and forgotten.

What I didn't expect to find at the border was a carnival atmosphere - a circus enacted with schoolboy competitiveness. It was more like a Disney cartoon than a horror film after all.

The Indian soldiers were the same size as their Pakistani counterparts and, right in front of me, the two armies paraded on their respective sides of the border, marching in unison. Then all the soldiers stopped. There was silence. One soldier emerged from each group. They had obviously been watching too much Monty Python - The Ministry of Silly Walks sketch in particular. They marched towards each other and, every fifth step, they kicked a foot up towards their heads to see who could kick the highest. Crowds of civilians and tourists on each side of the border come to watch this ceremony on a daily basis and cheer if one of their soldiers seems to have won out on the foot kicking.

Another soldier came forward and they stopped side by side at the border crossing. Looking towards their different gods, they started making a call – a single note – almost like an 'aaah' at the dentist. This went on and on as apprehension built in the audience.

The competition seemed to be about who could make a single note last the longest without breathing. The Pakistani soldier outdid the Indian one, and the crowd around me went wild.

And the next event in the school sports day challenge was to find out who could run up their flag the quickest.

This routine happens every day. Stern faces seem to mask a friendly rivalry. It reminded me of the cycle rides I do with Steve. But underpinning all this frivolity was a deeper undercurrent. To the north especially, people were being killed in gun fights and both sides were blaming the other for the explosions in cities. It was a nasty situation.

When we thought no-one was looking, we posed for pictures, kicking our legs as high as we could. Within the space of seconds, a large guard was looming over me. Bowing my head, I shook his hand and made for the sanctuary of the buildings.

Leaving the dry, desert landscape of Pakistan with its grey buildings and the men wrapped in grey or brown shawls, I walked through the border post separating the two countries. The Pakistani guard stamped my passport in a distracted manner without even looking at my visa.

As I popped my head out the other side, I was greeted by green, lush foliage, birds flying and the sounds of animals. I wanted to go back and see if the grey Pakistani side had changed too. One thing remained the same however – the friendliness of the people.

Five kilometres from the border, we were dragged off the road and through two gates decorated with flowers in colours I hadn't seen for some time. A big hotel had been decorated to the nines, and the guests were sitting at red plastic picnic tables. We were required to sit down and talk to the guests.

Dressed in my finest-looking, nastiest-smelling Lycra, I had been invited to participate in a Sikh wedding celebration. The colours of the men's turbans intoxicated me, or was it the whisky they plied me with? I'd never seen men gallivanting in such bright colours before. It felt wonderful. Nisa, dressed in her traditional Pakistani attire, was dragged over to the women's section whilst Aron, still queasy from his tummy bug, had to keep rejecting the whiskies which were then passed onto me.

The music started and we were surrounded by dancers pulsing and wiggling their bums and hips whilst gracefully snaking their hands through the air. The dance floor was crammed with men whilst the ladies looked on. It was as if the men were performing like the peacocks in the natural world. Bright colours and exuberant dancing.

It was amazing to think that in some Indian's wedding pictures there would be a guy with flowers all over his bike, wearing the tightest, shortest shorts ever. Surely they would wake up the next day with a nasty whisky hangover and look back and wonder who the hell he was.

Back on the bikes, we wobbled another fifty kilometres towards Amritsar, home of the Golden Temple. The traffic in town was horrendous. Aron and I were buffeted from pillar to post whilst Nisa led the way. At only five foot and riding a worn-out bicycle, she was in complete control. She even managed to hustle a bus off the road and onto the pavement. She was so strong and confident, I couldn't believe it.

Finding somewhere to leave our bikes, we made for the Golden Temple. We stopped off to have our feet washed in the gushing streams that ran between the street and the temple, and were told to cover our heads. Luckily Nisa had a scarf round her shoulders and was able to put it on my head. Aron had a woolly hat. I tried to copy the way the locals did it, and I thought I'd done a pretty good job creating a turban around my head. A soldier guarding the temple stopped me and pointed out that the top of my head was still visible, kindly correcting my headdress for me so that I felt quite regal in my first-ever turban as we strode over to the lake surrounding the Sikh temple.

Thousands of people are welcomed here every day. Your faith doesn't matter, you're wealth is irrelevant, your skin colour is beside the point. You are fed and watered - everything being prepared and served by volunteers - allowed to wash in the holy water (that others then choose to drink!), and invited to sleep there. This was my kind of religion. I lay down with a hand resting on Shirley's wheel and slept amongst the throbbing throng of people who had all been re-invigorated by feasting and washing in the holy waters.

Just north of Amritsar is Dharamsala where the Tibetan government lives out its exile, home of the Dalai Lama who once ruled over Tibet before he was forced to flee by the Chinese military. I hadn't been allowed into Tibet, so here was an opportunity to do a quick detour and experience something of what I had missed.

However, it required some very strenuous cycling into the foothills of the Himalayas. As I neared the town, monks appeared, dressed up and walking in procession up and down the hills. They held out their hands to give me high fives as I went by. Without this encouragement I don't think I would have made it up the tortuous ascents.

After the smog, the tension and the hardships of Pakistan, I dedicated myself to purification. I took a yoga class every day, cycled around the breathtaking mountainous countryside, ate *momos*, the food of the gods, and caught sight of the Dalai Lama who is ever-present in his adoptive new home.

Snow-topped mountains surround this bustling village and through the centre of it the monks flow like a river in their blood red gowns. It would not be the first river of blood some of these monks will have seen – slaughter, torture and assault occurred daily in Tibet once, and still do to an extent. Refugees arrive every day, having crossed the Himalayas by foot in gown and sandals. All have harrowing tales to tell.

Running up to me, a monk said he'd dreamt about me - a man in yellow on a bike - the previous night. In the dream, the Dalai Lama had told him to find me and look after me. He invited me to dinner and told me of his days of torture at the hands of the Chinese. He also gave me a bag full of gifts, including a signed picture of the Dalai Lama (a Tibetan's most prized possession). I couldn't refuse. I still have no idea what on earth happened during those few hours, but my life is richer somehow for the experience.

A group of Tibetans set up a school in town for refugee adults to learn English. Many of these people had seen nothing beyond their native villages in Tibet. Now ousted from their homes, they needed a new way to communicate with the locals. I felt it was my duty to get involved.

I arrived early as the staff were cooking for their teachers and pupils. They were making the customary *momos,* made with simple flour-and-water dough and filled with meat or vegetables, steamed or fried. A Swedish girl with long, flowing, plaited pigtails and blonde hair looked up at me and asked if I was a Viking with my red beard and blue eyes. She taught me some Vikingesque Swedish. *My sword is better than your sword. I like your helmet – where did you get it from? Let me drink your blood.* Knowing what would be on the menu, I'd bought some chocolate and we persuaded the cooks to make some chocolate momos. After dinner I spoke with a monk who had almost no grasp of English. Other Westerners were also conversing with Tibetan adults in line with their differing degrees of knowledge of English. The pupils were so grateful, it was almost embarrassing. It was fantastic to be able to help these people.

Later, one of the other teachers pulled out a bandolin - a cross between a banjo and mandolin. Rushing back to my dwellings, I collected my ukulele. A massive mini instrument jam session ensued. Towards the end of the night, people were pulling out their opium pipes and rolling dubious cigarettes – I hope they weren't trying to numb themselves to the music around them.

Feeling and looking fresher, I slept, ate, practised yoga, and sang and played with our new band - single to be released later this year should we get a deal, write a song and learn to play more than four chords.

We attended a protest against the Chinese occupation of Tibet, but I felt self-conscious walking with Tibetans and Westerners alike arm-in-arm screaming hatred towards the Chinese. Although we British didn't necessarily try to destroy ancient cultures, or commit torture, or practise mass genocide, we have occupied a large portion of the world until fairly recently and still will not allow the Falkland Islands to return to Argentine rule. It felt hypocritical.

* * *

After Dharamsala I saw a totally different side to India. In reaching the cities I passed through the slums where people were living in huts erected using sticks and polythene bags, and where to survive they had to sift through rubbish to find food, or collect enough plastic to sell to buy food. On the streets, they slept in rags, strewn left and right. As I passed south it got warmer but it was still very cold at night. These people took hours to stop shaking the following morning. Some didn't wake at all and lay in the streets for days until the smell got too much and someone cleared them away where they wouldn't bother passers-by.

In our hotel room, the price included a rat which clambered up the curtains and jumped from point to point. Then there were the bed bugs biting and savaging our bodies. We also had lizards which we welcomed to keep the mossies at bay, and mould of the scariest nature, its tentacles slithering down the walls like long fingers waiting to grab us and drag us to our doom.

When we entered cities the smog was unbelievable. Breathing was like sucking on an exhaust pipe - maybe worse. We could see about five metres and make out shapes only up to fifty metres away. It reminded me of scuba diving at thirty metres under, but without the hammerhead sharks. Instead we had cars whose lights acted like lasers in a disco and which cut through the smog like light sabres.

The setting sun was snatched into the mist like a fish catching surface flies. I had anticipated that some cities might be smoggy and had brought a fume mask normally worn by builders in the UK. The filter turned black immediately. We wore scarves round our faces at night and even tried poking cigarette filters up our noses to clean the air.

One night I couldn't sleep. The bugs were bigger than ever. Everything is big here (the cows are frighteningly large, like dinosaurs. No joke. They are huge). They kept jumping on my face (the bugs not the cows), landing in my eye sockets, my beard and my hair. I was constantly grabbing them and crushing them between my fingers with tremendous force, making sure they didn't bother me again.

Sander had met us that day in a café. He was very sick again, having passed through Pakistan. Aron was slowly getting better but remained very tired. I didn't want to switch on the light and wake them just because of a few bugs.

I put my roll matt down on my mattress to stop the bugs getting at me, but it made no difference - they just kept on coming. However, the noise from outside was a distraction - the deafening sound of the TV set.

I did manage to get a few hours' sleep in the end and I woke in the morning with a bladder full to bursting. Dashing to the toilet, I caught my reflection in the mirror as I passed. That wasn't right! I came back to the mirror and stopped. Suddenly my bladder was the least of my concerns. I had maggots in my beard and hair and on my face. I ran back to my bed. They were all over my pillow and the bed was covered with them. A constant stream of them was dropping from the rotting wooden beam above my bed. They hadn't been jumping, they'd been falling. Even after some serious grooming, the itching in my hair wouldn't go away. By the end of the following day it became too much. Taking my pen knife I cut my golden locks off, leaving me with a fairly short, shaggy mane.

But at least I knew there weren't maggots crawling in it.

Chapter 35

Sander, Nisa, Aron and I continued on our way across the Indian landscape. We were tired, and with tiredness came irritation. Whereas the attention of an entire village was fun at the outset, being watched by people standing perfectly still without saying a word - so many people that there was no way we could navigate our bikes through the hordes - soon became wearing.

It wasn't the staring, it was the lack of communication that drove us nuts. It drove Sander to genuine insanity and made Nisa feel very awkward. It was as if they wanted us to entertain them. I was sure we were entertaining them by being ourselves, but I needed to take it to a whole new level to alleviate the stress.

I became the ring master. My sole purpose was to entertain. Doing a little jig, I'd whisk Nisa off her feet with some ballroom dancing, sing a song, juggle available fruit, and then take Sander's cap and put a few rupees in it before asking them for money. Their reactions were hilarious. Some fled, some crossed their arms to protect themselves, but the majority just kept watching, which pushed us to try a succession of gambits to clear ourselves some space.

Swine 'flu was sweeping through Europe and we'd seen it on every news channel in India, so we'd burst into coughs and sneezes while wiping our noses and apologising for bringing the 'flu into their country. It worked a treat. At a local market we made up T-shirts carrying the legend 'Danger - Swine 'Flu Infected' written in both English and Hindi.

At other times I would keep my fume mask on and bark like a dog, scaring the people half to death, then pretend to be a policeman, with whistle and hand gestures, attempting to control both the people and the traffic.

It all seems a little mean looking back on it, but it got us through with sanity intact.

Sander took to explaining that we were Albanian brothers from the circus - sword swallowers and knife throwers ("I only sometimes make mistakes") - or we were escaped criminals, bank robbers and murderers.

The English speaker in the crowd would always command respect and would usually translate Sander word for word. He also, for some reason, never failed to remind people that, "if the monkeys start falling out of the trees, it's too hot."

We would then jump back on our bikes, cycling off in fits of giggles like school children.

Then a pervert on a motorbike came up alongside us, blowing kisses at Nisa and making rude gestures. It was about all Sander could handle, and he hurled himself and his bike at him, chasing him down the street.

We stopped in Ambala and searched for a place to stay. The town was one big rubbish tip. Sander tripped on a dead swollen rat in the road. Cows in India are supposed to have developed the capacity for digesting paper. Lining the streets, they ate the rubbish or ran from the rabid dogs that chased them. The smog and lack of sunlight was making our eyes red and skin pale, giving us the appearance of tragic vampire brides.

At every juice stall we carefully watched to make sure our juice wasn't diluted with water, although we were often not fast enough to stop them putting salt in it. It's perfectly normal here to put a few spoons of salt into your juice but, to our Western tastes, it was a foul habit.

We managed to grab two cheap rooms that were so small we had to sleep around our luggage, separated from one another by a makeshift wall. After wandering the town and finding the restaurant with the smallest number of flies in its pots, we lay on our beds chatting. Sander and I could converse with Nisa and Aron as easily as if there was nothing between the two rooms. For the most part there wasn't; just a board from eye level to the ground.

India seems to have the hugest number of beggars who are victims of severe disabilities or injuries. Blind, crippled and diseased, they tore our hearts from our chests. If we gave money to them, it would be taken by their pimp and, even if it wasn't, there were too many of them to have an impact – you'd need millions to fund them all.

We had to cycle round a guy lying in the road, looking like a child pretending to be a dead cockroach - lying on his back with his arms and legs rigid above his torso - the only difference being that this man was actually dead and left to lie in the street with no consideration at all - another victim of the Indian roads. This highlighted to us just how dangerous cycling through India was. People don't stop, even when they hit people, as the villagers have been known to come out and savage the car and its occupants if the victim is one of their own.

190

After coming across this dead body, Nisa and Aron packed their bikes on a bus and made for Nepal, and Sander flew on to Thailand. I had to continue on my planned route as I was doing it for the children. It was the only way I could persuade myself to put my life at risk any further, subjecting myself by the hour to thundering trucks, weaving cars, tuk-tuks travelling in the wrong direction, potholes and raised road surfaces.

* * *

The roads continued to take their toll on Shirley. Her seat was broken, meaning a sharp shard of metal jabbed into my bottom. I had a sore that ran from cheek to cheek and it was agony at all times.

There are hundreds of cycles in India, the majority being the three-wheeled rickshaw type, hence there are lots of bike shops. They are not quite Bicycle Richmond standard, but they mostly do the job. However, the cycle shacks didn't seem to be able to fix this particular problem. Each night I applied ointment but there was little point. The next day I would be on the bike again, and in pain again.

In Meerut I took a ride with a rickshaw driver but it was too painful watching him struggle with my weight. Making him stop, I pushed him into the seat at the back, to his bewilderment, and seized control of his vehicle. The rotation of the pedals was more eliptical like a rugby ball than circular like a soccer ball. The bike was in the worst condition. Chaos ensued as people fought to watch the idiot white guy with a really bad haircut cycling a local bike with an Indian in the passenger seat. Cars hooted their horns and trucks wavered off the road as their drivers looked over their shoulders – so business as usual on the streets of India.

* * *

As I rode south, working elephants started to appear and naughty monkeys plagued the road. It began to really feel like the India I'd seen in the movies. As I cycled along, a news channel pulled alongside and conducted an interview with me from a moving car.

I stopped at a café and the flies descended upon me, dragging themselves away from the cooking pots and utensils. Bird life freely feeds on the bulbous flies. Seeing meat hung from pegs in the midday heat wrapped in flies, I was suddenly vegetarian again.

After washing the pots with brown water, the cook brought over

191

my food with his thumb in my dhal. He removed it and wiped it on his never-been-washed apron. There was nowhere to wash my hands and the soapless spray handwash my mum had insisted on my using had been lost months ago. Dipping my hand into my food to take my first bite, I thought of the hundreds of hands I had shaken since waking that day and the number of people I had seen doing 'number twos' by the side of the road (there's no toilet paper in India – this is a hands-on approach). I was repulsed for a second but my hunger from a day's cycling got the better of me.

A mouse scuttled from beneath my chair and the obligatory swollen, pustulent rat lay in the gutter in the midday heat. It seemed to be moving but that was just the effect of the flies. The cows eat the fly-encrusted rubbish and they themselves are covered with flies.

It's probably hard for you to believe, I know, but I was sick. What was even harder to believe was that there was no vomiting or diarrhoea. I had 'man 'flu'. Why? When? How? My nose ran, I was coughing, and my throat was so sore.

Recognising me from the paper, my hotel owner gave me a fifty percent reduction. When I showered and dried myself, the towel was black with dirt. The smog and dirt mixing with my sweat from the heat was a terrible concoction to get off my skin.

Needing money, I went round every cash machine in the town. My card was rejected from the first, and the second, and the third. Here we go again. At one of the last ones, I heard it whirring and cheered as if I'd won the jackpot, jumping around the cubical and hammering my fists on the wall. A man ran in with a shotgun to see what the matter was. That soon shut me up. A receipt popped out of the cash drawer. "Unable to process".

Chapter 36

Ditching Shirley in the hallway, I was shown up to the viewing gallery on top of the hotel. Meanwhile everyone else in Agra, the home of the Taj Mahal, was making their way to the top of their own hotel. The sun was just about to set, leaving a magnificent glow over the shining white dome of the Taj.

The hotels vie with each other continuously to get the best view of the Taj. One hotel builds another floor and all those behind it have to do the same to protect their view. I slumped into a chair next to another Brit who was slowly polishing off the hotel's supply of booze, and ordered one of everything on the menu. The Taj looked quite small from where we were, and surprisingly unimpressive.

I wondered to myself whether I'd bother paying the 700R to see it. Locals pay 50R for the same honour. The price seemed to have become a little over-inflated for the foreign tourists. My viewing buddy was equally unimpressed. He was here for the birds. As green parakeets flew over our heads, he named each variety that is present in India. He too was travelling by bicycle, the 'Local Hero' variety, cycling a few miles each day to get to new vantage point to watch more birds.

Despite the fact that the Taj was relatively unimpressive, the view above the city was spectacular. Boys were whistling and whooping on top of buildings to get flocks of pigeons to do an array of acrobatic swoops before returning to their home buildings. Pigeons belonging to different people merged and then parted as the commands flew through the air like radio signals. Troops of monkeys jumped from building to building. Others sat and groomed each other whilst their youngsters fought and grappled on the edge of fifty foot ledges.

I was also joined by Hans and Sophie, a German / Irish couple who were decorated in an array of piercings and tattoos and who had connected their iPod up to speakers, pounding beat box music across the city. An Israeli song came on and a girl ran from her room to be comforted by her homeland music. All three were travelling India and smoking as much of the annual production of passing marijuana plantations as they could. We stayed up all night sharing our experiences and adventures. People still stared in disbelief at the journey I had undertaken but, now that I was in India, they were starting to realise that it was possible, and that I would make it, which was comforting.

.

When I awoke the next morning to see the sunrise, I glanced up at the viewing gallery from below. There were people up there reading the menus and I fancied some company. As I climbed the stairs, I noticed that these people were very small and quite hairy. The monkeys from the previous night were sitting in the exact same positions the guys and I had occupied, holding the menus in front of them as if they were reading them. One had his menu upside down. He was clearly showing off. A holler came from the kitchen below followed by a crashing of steel pans, and the monkeys scampered off, tearing and throwing the menus around as they left.

At ground level, just outside of the hostel, there was a cow that seemed to be meditating. Twelve hours later it was in the exact same spot. It was no doubt getting in the way of the owner's business but, as cows are sacred in India, it was allowed to stay until it decided to leave.

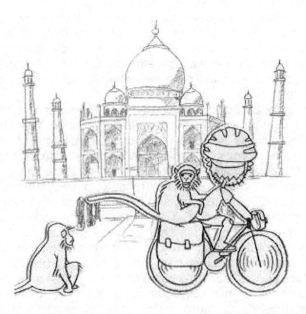

I sat in the centre of the old town waiting for a chai to be served and was greeted by a holy man who blessed me in Hindi before kissing my hand. He had a bright twinkle in his eye and, when he went to kiss my hand again, he bit down on it, drawing blood. Before

I could even begin to decide whether to punch him or run, a monkey jumped from high above onto an electric power pylon. The pylon exploded, sending three prongs of lightning shooting around me. Happy to see the monkey scamper off, I looked around. The holy man had disappeared.

Dressed in beautiful blue uniforms, a group of school children caught my eye and I followed them up the nearby steps near to their school, taking pictures of them and conversing with them in different languages. Sitting a few metres from the stairs, a group of men beckoned me over but I was too busy with the children and monkeys to pay them any attention. The school had a wonderful view of the Taj Mahal. I thought how lucky these children were to have that inspiration in their backyard. On closer inspection, they also had a great view of the men injecting heroin into their crutches and legs. One man noticed my shock and gave me a full frontal of him shooting up.

The heat during the day was becoming intolerable, so I decided to 'go native' and buy the local *lungi, a* sheet that is worn like a skirt in a number of different ways. If David Beckham can do it with a sarong, then Danny Bent can do it with a lungi.

I decided that it would be rude to visit Agra and only see the Taj from afar, so I walked down the street towards the entrance. Pestered by guides trying to make a living at the country's most visited tourist attraction, I strolled forward, avoiding the meditating cow. People tried to entice me into their hotels with calls of marijuana and beer, and I thought it strange that no-one offered me a bed or a good meal.

On my left I had a boy trying to sell me miniature Tajs; on my right were two guides fighting for my trade. When they realised I wasn't buying, they hurled insults at me. In England I would have been stressed by this attention, the peppering of invites and insults, but not here. I realised how accustomed to the attention I'd become. It just washed off my back, but I understood the reputation Agra had. "The city is horrible - arrive and leave in the same day," I'd been told more than once a day since arriving in India. Now this attention was my bread and butter. I needed it. Without it, I'd feel like a movie star going from Hollywood blockbuster to detergent commercials.

After a scrummage at the ticket office, I walked through the majestic gates to the Taj and stopped dead in my tracks. There were long lines of fountains leading to a round dome, surrounded by four pillars. It looked like a long lost friend, so familiar to the eye, as if I had known every detail before I'd even arrived. It was amazing. I stood for minutes just gazing. I looked around and saw the same look in everyone's eyes. The entrance was huge and opened into a clearing which I'm sure was engineered so that people had a chance to just stop and soak it up.

It is one of the most recognizable structures in the world. It was built by Mughal Emperor Shah Jahan in memory of his third wife, Mumtaz Mahal. It is widely considered as one of the most beautiful buildings in the world and stands as a symbol of eternal love.

Twenty-two thousand workers and one thousand elephants built it between 1631 and 1653, whereupon the emperor gave the order for the workers' hands to be chopped off so no-one could make anything like it again.

Most of the tourists around me were Indians. They told me that, "Domestic tourism is very big in India", speaking with that beautiful Indian twang where every syllable is rounded out, and with the accompanying head wobbling that I tried my hardest to perfect during my stay in India.

These tourists, after tearing their eyes away from their beloved Taj, soon noticed the white man in the lungi. In the same way as I'd gazed at the Taj, they gazed at me, and the cameras started to go off. Groups of people gathered round me wanting to pose with me for pictures, including the gardeners pruning the roses who asked me to hold their tools and immediately trod all over the sacred gardens in their haste to appear by my side. Then a monkey jumped over my head. This was something else.

One minute India is beautiful - A-Ma-Zing, magical, tantalising - the next it's nasty, repulsive, vile and angry but, before you know it, it's back to being mystical, tender, wonderful and breathtaking again.

* * *

Men on motorbikes thought it was fun to ride into my handlebars and wheels. Buses played with my life like babies with a rag doll. Children threw stones at my head and, if I stopped, they ran for cover. Cheeky things.

Men made dirty homosexual hand gestures at me. They have grown up surrounded by men, starved of female attention. They are forced to marry a woman they don't even know, who could end up being a bit of a minger or not their type at all and, having totally different interests, they end up despising each other. Is it any wonder they turn to each other for affection and love? And I guess a white, Milky Bar Kid is a new delight.

In fact I noticed an inverse correlation between the number of women in a village and the levels of aggression in the men - more women less aggression, and vice-versa.

In some parts of Pakistan, as I have already observed, the women were not allowed to leave the house. In rural India they are forced to do ALL the work, including mixing cement and working in the fields, while the men sit around chatting and smoking, their only role being to ensure that the women keep up the expected rate of work. By the evening the women are walking back from the fields carrying a huge weight of logs or sticks on their heads. The man walks behind them with an ominous stick. In the end I became so frustrated at their laziness that I would stop and shout to them as I went past, "Working hard? Busy as usual?".

How can this be the case in a country where the first female Prime Minister, Indira Gandhi, was in power almost twenty years before Margaret Thatcher, Britain's first woman Prime Minister. Surely she would have advanced women's rights.

'*Show me the real India*', I called to the universe.

I'd left the beautiful Taj and the bustling Agra, with its town filled with foreign and Indian tourists, and locals who would sell their own mother to a tourist for the right price. '*Best mother in all of India. I give you good price*' – with more head waggling.

The smog seemed to be chasing me and my lungs were hurting. I occasionally coughed up nasty brown sludge.

Red dusty roads cutting between rock formations that wouldn't look out of place in the Australian outback lay before me. Somehow bright yellow rapeseed (my home town, Canewdon's, finest export) managed to flourish here, leaving a wonderful smell and contrast with the red rocks. The red then turned to bright, lush green as agriculture kicked in. Extensive and complex irrigation streams had been cut into the earth to make it possible. Kevin of '*I've eaten marijuana and can't tell if I'm breathing*' fame, from Gilgit, wrote to me telling me how he'd camped in one of these fields. At two in the morning his tent was floating in half a foot of water. In true Irish laid-back style he went back to enjoying his waterbed. We cyclists get tired you know.

The green farmland turned to palm tree jungle, bejewelled with pink and red flowers. The ruined ghost city of Fatehpur peeked out from the undergrowth.

Stopping, I went tiger hunting, intending to shoot them only with my camera. We saw monkeys, all sorts of birds, deer, a leopard kill, and crocodiles, but no tigers. I continued to keep my eyes peeled, except when I was in my tent where, if I had heard a roar, my strategy would have been to hide in my sleeping bag and hope for the best (after kung fu chopping the little blighter and subjecting him to a judo throw, of course. I'm a tough guy. You know that).

As I left Ranthambhore, I passed ladies in luminous dress. Rajasthan is famous for its saris. Carts pulled by camels filled the roads. I saw one that had stopped at a petrol pump. The owner was filling a tank of fuel for his house but at first glance it looked like he was filling the camel up. The home he was taking the fuel to was built of mud bricks and almost certainly had a buffalo roped up outside to provide milk for all the occupants.

A motorcyclist in a clown mask flew past in the opposite direction, carrying his two mates and destroying my last hopes of arriving without incident in Chembakolli.

Never put your camera down, never take your eyes off the road. India is very much alive and not afraid to show it.

Chapter 37

I stopped to buy the Coke and crisps which were what I was eating for breakfast after recent bouts of sickness of the, '*Oh no, how do I get to a phone to call the ambulance without leaving a nasty trail?*' variety, and all business in the village stopped too. Motorbikes pulled over with anything up to four additional passengers, shops emptied, cafés were vacated leaving bills unpaid, and children ran to practise their smatterings of English. These villages don't see Westerners very often.

You can normally tell how long it has been since a foreigner has been around by the ages of the children who burst into tears at the sight of the 'white devil'. Normally it is three to six years.

For someone who loves children and often finds their company more appealing than that of adults, I find this experience surprisingly rewarding. I'm the only white man these children have EVER seen. Normally a few massive smiles and a song can prise them away from behind their fathers' legs, but any fast movements on my part send them scuttling off again.

While I chatted with the kids, the gathering got bigger and bigger. By now I couldn't see anything other than eyes peering at me. If I were to eat lunch, it would remain this way until I picked my bike back up and pushed my way through as politely as possible using my basic Hindi. Having people watch you eat isn't the nicest thing normally, but if they weren't there I'd have been lonely.

As I passed through a village, a cow in front of me did the deed right ahead of me. A woman whipped out of the nearest hut and scooped it up, making it into what can only be described as a huge chocolate button. It would then be left outside the house, or on the roadside, to dry and be used as fuel for the fire. Villages that looked like something from Hansel and Gretel, chocolate button houses, tended to have particularly keen gatherers of cow dung. They looked good enough to eat.

When I was a child, my dad claimed to have been the discus record holder at his school. He would demonstrate his ability to us by picking up cowpats as we walked in the Peak District and he would fire them like bullets as far as we could see. Unlucky bystanders would dive for cover as the stinky discs flew all around them.

A super-attractive girl blew me a kiss. What a highlight. It was my closest encounter with a female in months and it felt GOOD! I was ready to settle down, get married and have kids with her within the year. Shirley, however, was having none of it and forcefully carried me off (albeit kicking and screaming) to my next destination, Bundi, the blue city.

I was glad she had. Bundi is a bustling town drenched in colour, surrounded by an ancient palace in the hills and a putrid lake on the other side.

* * *

I arrived late at night to find markets alive and lit with all sorts of colours. Bundi is a new stop on the tourist map. There weren't many tourists yet but the locals were keen and had set up several hotels, home stays and restaurants in anticipation of a boom. And a boom there surely would be. It was stunning and sitting on top of a mountain above it was an illuminated fort.

I checked into Mama's, a home stay owned by the infamous Mama, *Mother*. I was told to sit myself down with the other travellers who were all waiting for their feeding time, and not to move. One girl tried to go to the toilet but was slammed back into her seat by the small but feisty lady.

When the food came, it didn't stop. We were all treated to *thali*. A thali is a selection of different dishes, usually served in small bowls on a round tray. The round tray is generally made of steel with multiple compartments. Our trays were filled to the brim with dhal, rice, vegetables, chapatti, curd (yoghurt), and chutneys and pickles. By the time we'd finished we had no choice but to stay seated. We were wedged into our seats. Groans echoed around the room as expanded bellies gurgled and complained at the strain. A French couple travelling with their children round the world for a year fell asleep on the spot, allowing the children to explore the house.

Stepping out of the front door, I realised how the city had acquired its nickname. It sloped away from the building we were in and every building was painted the same blue colour. Kites flew all over the city from every rooftop. Boys did battle against each other and kite runners chased those that had been cut down.

Kathleen and Katherine were distracted by jewellery shops, so I walked over to a boy, Gulfam, meaning 'colour', on a roof who invited me to come up and join him, offering me the string to the kites. My nephew, Isaac, would tell you that I was the best kite flyer in the world, so I confidently took the string. A few sharp tugs would

200

normally see the kite soar into the air, however, these kites require skill. The first tug took it into the air; the second turned it and sent it crashing to the earth at the feet of the girls as they came from the market stall. They picked it up and, with some coaching from my new friend, I managed to get it into the air again. The skill is that you have to tug as the top is pointing upwards, then allow it to spin and tug again when it is again facing upwards. Another kite came into sight and the strings were quickly taken from me. The other kite wanted to battle. The battle lasted for about five minutes and, unfortunately, Gulfam had his string cut and his kite floated off into the distance as the kite runners (his younger brothers) ran off to retrieve it.

That night we all headed up to see the sunset from the fort overlooking the town. On the way up, an Indian man tried to sell us a stick. It looked like a very nice and sturdy stick but we thought we were OK for now. Strange man. Who in their right mind buys a stick?

As the sun began to drop, the monkeys poured out of every orifice in the fort - from cracks, from doors and over walls. It was almost like an old-fashioned horror film before chainsaws, guns and stacks of ketchup take over – 'The Birds' maybe; 'The Monkeys'. There were thousands of them. The youngsters played on the walls. The adults sat and de-ticked each other or watched the sun disappear. As the numbers increased, a few males started hissing at us. A particularly brave one took the bag attached to my rucksack and started eating the fruit I'd bought myself. There were only three people up there, Kathleen, Katherine and I, and Katherine had gone. We looked everywhere. The fort was so huge and with so many different demolished rooms that, although we shouted out, we couldn't see or hear her. We grew nervous. It was almost completely dark. After shouting for a few more minutes, we decided to head down. Monkeys lined every path. We had to weave in and out of them. On the way down we saw the stick seller duelling a large male monkey with his stick – now we understood why people bought them. We heard a shout from the café below. Katherine was there and had three ice creams lined up and waiting for us.

The next day I walked around town and had the ruby from Pakistan made into an ear stud. The silver from India and the red from Pakistan became my symbol of peace between the two nations.

It was Eli's Birthday. Eli was a guy from the States who'd spent his time in Bundi learning from Mama how to cook. She had baked a cake for him. In celebration, I bought a turban and headed back. Our normal belly-filling thali was followed by cake (which tasted like washing powder), and by rum and beers in the garden (Mama wouldn't allow beer in the house, even though her husband was selling it on the black market). Mama's daughter, Saatchi, joined us tonight with her lucky white rat. In the Karni Mata Temple, near the city of Deshnoke, rats are sacred. If you go there, the temple is overrun with rats. If you see a white one you will be blessed with luck. Saatchi called me 'turban man', quite a regal name, I thought.

* * *

Travelling across India you can't help but notice the number of very young children working in cafés as chai wallahs and running errands - doing anything, in fact, except being at school. If I had decided I wouldn't eat anywhere which employed child labour, I would have starved to death.

They serve you delicious food with the most amazing smiles and you can't help but want to tip them. I guess this was originally a cynical commercial tactic that became second nature. However, by giving them even a small tip, you encourage their fathers to keep them out of school all the more. I imagined that everything I was giving them was taken off them by their fathers, uncles, or brothers who ran the café, so I decided to start using some tricks of my own. I'd distract the adults with idle chit chat and, at the same time, pass a note behind my back to the boys. The children only needed a moment to have it in their pocket and be acting as if nothing had happened. It probably made no odds but it made me feel a little better.

From Bundi it was a short journey to Udaipur in the bottom left corner of the tourist triangle, completed by the adjoining vertices of Agra and Judaipur.

Udaipur is also known as the city of lakes. 'Octopussy' was filmed here. In the surrounding desert, Bond heroically rescued Octopussy from an aeroplane which resulted in Gobinda falling to his death. The lake and palace were also used as perfect settings for the film.

Down by the lake, local people were washing themselves and their clothes. The mornings are alternately reserved for men or women to bathe. By the side of the banks, two spiritual men were playing their *kamayacha*, a stringed instrument played with a bow which makes a low tone. After filming a quick Happy Christmas video for the children at school, and friends, I started dancing with the local children to the music. I'd given the local children mini plastic instruments as they waited for their mums to finish the washing, and with my ukulele we played along with the men.

Some time later a male arrived whom I assumed was some of the the children's dad. The mums shouted at the kids to come away from me and sit by them. It felt strange to be left alone like that. I walked away with my head down. I didn't like to think I'd got the ladies into trouble.

I'd developed a really bad stomach again. Squatting above the hostel 'hole in the floor' toilet, I emptied my bowels. My stomach gurgled and pains shot through me. It was made worse by the fact that the kind architects had made the wall to the toilet mirrored so I could see my face contorting in pain. They had also thoughtfully built a nice shelf in the toilet – just above the hole. So depleted, sick and tired, I stood to leave, only to smash my head on the shelf, knocking me back towards my waste.

The hostel owner pointed us in the direction of a Raj music festival. It was a strange affair. Performing to the tabla, a bol (drums) and the harmonium (an Indian piano powered by air, played with one hand whilst the other pushes the hand-operated bellows), a woman carried an ever-increasing number of pots on her head. There was also a puppet show. Udaipur is famed for its puppets and this was no ordinary show. The dolls danced as their strings were twitched. At the finale, a puppet played 'keepie uppie' with its own head. Quite extraordinary.

* * *

Leaving Rajahstan, I entered Gujarat. The race riots of 2003 between the Hindu and Muslim people were centred here. People went out and butchered neighbours, co-workers and friends if they were not from their religion. Most of the one thousand who lost their lives were Muslim and sources say that the police condoned their murder.

The state, which is on the west coast of India, encompasses major sites of the ancient Indus Valley Civilisation of 3,300BC.

Stopping in a very small shop in the middle of nowhere, I made friends with the son and daughter of the shop owner. They initially cried when they saw me, but polystyrene planes soon bought their affection. I was sitting back enjoying watching them play nicely among the quiet surroundings when a man appeared to my right. He was staring at me but in a slightly unusual way. He seemed to be looking in my ear.

"Dirty."

He pulled out his little wooden box and before I could say *'Please don't put that painfully long needle into my ear'* he had already extracted his first potato. After retrieving several more (it's been a good harvest this year), he said I needed medicine. Pouring it into my ears, he shook my head one way and then the other. Tweezers were produced and he pulled something looking like my ear drum out of my ear canal. Repeating the procedure in the other ear, he gave me back my habitual 20:20 hearing and now, when buses hooted their horns, it hurt my head even more. Great.

As I passed through the lush green countryside, I understood why Gujarat had one of the fastest-growing economies in India.

A tuk-tuk meant for three people and its driver swept by me ferrying twenty-five children back from school. It was nice to see the children in a mixed-sex vehicle. Perhaps this practice would lessen the divide between women and men as they grow up.

Further on, men were sitting under their trucks, eating a picnic thali which looked very enticing, whilst sheltering from the sun which was getting hotter and hotter as I cycled towards the equator.

I found my way onto a highway with six lanes of traffic. The outside lane, normally reserved for the speeding vehicles, was filled with cows with horns as big as their legs. It's a cow's life here in India – if they want to hang out in the fast lane they damn well do it and no amount of hooting of horns will budge them. The next lane was fairly normal – for an Asian road - just very fast-moving traffic swerving left and right. The third and outside lane was the most interesting. Really I should have said there were eight lanes as the outside lane was again used for two-way traffic. In one direction (normally the wrong direction) I could see herds of cow / goats / sheep, bikes, tuk-tuks, rampaging buses, trucks, motorbikes, industrial vehicles, camels, the odd elephant and carts. In the other direction (the correct direction) was the odd tuk-tuk banished from the faster lanes by a careering bus, and a lone English cyclist fighting tooth and nail for his little strip of tarmac, and his life.

Chapter 38

I arrived in Ahmedabad, the largest city in Gujarat, under the cover of darkness. The old town was erupting. A festival fuse had been lit and it was going off, big time. Wherever you are in India it seems at least one festival is happening on a daily basis. With the range of religions in India, and with such high family and social values, it is hardly surprising.

This one was a Muslim one, celebrating the birth of the prophet Muhammad. People were drumming and dancing themselves into a frenzy. Then, when I joined in with both, it got totally out of control.

It was fun to begin with, dancing and drumming with crowds of Indians. But as more and more people got involved and breathing became a struggle, I started to get scared, my smile fell away, and I started to fight. My clothes and my flesh were being grabbed and pulled in a million directions. Each person wanted the white man to be part of what they were doing. I could feel my clothes tearing and my joints loosening. I'd gone too far this time. Why hadn't I kept away?

Pushing, shoving, pulling, and tugging myself free of their grasps, I saw a gap and moved swiftly up an adjacent street. The carnival was heading in the opposite direction so I felt I was safe. But no. The carnival split in two. The people in front of me headed in the direction they'd originally planned and the half behind me changed and followed the white guy who was playing drums like Phil Collins and dancing like Michael Jackson.

It was like a movie chase scene but at a fast walking pace. Taking a few lefts and rights down side streets wide enough for just two or three people, and eventually finding myself lost but free from the crowd, I looked behind me to check that all was clear. I sighed and relaxed, turning to make out where I was, only to see them coming at me from the opposite direction as they enveloped me like ocean currents.

A group of girls caught my attention as the carnival wave swept by me and I was dragged into a café. They were four stunning French girls, students at the local university on an exchange programme, and they invited me back for a French meal. We arrived at their lecturer's home as they weren't allowed boys in their university accommodation. The lecturer, another French lady, Manoushka, invited us all in and I was cooked up a delicious French fish meal as we jammed on the guitar and ukulele.

Although I was still quite rubbish at it, I'd started making up lyrics to chord sequences. I made one up about the French Connection, which they recorded and cheered at the finale.

The girls were all studying the arts - some fashion, some animation. I couldn't believe my luck to have fallen in with these guys. They asked me to stay, and Manoushka offered me a mat on the floor for a while. Let's be honest - what man could possibly say no? Another festival was creeping up on us and I couldn't imagine a better crowd to spend it with.

Each day, as I walked down to buy chai or supplies for my studying companions, the children from the slum would run and fling themselves at me, wrapping their arms and legs around my waist. The women of the slums, nursing newly-born children, had different eyes to the other women in India. Whether it was their caste or lack of protection from the sun, their eyes shone like balls of fire. I was in heaven, living with five gorgeous girls and adopted by a slum that thought of me as one of the family.

I continued my yoga which I was convinced was serving to relieve my aching muscles. As I walked through the slum with Minna, Sandra and my camera, we were welcomed into a house for tea. They got the milk from the goat tethered just outside. I asked if I could have a go and the udders were thrust into my hands. The goat didn't attack me and I managed to get enough milk for tea, so I felt pretty pleased with myself.

That night the celebrations for Holi began, even though the festival wasn't until the next day. We danced round a fire with the slum children and then back at the university. I'd dressed in a white lungi and *kurta* (the over-sized shirts) that I'd bought my dad for a present. Playing with *fire poi* (two balls of fire on the end of chains), I managed to set myself alight without noticing. Sandra came running over to me with fear on her face, I had no idea why, and ran into one of the sticks, setting her jumper alight. I then realised my naughty bits were getting warm and saw that my lungi was alight. Rolling in sand and patting helped immensely, although Dad's outfit was somewhat ruined.

Finally, at the end of a chaotic day, one of the boys who'd been drumming came and rubbed a few handfuls of coloured powder onto my head and beard. Holi had begun!

Holi is a festival in memory of the miraculous escape that young Prahlad accomplished when Demoness Holika carried him into the fire. Holika was burnt but Prahlad, a staunch devotee of the god Vishnu (the supreme god in Hinduism), escaped without any injuries owing to his unshakable devotion. It is celebrated by people throwing coloured powder and coloured water at each other. What other way could there be? The painting doesn't start until everyone from children to old people have drunk *lassie*. A special lassie. Or *bang lassie* - marijuana in a milk shake, served from the university canteen in the morning.

I was up way before the students, so took the time to paint my nails and add eyeliner. It's not traditional but I thought it'd be fun, and the more colour the better in my books. I could hear the kids screaming outside and ran to grab one of my pump-action water pistols – I'd bought seven, slowly finding bigger and bigger ones as I traversed the city. I had also spent the morning filling up balloons with water, so I equipped myself with a bag of those.

I charged outside with a few bags of powder attached to my belt, ready to do a Rambo on these kids, but I had severely underestimated their ability and grace. I was on the floor, covered in every colour under the sun and soaking wet, before I could say, "Tally Ho-li".

The commotion raised the dead and students alike, and together we fought. I'd been looking forward to playing with the kids in the slum I'd met the previous day and formed a small band to tackle them.

Boooom! We hit them hard. We had the upper hand initially because they were in poor condition and didn't have the money to buy paint or the water to add it to, but when we shared our goodies, the slum erupted into the brightest display since the Big Bang. It was like a colourful snowball fight in thirty-five degree heat.

* * *

After the festival there was more of India to see and I needed to get going if I wanted to get to Mumbai to celebrate Christmas.

As I left the university, the children from the slum ran alongside my bike until I slowed to a stop, at which point they all dived on me for cuddles. Leaving those children broke my heart.

On the way down the coast I got my first taste of the Portuguese colonial effect, Daman. I was expecting to find perfect beaches with crowds of people having fun on them, bodies everywhere, but the bodies were of the hoofed variety. It was the cows who were enjoying themselves at this beach resort, although there were also a handful of Indians spending time with their families there, the women in their beautiful saris I had become accustomed to. Staying the night, I sampled the port of colonialists past. It made me feel like an alcoholic, sipping it in one of the seedy bars and I soon took off back to the hostel.

Moving alongside the belching trucks, cars, and over-loaded rickshaws, I covered my mouth as a bus burped, covering my face with soot. Along the roadside was arranged a startling array of material. The people living in the slums were hanging out their clothes to dry on the railings after washing them down at the *ghat*.

It was December the 23rd – I really wanted to arrive in the city to give me a chance of finding some friendly faces to celebrate Christmas with. I'm the world's biggest fan of Christmas and was already feeling a pang of sadness for not being around for Anya, my much-loved niece's, first one.

The going was tough and I was falling behind a schedule I'd made out for myself to try to get there on time. A lorry pulled alongside and the driver's partner hung out of the window and asked me to hold on. I couldn't help myself. I did. He sped up to one hundred kilometres per hour as I hung on for dear life. The truck swerved round slower vehicles and animals and I, in addition, swerved round the potholes.

It was the most dangerous thing I have ever done. I'm shocked, looking back, that I put my life at risk merely to find a friendly face on Christmas Day. But, by this point, life had taken on a different meaning. Dangers and annoyances ceased to exist. After a short time, my ride slowed. I was disappointed that it was over. The driver leant out this time and shouted, "Chai?"

Why not?

They wouldn't allow me to buy the tea. Instead, they gave me a whole drink for myself while the driver poured half of his into the saucer and shared it with his partner. It was so wonderful to see them sharing. I'd taken to drinking from the saucer too. It helped cool the scalding liquid. Until fifty years ago this was not an uncommon practice in Britain but is now considered a breach of etiquette.

I hung on again and off we went. Fifty kilometres from Mumbai we hit a city. The traffic got out of hand and I had to say goodbye to my ride. The smog was horrendous. The traffic appalling. I pedalled hard to get out of this city and looked forward to arriving in Mumbai.

Unfortunately this was Mumbai.

208

Chapter 39

Weaving in and out of the stationary traffic, I tried to keep my eyes on the road but couldn't help noticing the life on the sidewalks. Mini tent structures were set up as houses for families, and mothers sat cooking over small stoves or fires whilst their children washed in the gutter water.

Skyscrapers towered above these people, housing industries powering a world standard nuclear program and a leading space programme. I found it hard to come to terms with what I was seeing; people living in slum tents in the countryside didn't seem as bad as this. The people who work in these offices, people who have six-figure salaries, have to walk past this every day on their way into work.

Between these imposing concrete structures was something altogether more impressive. Using wood, corrugated iron, plastic and cloth, people have created a whole city at street level - the slums. Twenty-five million people live here, turning over two hundred and fifty million dollars a year. They recycle everything and they live amongst vermin.

I passed by the Western Railway cricket fields. Seven different games were proceeding on a pitch the size of a normal cricket ground. Others were practising in the nets. It was rammed with those who shared one thing in common, cricket, bringing all types of people together - men and boys, rich and poor. The Indians love it.

As I arrived in Colaba I saw a café well-known to all travel readers – Leopold's – a café housing the good, the bad and the ugly, the focal point of the book 'Shantaram' which is found in every good backpacker's rucksack. Outside, locals were doing everything they could to get a rupee from passers-by - shining shoes, selling drums, finding people hotels or a taxi ride or a parking space or a souvenir. I moved inside, past the shotgun-wielding guards, to escape the touts outside, and grabbed a beer.

The bullet craters from November 26th 2008 still show on the walls, the day Leopold's was riddled with bullets that ripped bodies and ended lives. It was one target among many in this city as the Taliban unleashed themselves on India.

Looking round I saw groups of tourists, businessmen, gangsters and facilitators. If you want anything, this is the café to go to - drugs, girls, a hitman, rock 'n' roll. Unfortunately the people I sat with had come to India for one reason. Girls.

The Ministry of Women and Child Development reported the presence of 2.8 million sex workers in India as a whole. That's well over the population of Greater Manchester. Most enter the trade before they are eighteen years old. Mumbai alone has two hundred thousand prostitutes working the streets or brothels, the largest sex industry in Asia. It is estimated that fifty percent of this population - yes, half - have HIV.

Most of the research done by Sanlaap indicates that the majority of sex workers in India work as prostitutes because they lack the resources to support themselves or their children. Most do not choose this profession; it is forced on them, often after the break-up of their marriage or after being disowned and thrown out of their homes by their families.

* * *

I left Leopold's swiftly and checked into a quiet hotel before going back out on the streets again to see what Christmas would bring. I met more Brits getting wasted – they'd come because of the cheap beer. *Come on, Brothers, India is beautiful. At least experience some of the local delights.* I guess they would argue that they were.

As I walked down the street, losing hope and anticipating a Christmas in my room, an arm tattooed from wrist to shoulder waved past me. The tattoo depicted the Buddha and the lotus flower. At the end of the arm was a girl with short dark hair. Angela. After some discussion, I found that she was studying at the same university as Sandra and gang, but had been travelling elsewhere in the country when I was there. She'd also been at the Golden Temple on the same day as me. She'd seen my bike but I'd left before we'd met.

It was Christmas Eve and we went to a quiet bar up the road. It didn't stay quiet for too long. In my little backpack I had all the instruments that I had been playing with the kids on my journey and some rocket balloons that kids had chased throughout Asia. Soon the balloons were shooting around the bar and locals and Westerners alike were playing horns, whistles and kazoos.

Angela was feisty, pushing unwanted attention away and arguing with those she considered to be speaking rubbish. She was sharp, and not afraid to cut people.

She came back to my hotel and we stayed on the balcony sharing stories, dreams, and wishes. She was a juggler, an artist and a toy maker, giving her toys to Indian children to play with. As more stories came forth, my heart melted.

A Japanese lady came out of her room and asked us to tone it down. I could see the twinkle in Angela's eyes and the tension in her face. As she began to give the lady a mouthful, I leaned forward and put my lips against hers. It muffled her voice and the Japanese girl walked back inside. I pulled away as soon as she'd gone, but Angela's arms wrapped themselves around me and my lips were ambushed. Christmas was only four hours old but I'd got everything I wanted already. Thanks, Santa!

As we tumbled into my room, I noticed Shirley leaning against the sideboard. As my shirt came off, I threw it over her. I didn't want her to watch.

* * *

The next morning, tears were rolling down my cheeks. I held my hand over my eyes to avoid people's gaze as they looked on awestruck. They thought I was sick. I wasn't sick, and I wasn't unhappy. Angela put her arm round me to comfort me.

I was in the biggest slum in Asia. Deravi slum.

I'd met some photographers here for a shoot for the national press, and had had to leave my bike as the paths between the houses had narrowed so much that Shirley's handlebars were pulling down the corrugated houses. My senses were on overload - incense mixed with raw sewage. Banging house music deafened all conversation but I turned another corner and the music died, and I could hear the kids playing cricket on the rubbish dump, squealing and arguing whether it was LBW or not. Saris flashed past me and kids' dirty colourful toys were being hugged intensely.

We'd been invited into a house which was no bigger than a storeroom. Five to ten people typically shared these sorts of houses. Kitchen, storage and beds were all in a space about the size of a queen-size mattress. A girl lay in the tiny bed. She was so skinny that she looked like Ginger, the mummy in the British Museum. She was just skin and bone. A tear rolled down her cheek with the effort it took to look up and see the aliens who had entered her home. Angela had her bright tattoo down her left arm and piercings, and carried the looks of a professional model. I had the brightest ginger beard and blue eyes, and a stupid grin on my face, that could only be associated with something from another world.

Seeing this girl was the only low point of the visit. ActionAid had really tried to give me an insight into what life was like in the slum. I was impressed how well they lived in these buildings, if you could call them that. They looked like a strong wind would flatten the lot (luckily I was able to handle curries a bit better by now, so my wind wasn't going to be a problem). The children were all happy and enjoyed treating me like a climbing frame, and chasing the balloons that I fired all over the slum.

My tears were falling because I was back in the charity's office and they were telling me how the money I had raised was being used in the slum. Abhi, a local aid worker, translated what the women were saying, section by section. Part of the money was funding a trade union run by women for women. I heard graphic stories of how initially the women were beaten and verbally abused by their husbands and society for joining and creating such a thing. Bano (the team leader) was speaking. The emotion was etched on her face and I could feel it in my body. Abhi translated, "These women stuck with it and kept working and then the results came..."

It felt like a movie. I knew what was coming next and burst into tears. All the emotion I felt from the trip ripped through me. I was uncontrollable. I tried to pull myself together because I wanted to hear the results which were that people realised these women were performing far better than the men ever had, forcing their husbands to change their attitudes. They began to stay at home with the kids on the days the women needed to work. The women's status in society was now sky-high.

Tears were still blurring my vision. I apologised for being silly. The squalor these people lived in, the disease, the lack of education, the way children and women were treated in India - what a difference the charity was making. What a difference we had already made by donating money to ActionAid. One pound here travels a hundred times the distance it does in the UK. Five pounds is enough for a month's wage for one of these workers.

As we walked back through the slum again, Abhi told me that the children were calling me Father Christmas. Angela seized on the nickname and, for the rest of our time together, I was Papa Noël.

Angela returned to her hostel. I was on my way to another charity gig. All the children of this slum were putting on a performance for children from other slums. It was another programme organised by the children but funded by the charity. Young females from the slums of Mumbai, and surrounding towns, had put together a set of objectives that they wanted to achieve, such as a right to work, safety in their homes and educational rights.

The catch was that anyone who came had to attend the AIDS education programme. It was wonderfully simple. Children had fun and got the education that they might not have received from their families or at school.

One of the young men helping at the festival was Naresh. He wanted me to meet his mum and dad. When I said I would like to, he took me through the slums. Weaving in and out of alleyways and buildings, he kept reiterating that his house was small and that it wasn't very nice. He was very worried how I would react. On arrival, it was indeed small, but it was amazingly clean and I was served an excellent cup of tea and some curry by his mum. By this point it was starting to get late and his mother asked if I wanted to stay. Naresh's face fell. *As if a white man would stay here, Mum.* I would have to share with him and Zubed, his brother.

I was happy to. "Of course," I said, "it would be an honour."

Roll mats were produced and we lay on our straw mattresses on the floor. The three of us side by side were sharing a room that in the West would be a cupboard. The boys were asleep in no time. I was left thinking about life in this place. Who would invite a stranger to dinner in the UK, let alone ask them to stay over?

I met Angela at Leopold's the next morning. I'd been invited by Naresh to stay as long as I liked. At the table next to us was a group of Russians who were still out from the night before and still drinking. One was under the table being sick and another ordered us beers, prawns and a kebab. Fair enough. Thanks. Angela was leaving for Goa in the afternoon for New Year celebrations.

After Angela had gone, I decided to take up Naresh's offer and stay for a few more days in the slum. I'd been savaged by bed bugs and treated like scum in the most popular hostel in all of Mumbai, so it was a win-win situation. Dharavi slum may be the biggest in all of Asia, playing a crucial role in the book 'Shantaram', but it is home to some of the biggest smiles in the world.

That night there was the obligatory festival and the crazy juice had entered every male in town. Everyone wanted to shake my hand and, as ever in India, a cup of tea needed to be drunk in every house. Ending the evening hanging out with young men sitting in a makeshift hut, I was accorded the only seat. I was introduced to everyone's nicknames which all related to their professions. "Bike Boy" sold knick-knacks on his bike, "Samosa" sold, you guessed it, samosas to commuters. Everyone was fluent in English. They wanted to see me dance, and then regretted it. They wanted to hear me sing, and then regretted that too. What could this stupid English guy do? I smiled.

They were standing for leadership of the youth council and I was pleased and proud to hear later that they won the position and were already putting plans into action to help the youths in the slum.

Chapter 40

As Angela was already in Goa, and hearing that the French Connection gang were all there too, I wanted to arrive as soon as possible. A straight road led me most of the way and I stopped in trucking cafés to eat and sleep underneath their tables. Shirley's chain fell off, her front wheel started to wobble, her panniers kept being dislodged by the smallest bumps. It was as if she was trying to stop me getting there. Was she jealous?

Goa is another ex-Portuguese colony. Swaying palms, white sands and sparkling waters - the three essential elements that attract two million visitors annually to Goa's balmy shores - are plentiful in this tiny, glorious slice of India, hugging the country's western coastline and bounded by the Arabian Sea.

It was time to forget about the fact I was missing family and friends as they celebrated Christmas and New Year, to forget the pain of the saddle, to put aside thoughts of the suffering in all the countries I had visited - the homeless, the dying, the deformed, the handicapped, the diseased, the repressed, the child labourers, the starving, the torturers and the tortured.

People flock to Goa in their thousands during the festivities to enjoy the cheap drinks, the parties, the sand, the blue seas and the coconuts. I had decided I wasn't going to miss one piece of it.

I met Angela in town and we went straight to the beach. Within minutes we found ourselves with soft sand between our toes and being welcomed by dolphins leaping and playing on the horizon.

It was New Year's Eve. Clubbing to horrendous techno, we jumped around like the monkeys I'd seen in the trees on the way down, made friends with our silliness, performed makeshift break dancing on the sand and juggled fire. The domestic tourists were getting some well-earned entertainment in the shape and form of a Spanish fire fairy, Papa Noël and friends. I ended the night sleeping in a fishing boat wearing a motorcycle helmet as the sun rose above me.

* * *

Goa is a place where the arts meet spiritualism. Yoga, meditation and martial arts classes covered the beach in the morning. Ayurvedic medicine centres, tattoo parlours, markets selling trendy Indian clothing, music studios and sumptuous restaurants selling fish fresh from the sea plied their trade on the coastal path.

I dived right in and was to be found every evening with Lucy and Alastair doing stick martial arts on the beach. It may be beautiful and graceful, like dancing, but it does give you a few more bruises and fat lips. As the days wore on, our numbers started to swell.

One particular night, Natalia, a yoga teacher from the Ukraine, and Rafi, her Indian sidekick, came and said they'd join us after 'laughing therapy'. What? Laughing therapy? I couldn't miss this.

Five minutes later we started the therapy on the beach surrounded by regular holidaymakers. Laughing for five or ten minutes at a stretch, I think it was the first class I've ever excelled at. Rafi and Nat had bundles of energy that seemed to light up anyone they came across. I then went on to Stick Club (the first rule of Stick Club: no-one talks about Stick Club), and found I still couldn't stop myself laughing. Even when Lucy caught me with an upstroke which cracked my jaw and left me lying on the floor, my blood dripping onto the sand, I couldn't help but let out a prolonged snigger. Even now, writing these words, I'm giggling to myself. Laughing therapy - it works.

The following day it was suggested that we meet at four to give sweets out on the beach to spread love and happiness. I'd just bought an orgasmatron, a cluster of wires that are used to massage the head. It does just what it says on the can. Bringing that along too, we traversed the beach bringing smiles to people's faces and sweetness to their bellies, whilst promoting the laughing therapy session which would take place later in the afternoon.

That night I'd been asked to lead a class in animal balloon making, the second class I have ever excelled in. Monkeys, elephants, tigers, palm trees and flowers littered the venue. It looked like the jungle Goa used to be before tourism moved in. Fifteen people came, including Rafi and Natalia. Such a compliment.

* * *

People warn of the potential for thievery in India. 'Slumdog Millionaire' reiterates the risks faced. From my own experiences, this sounded like twaddle. I didn't lock my room at night or when I went out. I had accidentally left my bag open outside my room in a busy cheap hotel in the city with all the valuables visible and nothing had happened. My wallet fell from my bag and about five cars stopped to tell me. Cleaners came into my room with thousands of rupees (months of salary) lying on the bed amongst the mess, and they just stacked them all nicely and I was sure the idea to take them hadn't even entered their heads.

I had got it into my head that everyone was honest and decent.

So I was devastated to be blatantly robbed whilst on the beach. Stupidly I had left my bag open with my wallet, SLR camera, video camera, $200 and ten thousand rupees of notes in it. I was planning to do some stick martial arts, so I had also left my bamboo rod next to it.

I left it for maybe one minute as I paddled in the sea and looked at the fishermen. When I got back, it was gone.

I searched everywhere. I asked anyone nearby if they'd seen the scoundrel who'd taken it. I could see my stick's imprint in the sand. After a fruitless search, I had to face facts – my stick was gone forever. My bag and all my valuables were still there.

217

* * *

Angela and I headed further south to meet the French Connection. At a local Nepalese bar we all celebrated by drinking rum before retreating back to the jungle where Angela and I had put our hammocks up between palm trees, leaving our bags in the sand. We stayed for five days, waking to the sun, diving into the sea, chillaxing and drinking. We ate fresh fish, caught off the beach and cooked in front of us, and devoured platters of fresh fruit. I was trying to recover my strength and energy.

My partner in crime from the UK, Michael Jackson (yes, that is his real name and, no, he doesn't wear a white glove), had booked a holiday in India with twenty of his buddies. They arrived in Goa totally fired up and excited. The charms of India had seduced them already. With three of their group celebrating birthdays over the space of three days, they had a whole day of fun planned.

It started with Indian Olympics. What, you don't know what they are? They are track and field events, with an Indian twist. Splitting into teams of five, the first event was the 'onion bhaji and spoon race' (a variety of egg-and-spoon race). Next came 'throw the chapatti' (a flat discus-type bread). The 'balance the curry on your head' race was next, followed by the finale - the elephant riding race. My team won all but the elephant race, but with no thanks to me. I was useless.

After the games we had a full team photo – the French Connection, Angela, the Jackson crew and me. Even though most of us hadn't been in India more than two days, I was still the whitest person in the photo by far.

We had booked a club for our gang to have a Bollywood bad taste party to recuperate from this strenuous activity. You can imagine everyone dressed in a variety of Indian coloured clothing. The scary thing was that I had clothes like that in my rucksack to wear on a daily basis.

With a bit of help from my mum, I'd managed to get some decent ingredients for my dress sent out with Mike and, with the Fire Fairy being an artist 'n' all, I was in luck. Just as the food was being served at the party, a tiger roared on the beach. People climbed palm trees to escape, grabbed their children and ran to their shacks, and launched boats into the water to put a barrier between themselves and this fearsome tiger. Dogs howled and cows ran from their comfy sand seats. Angela had painted me from head to foot as a tiger, and I have to say I looked awesome.

Mucho dancing, free beers, congas, singing and photos with everyone in Goa ensued. A rather voluptuous Swedish girl wanted me to use my hands to paint her body in the same fashion. I looked at Angela who had somehow made a blow-up swan and some face paint look like something you might find on a Parisian catwalk. She gave me a nod and a smile and I got to work. It was a tough job but someone had to do it. So the tiger had a tigress and that meant more photos and more free drinks.

The next morning I awoke in my hammock with one hand on Angela and surrounded by a group of people. Through blurred eyes I couldn't work out what was wrong. They were all staring at me. Looking down I saw the paint and realised I should have washed it off last night. Prowling down to the water's edge, to the surprise of sunbathers and joggers, I took a bath. Oh dear! It wasn't permanent but it lasted a few days.

* * *

Whilst the UK had the worst winter in history, we had some tough times too - swimming with dolphins, surfing, kayaking, jogging on the beach and cycling to perfect jungle towns. One kilometre from the beach, Goa turns back to being India, barring the fact that Catholic churches occupy the towns rather than temples.

Everyone was having a wonderful time except Shirley, who was sitting in the same spot for over a week. She'd got a layer of dust and sand on her and had acquired an expression of forlorn rejection.

In the end sadness descended on my world. Angela decided to leave. She left me a note saying she didn't like the feeling of hurt that had been creeping up on her. Worrying about the pain she'd feel when we parted, in typical Angela fashion she had confronted it head-on, packed her bags and left.

So the next morning it was back to me and Shirley. I felt guilty for coming back to her only when Angela had gone, so I brought her a token to make it easier, some oil to lubricate her to make the rest of the ride more pleasurable. I tenderly wiped her down and pumped up her tyres. It felt good to be back, just the two of us. It's how it'd been the whole way. We knew we could rely on each other. As my and her memory of Angela floated away on the currents of the sea, Shirley slowly softened and started to purr as I span her pedals.

Chapter 41

On the balmy morning of the 27th of September 1953, in a small, poor fishing village – Parayakadavu, in the Quilon district of Kerala - a baby girl was born. Her parents gave her the name Sudhamani. She came into this world not in tears as babies usually do, but with a beaming smile on her face, as if professing the joy and bliss she was to bring to the world.

Sudhamani spent the years of her childhood and teens immersed in intense spiritual practices in order to present a living example to the world. Even as a small child, she could often be found absorbed in deep meditation, totally oblivious of her surroundings. By the age of five, she had already begun composing devotional songs laden with deep mystical insight.

Another quality Sudhamani manifested from this tender age was her love and compassion towards her fellow human beings. Though only a child, Sudhamani did whatever she could to ease the suffering of her elderly neighbours. She washed their clothes, bathed them and even brought them food and clothing from her own home. This habit of giving away things from her family's house landed her in deep trouble, however, no amount of physical abuse or punishment could stop the expression of her inherent compassion. She later said, "An unbroken stream of Love flows from me towards all beings in the cosmos. That is my inborn nature."

'Amma', as she is known all over the world today, has inspired and started innumerable humanitarian services. She has earned international recognition for her outstanding contributions to the world community. She is recognised as an extraordinary spiritual leader by the United Nations and by the people all over the world.

Though Amma makes no claims for herself, those who watch her closely notice that she is the greatest example of her teaching. Her disciples and believers take in her teachings simply by watching her.

For the past thirty-five years, Amma has dedicated her life to the uplifting of suffering humanity through the simplest of gestures – an embrace. In this intimate manner Amma has blessed and consoled more than twenty-five million people throughout the world.

When someone asked Amma why she receives every person who comes to her in a loving embrace, Amma replied, "If you ask the river, 'Why do you flow?', what can it say?"

Amma spends most of her waking hours receiving the distressed and all who come to her for comfort, day after day without a break.

A New Yorker recently said, "Amma's hug is the greatest humanitarian work, in my opinion. I believe that her embrace gives the inspiration and the strength for all other humanitarian work which spreads the message of love and compassion."

* * *

I was coated in a greasy white layer of Factor Ginger sun cream, and droplets of sweat ran down my face before making a leap to land on Shirley's handlebars where they'd sit drying out in the fierce heat. The temperatures rose to well over forty degrees and my brain, still protected by my helmet, boiled in its casing. I found myself wondering why I had left the calm sands and cooling waters of Agonda Beach, the fun times, my friends, and the Nepalese boys who'd been so wonderful to me. But deep down I knew why. Tomorrow I had a meeting with destiny.

Amma, the hugging mother, had always been on my radar. She is a lady who travels the world giving energy and hope through the simplicity of a hug. This is my kind of lady. The mother hugger.

She had been in Gokana for a week, and tomorrow was her last day before beginning another world tour. I couldn't be so close to her in her home nation without going to see her. With the heat eating away at my energy levels, I needed to take as much as I could from her hug.

Gokana, located on the coast and surrounded by lush, green forest, is a Mecca for the spiritual traveller. When I arrived I saw a beautiful village ruined by Western influences - heaps of rubbish that the local people weren't ready to deal with, Westerners pushing through the streets ignoring the local man squatting on his hind feet looking to sell small tokens to feed his family, Westernised restaurants full to the brim. People seemed to be missing the point. So preoccupied with their own quest for enlightenment, they were ignoring the people around them at best, being outright rude at worst.

Leaving Shirley in the shade, I made sure she was comfortable before I headed off, carrying my staff with a number of blow up monkeys attached to each end. I met Kathleen, a Chinese girl with dark pools in her eyes that made you feel as though you could dive right in. She was standing open-mouthed, staring, looking on at the whirlwind of white-clothed Westerners brushing past her on either side and tutting that she was in their way. I put a hand on her shoulder and asked in pidgin English, "You OK?" She turned to me and I almost fell over when she replied in a strong Geordie accent "Ahm OK, but ahm not sure aboot these fowk, ye knaa what ah mean, leik?" nodding towards the white ants busying themselves.

We stopped and looked at each other. Did we really want to submit ourselves to this?

Entirely sceptical, Kathleen and I stepped into Amma's ashram, a temple built to house the hundreds of people that come to visit Amma when she's in town. The ashram was like the ants' nest. Westerners dressed in white, looking like their farts don't stink, and looking down upon those who arrive with animal balloons all over their new bamboo stick dressed in every colour under the rainbow with feral ginger beards.

The ashram had history beatifically enshrouded within it. The sight of so many Westerners fussing over the ancient Indian ashram was surreal and we whipped out our paparazzi cameras to capture the moment.

A voice came from behind us, "Please put your cameras down". We turned to see a girl in white about our age looking ferociously cross, "And delete your pictures or you'll have bad karma."

Bad Karma for appreciating the beauty? The hard-nosed woman, let's call her 'Bitch Face from Hell' (BFFH), was clearly unimpressed.

Kathleen stood incredulously and slowly opened her mouth to respond. "Forget about it," I told her. I knew it was going to be a bit like a circus in here and had kept telling myself that I was there only to experience one second – the hug.

We entered the hall where Amma performs her *Dasham* (her hugging *Cocoon*), to be greeted by wonderful live music and gorgeous food to fill our bellies after long journeys. Washing our plates and leaving them for the next people to come in, we then joined the back of a huge queue that wove round the ashram, ending at the feet of a rather short and tubby lady - Amma. As we weren't staying the night at the ashram, we were allowed to queue with the Indians during the day, something which turned the noses of those in white up further.

In the queue I whipped out the orgasmatron and proceeded to spread some love. Even those who weren't being touched smiled and laughed, watching as Indian ladies rolled their eyes in ecstasy as the thin, metal arms encased their heads. I began to gather a crowd as people looked to be entertained as they waited. Suddenly there was a tap on my shoulder. "This is not allowed – you are obstructing my view of Amma." I'd managed to piss off BFFH #2. I looked where Amma was, just a spot in the distance amongst many others.

Two hours passed and we were getting close. We could feel the excitement. I'd told Anju next to me that I had cycled here from England and she and her friends were gathered round me in an excited gaggle asking questions and poking fun at my freckled skin. I'd made Amma a bouquet of flowers out of balloons and, sure enough, I was told off by BFFH #3, #4 and #5 who insisted that bringing balloons into the ashram was, you guessed it, bad karma. These guys were so at peace.

All the BFFHs (1-5, plus a lot more) were all fighting each other to be part of the entourage that sat behind Amma, struggling to get a spot within four metres of her, and then desperately striving not to be pushed aside by another BFFH by slowly digging knees and elbows into other people's backs to get that inch closer as thousands of people came to have their hug. One second, maybe two if she likes you. Again I found myself wondering why we were there whilst we passed in front of these people.

As in many religions and in the animal kingdom, keeping your head below those above you is paramount. As I got close to Amma, Indian ladies touched my shoulders and helped me to my knees. Looking up, I could see into Amma's eyes and feel the strength in them. I handed her the flowers. She beamed and gave them to the person beside her, asking for them to be put into her bedroom. Wow!

As she put her arms around me, I have to say it felt wonderful (but you know I do love hugs). She sang a soft mantra into my ear. The notes resonated in my mind and brought peace and comfort. Surely my time was up; but she was still holding me in her arms. I could feel the eyes of the BFFHs boring into my head. Keeping my eyes closed, I let the hug linger. I started to feel awkward but it was too nice to let go. I could make out odd words as Anju told her that I'd cycled from England. She let me go. As I stood to leave, I was forced back to my knees by hands behind me. Touching my head, she fed me chocolate, putting it into my mouth as if I were a Greek god. She then summoned everyone in the ashram to give me a cheer and a clap. Wow, wow, wow!

Finally I was allowed to get up and, with my head bowed, I self-consciously made my way back. Another hand grabbed me from behind. It was Anju. She had a fierce grip for a tiny lady. She said

Amma had asked her to tell me she wanted me to sit next to her. So Amma's guards pointed at the many BFFHs and told them to move aside to allow me through next to Amma, to share our energies.

I was sitting next to one of the most highly respected spiritualists in the world. I couldn't help but smile.

Bad Karma my ass!

Chapter 42

As I sat there, I witnessed a disabled and blind band come to the ashram to sing and play music. It was some of the most amazing music I'd ever heard. Deprived of their sight, their hearing had become finely attuned, and the notes that emanated from this huddle of people, dressed in rags, who had to be lifted into position because of the deformities to their legs was the perfect end to the most spiritual of experiences. My emotions rose and fell like a ship riding a storm-ridden ocean.

Wrapped in the protective arm of Amma, I felt relaxation sweep over me, completeness. Kathleen winked at me and waved as she left the ashram. That night she was hoping to set off back to her original homeland, China. After witnessing the beauty that Amma's hugs were bringing to those who came to see her, I stood up, to the surprise of the people around me. I was really enjoying sitting with her but I had my own journey to complete, my own cause to give MY energy to. Back on my bike, I managed to cycle in the relative cool of the evening until darkness descended.

A man I used to work with in the city, Robert, had seen my story in the paper and had paid £300 into my account, telling me to buy myself a nice meal. £300 would feed me for a year in India. I made a pact there and then that every time I ate from now on I would treat someone else to food as well. A man sat in the street as I entered a café. I invited him to eat with me. As he sat at my table, the owner tried to shoo him away, but I told them he was with me. Now in Karnataka the local language is Kannada. My English and basic Hindi were useless. A fantastic game of charades told me that my guest had four children, a small house and no job. I, in turn, told him, unintentionally that I was from space, I liked to ride camels and I didn't have a job either.

The following day, as I moved inland, I found myself in the hills. I needed to drink constantly to remain hydrated and my head pounded with the intense heat. I mulled memories of the past weeks, and I was angry at myself for having spent so long in Goa. I'd wasted a lot of time being a bum. If I wanted to arrive at the school within a week, I had to ride every day, all day. It would have been so nice to relax in the shade during the hottest hours, but instead I had to plod on.

Setting off early so that I could avoid the heat, I'd arrive in cafés at midday, order a thali, put my head on the dirty table and pass out until the food arrived. As I got further into the jungle, the thali would arrive on a banana leaf, the rice would be dolloped from a bucket, and an array of curries would adorn it.

In one of the cafés I met a self-hypnotist from Germany who taught me how to hypnotise myself by concentrating on squeezing an imaginary ball in my hands and evoking the feeling I wanted to achieve. I wanted to cool down, so I imagined cool rivers, freshly-squeezed lemonade poured over cubes of ice and ladies in bikinis fanning me. I'm not sure if it was down to the bikinis, but it had absolutely no effect.

As more hills lined my way, it got harder and harder to make progress under the unrelenting sun. My sweat dripped continuously onto Shirley and I couldn't help being a little embarrassed. I would cycle in the midday heat, wobbling from one side of the road to another as my brain cooked, but she kept me safe. I developed a headache that I couldn't lose - sunburn, sunstroke. The last days were the hardest by far. But I wasn't going to miss my deadline. As I crept closer and closer to Chembakolli my emotions built up.

I arrived in Mysore, my penultimate destination. I thought I'd go and enjoy the sights and sounds of India there. Outside my hotel I met Darpan, a motorised rickshaw driver. He couldn't believe I'd never seen a *beedi* (Indian cigarette) rolled, or an incense stick made, nor smelt the oils Mysore is famed for. He said it was as though God had put us together. He was a man who knew his way around town, I was lucky. He knew where beedies were made, where the incense could be tested and the most legitimate oil presser in town. He would also take a big cut of anything I spent.

On the rickshaw we laughed about his being a businessman. We saw the beedi factory, a small room in a flat where twenty people squatted making a pile of beedies two metres in circumference and one metre high - cigarettes made from one leaf of tobacco rolled then tied with a red thread. We went to the oil press where I tested every oil until I smelt like a flower shop and I was forced to buy one that supposedly increased my male virility by a factor of five. I told him to ask my wife Shirley if I needed it. Back at the market, I was taken inside a store and shown how to make my own incense stick which I was allowed to keep, and still display alongside the menthol black sandalwood oil. As we left the market, he asked if I'd ever driven a rickshaw.

"Of course not. We don't have them in England."

"Would you like to try now?"

Within minutes I was whizzing past all the places we'd been to, leading a particularly vocal passenger, Darpan, who was shouting to his friends as we cruised past like rude boys on Southend Seafront.

As I got bored of driving the rickshaw and switched places with Darpan, my mind turned to my future. It was so up in the air and I had no idea how it was going to come to land. I caught sight of an older Western lady crossing the road, so I jumped out of the cab, paid my bill and caught up with her. After a few seconds of small talk, there was a connection and I felt we just had to have a hug.

Embarrassed about our embrace after so few words spoken, we went our separate ways only to bump into each other later and to start on a profound conversation. She was another spiritual lady. Where do they all come from? She reassured me that I was on the right path and, without knowing my issues at all, said she felt clarity was coming my way over the next week. As for love, for that I had to be patient, as ever!

A few hours before I was due to leave on the last leg of my journey, I was lying listening to music and we were still chatting. Each word connected with my every thought. She asked me if I was spiritual. It was one of those questions she already knew the answer to.

"Nah," I replied, "I'm not into that kind of stuff."

"The kind of stuff we've been talking about passionately for the past eight hours?" she replied smiling.

"Oh?"

I'm Danger Dan – nerdy, clumsy, loud, ungraceful, stupid. My farts stink. Spiritual? Come on, get real – I like bikes. No?

Chapter 43

I switched on the video camera with bleary eyes for my last video diary. The usual red light flashed to let me know it was recording. I was sitting on the edge of a checked mattress with the usual stains I'd come to expect engrained within the fibres. A couple of mosquitoes were circling me with intent. There was a commotion outside as a man selling pots and pans was escorted away by the police. I looked back at my camera and still the light was flashing. I got as far as, "This is my last..." before emotion dried me up. I couldn't speak. Choking down a sob, I grabbed the camera and swept the room with it, recognising that I was starting the last day in the same manner I had the first - surrounded by kit. Just like me, it looked a little older, sun-blemished and in need of a deep soak, but it had made it over fourteen thousand nine hundred kilometres, halfway across the world, crossing fourteen countries in six months and two days.

There were only one hundred kilometres to go, meaning I'd be in Vidyadaya School in Gudalur today. I should be celebrating tonight. I wondered whether I would be able to in the heart of the jungle. Who would I celebrate with? I didn't know anyone, and who would be interested anyway? I had been passing through the jungle for over a week and hadn't been able to contact anyone. I worried about interrupting the school's education programme and about how I would introduce myself if I were to visit the classrooms. What would I say? I couldn't speak one word of the tribal language used in the area. I began to question my motives for doing the ride and what it had achieved. Did anyone care?

For the 188th time I rammed the kit into my panniers and dragged my bike down the stairs.

Sitting outside the hostel, with Shirley by my side, I felt I needed to talk to her; to let her know how I was feeling. Would she and I find ourselves in this position again? Would she forget me now the adventure was coming to an end? I casually flicked a bit of dirt off her handlebars. She looked so pretty cloaked in flowers.

"This is our last day together. Our last adventure."

I ran a finger along her top tube. I knew every dent, every scratch, every curve. We had been through so much together, Shirley and I.

She said nothing, but I knew she was listening. Her lack of outward emotion did nothing to deaden my own as I swung my leg over her for our last assault; the final leg of our journey.

The air in Mysore was rich with the smell of the spices and herbs of the street vendors setting up shop. All creatures great and small came out to see us on our way. Workers knee deep in road waved and cheered as we cycled by. A gaggle of monks cheered and bowed as the breeze from Shirley made ripples in their robes. Boys, on their way to school on single-speed bikes that were far too big for them, raced alongside calling, "Mr, Mr," before dropping back. My constant companion, the swift, returned to surf my slipstream for a few hundred yards before flying off into the Maharaja's Palace under the radiant blue sky.

After thirty kilometres, a car stopped and, in faltering English, a lady with a pea green and luminous pink sari said, "From Chembakolli," before draping a flower reef made of yellow marigolds around my neck. For the second time today I was struck dumb and couldn't say a word. I fumbled to push emotion aside to allow the words out and eventually managed a pathetic, "Thank you", but she had already jumped back in her car and was driving off in the direction I'd come, hooting her horn and waving in the rear-view mirror.

A few hundred metres further on a group of monkeys sitting in the road showed their teeth and hissed as I came closer but, as I drove by, they broke out into a playful game of chase through the trees above my head. A large male sat with his knuckles on the floor, shaking his head and watching the white man cycling a bike looking like a horticultural show on acid through the open jungle.

"Is this how people behave in Europe? How very uncouth."

I was beckoned over for tea by a group of men who took the opportunity to down tools and get some much-needed rest and entertainment. As we sat on handmade stools around a table with each leg of different lengths, causing our tea to slosh from cup to saucer, I imagined I was Alice in Wonderland, or was I the Mad Hatter? And who was the March Hare? I saw no Dormouse; only a rat the size of a small dog. The men didn't speak English but this didn't stop them telling me their life stories in Kannada, and my thoroughly enjoying their accounts.

I finished off my cup and supped what remained in the saucer. I was torn; I wanted to stay and chat, and savour the taste of tea on the road because I didn't want my journey to end but, at the same time, I had the utmost desire to complete my task, to get off my bike, and never to cycle again.

I was also worried about the next leg of my journey through the Kalakad Mundanthurai tiger reserve. Did I want to see a tiger or not? Of course I'd love to see the fiercest animal of them all, the most intricately beautiful, my favourite creature. All those people who had rubbed my nose in it for not having seen one yet, when they had come across two or three, still bugged me. I'd have loved to post a picture home of a real one after dressing up as a tiger at the party in Goa. But now was not the time. Probably best to see them through a Jeep window rather than up close and personal.

I began to see signs advertising the reserve. I'd read that it had the highest concentration of tigers in any part of India, and that it was common to see them prowling by the sides of the road that passed through the park. I started imagining what I would do if confronted by the two-ton beast. What if it had cubs that were hungry? Shirley shuddered beneath me – I knew she could feel it too.

With my heart beating hard and mouth dry, I made my way up to the park entrance. A very kindly-spoken man, with a well-groomed white beard and khaki uniform, instructed me that it was too dangerous. I said I didn't mind and that I had to go through. A shake of the head and deeply sorrowful eyes said, "No way". He followed this up with, "Tigers, elephants. Too slow," pointing at Shirley.

I looked at my map and there was an alternative route. It was a diversion of about a hundred and sixty kilometres. I'd never make it to the school today. I hung my head and let the exhaustion flow through my body. My hopes of arriving today had grown wings and disappeared off with the parakeets, disturbed by the motorbikes revving their engines in the distance.

The motorbikes were driving through the park at a tremendous pace, kicking up a dust cloud that followed in their wake. As they got closer, I could make out four men, all riding on black Royal Enfields in black leathers, black helmets and tinted visors. I'm not the biggest fan of motorbikes but these classic machines turned my head. They were sleek and curvy, and exuded testosterone, the most popular motorbikes in India and every Westerner's choice of machine for engine-powered touring. They tore past and I returned to analysing my map whilst spitting dust and expletives. The screeching of rubber grabbed my attention as the bikes turned and accelerated back towards me. The scream of the engines subsided to a low chug as they pulled to a halt. The dust clouds caught up with them, blinding us momentarily before passing on to trouble someone else. A visor was opened and a dust-encrusted face revealed. As he smiled his dust mask cracked and pearly-white teeth lit up his face.

"Danny?"

"Yes."

"I'm Stan and this is your Royal Escort."

I was stunned. I couldn't believe it. Who? Why? Where? What? My questions would have to wait.

Baksheesh was handed over to the park guard who took it with the practised flick of the wrist that has you questioning whether a transaction actually took place.

This day was surely the most dangerous stretch of my journey – the Taliban, wild dogs, stone-throwing kids, crazy truck drivers, pan-fuelled nut jobs – they paled into insignificance as Shirley and I entered this wildlife park containing the largest numbers of elephants and tigers in India, one motorbike to my left flank, one on my right, and two behind guarding the rear.

My pupils were dilated as I searched every inch of the undergrowth looking for tigers. Stan pulled alongside me and above the roar of his Enfield he asked why I looked so concerned.

"How often do tigers kill humans?"

He replied that I didn't have to worry about tigers. I sighed with relief. "It's the elephants you really need to worry about." I remembered the story of the tourist killed in Chembakolli one month previously. "But you won't see them at this time of day."

With only slightly less anxiety, I carried on.

Two minutes later the motorbikes hit the brakes and I ran into the back of Stan, making his already-loose number plate fall to the floor. As he leaned over to pick it up and pop it in his pocket, I noticed why we had stopped. Ahead of us in the distance there was a herd of elephants by the left-hand side of the road.

"Problem," he said, wobbling his head from side to side. His three colleagues all mirrored the wobble of the head enthusiastically. That pretty much meant it was serious. Great!

They formed a huddle and I wondered if they were talking about their insurance and risk management policy towards cycle tourists.

Stan walked calmly up to me and stated, "We've decided. You need to stay right and go fast."

Motorcycles go fast, cars go fast, Jeeps go fast. Shirley was a plodder; she didn't go fast. That was one of the reasons I cared for her so much. I bent over and asked her if she thought she could make it. Stan stood patiently and waited for me to answer. After a moment I responded, "We'll give it a go." Stan smiled again and flipped his visor down again.

As we set off towards the elephants, they looked up and noticed us. I imagined us locking eyes and taking up the challenge, like a completely skewed boxing match weigh-in. Keeping to the right, I put the pedal down. My lungs and thighs screamed in a harmony that would have been beautiful had I not been in excruciating pain. I passed by the elephants so closely that I could smell freshly-laid dung the size of a football that lay at the feet of one of the larger elephants. I imagined them turning and charging, small saplings crashing to the floor, stones jumping as the ground rumbled under their weight, the thunder as their rounded feet pounded the earth. The motorbikes had accelerated on. I didn't want to die, not this close, not now...

As the undergrowth flew by, a familiar noise caught my attention and, as I looked to my left, I saw four motorcyclists in hysterics. I looked back and the elephants were still calmly grazing on the finer tips of the fresh bush.

"You should've seen your face," they sniggered.

"I wish I could have seen yours," I retorted.

As I left the park and continued, I was joined by more cyclists and motorcyclists. Our number was increasing, as was the number of flower wreaths round my neck. I was surprised by how heavy flowers could be as they dragged me down towards the earth.

Gudalur is generally a very quiet area and the commotion brought people from their houses, some of whom, without reason, grabbed their own bikes to join the procession. Poking fun at each other, the convoy drifted on at a steady tempo. Only the motorbikes accelerated and broke rapidly, showing their status amongst the other bikers.

Shirley was the centre of attention. Everyone wanted to touch her, to flick the switches of her gears, to stand on her pedals, to stroke her flowers, but she was mine for now. I was savouring every last moment.

As we passed an opening in the bush, I could hear a regular drum beat in the distance and wondered if it was my heart in my ears or the fast-approaching monsoon. Within weeks this road could be like a river, the houses flooded, stock washed away.

I was told there was about a kilometre to go as we rounded a sharp bend. We pulled out of the turn and I could see a huge crowd gathered in the distance - children, men and women, all dressed in colourful traditional dress - singing and playing drums. Another festival. It made me smile as I wondered what it was in aid of this time. As I got closer, the noise increased as the drummers became more frantic in their efforts.

I could see their faces now. They were mostly tribal people, but there were others in Western dress. When I got close enough to read the signs, I saw it was some sort of birthday they were celebrating. It seemed strange to see them using the Roman alphabet. 'Happy Birthday', 'Congratulations'. A little closer and I could make out my 'Velo Love' logo, the symbol of my trip, in the hands of every child. Some held it upside down, others on its side, but there was no mistaking it. These people were here for me!

In all the excitement of the journey, I'd forgotten it was my thirty-first birthday – twenty years since I had first dreamed up the idea of cycling around the world to help people.

I was greeted by a carnival of thronging bodies. School children danced and weaved, tribal leaders waved flags and local journalists shot pictures as mothers, fathers, visitors and workers drummed, sang, cheered, and held banners. I picked up a boy no older than six and placed him on the seat of my bike, and we danced all the way up the red clay road, through the tea plantations, to the local school where cake was to be handed out to one and all.

As we arrived, I could see the simple school had been decorated with more posters, signs and well wishes. I wanted to be articulate, to thank them for everything they had done, to tell them of my adventures, and to pass on messages from the children in England. All I could do was crouch down beside Shirley and cry. Tears of joy were rolling down my cheeks. I'd done it. I'd cycled fifteen thousand kilometres from England to India. I'd lived my dream.

Postscript

Chembakolli, the village that inspired my trip, where the children come to the Vidyadaya School.

Westerners aren't allowed into the tribal area. Not even Indians are allowed in unless they have ancestry there. As an elephant had killed a trespassing tourist there, I had been told that I wouldn't be allowed to visit it. It was too dangerous.

So when I was told we were going anyway, I was totally dumbfounded, apprehensive and excited. Knowing my arrival was imminent, the village leaders and elders, and spiritualists, had got together and decided in one day of talking that I could make a visit. The next day they decided that I could have a 'sleep over.'

And they wanted me to cycle in ...

So, mounting Shirley, we set off again, deep into the jungle. Villages got simpler, then simpler still, and then we were in the jungle and my guides on motorbikes had to leave their machines and follow by foot.

After a few minutes, the undergrowth parted and opened onto a small clearing where there were two buildings - a nursery and a temple - both made of mud with straw roofs. In the distance I could hear children and make out houses dotted into the hillside. Women carried water from the stream up to their houses, some of which were miles away.

I had seen 'Avatar' in 3D in Mumbai over Christmas, and Chembakolli had many similarities, not least the sacred tree in the middle of the village.

I visited the families and was welcomed with tea (as usual) and smiles. Some kept their distance from the 'strange one', others were transfixed. I saw some children with scabies but the hospital, funded by Accord - a partner of ActionAid in India, had given them the necessary medicines to effect a cure.

Night was drawing in, so we made our way up the hillside, climbing roots and avoiding vines and palms. At the top, the chief's house was the same as all the others - simple, clean and friendly.

We lit a fire immediately to keep the wild animals away and, after chatting for hours by firelight (there was no electricity), I was brought a gourmet meal cooked over a fire in the kitchen. Lying down on the mud veranda, the head teacher of Vidyadaya School and I settled in for the night. It was surprisingly cool after the heat of the day, and the call of the wild lulled me to sleep as birds made their nests and beasts began to hunt by night.

I was woken in the pitch dark by the chieftain who was announcing excitedly, "Listen. Tiger."

Oh my goodness, there was a tiger close-by.

He explained it was some way off. Thank goodness. The only protection I had was my sleeping bag and I'd even forgotten my mosquito repellent which would probably not have been much use against the King of the Jungle. I lay and listened a bit longer but the tranquillity had me at its mercy and I was asleep before I knew it.

A few hours later, I jumped out of my sleeping bag. The dog was going crazy, I switched on my torch and saw a leopard disappearing into the jungle. A leopard had become attached to the chief's cow. I liked to think two creatures from separate worlds had fallen in love, but the reality was probably a little more gruesome. The leopard, unlike the Indian human population, wanted beef on the menu. It had been within two metres of me. This wildest of creatures was one pounce from having Mr Bent à la carte.

Again I slipped off to sleep, lying on the hard floor with wild ideas in my head. When I awoke in the morning, I was surrounded by children. A gazillion balloon animals and flowers later, when they were all happy, I was allowed to go for a tour.

I walked down the steep hillside, stopping in at many of the hundred and fifty houses that constituted the village. Then, by another simple temple, we met another chief who had his bow and arrow on him. We practised shooting my shoes (they were off my feet at this point). After a while, a youth took the bow and wanted to show what he could do. He fired one shot and a tiny bird fell from the canopy way above us. The young children scampered off to retrieve the tiny bird and the arrow.

I felt a bit guilty. Did a bird have to die just because I was here. "What will you do with it?" I asked.

"Eat it," they responded as if I were an idiot.

A fire was rustled up and the bird was plucked and gutted and just thrown on. It was barely larger than a wren, but we all took a piece. I had both breasts (about the size of a penny), as the guest.

It was my turn to pluck the second bird to fall. I didn't want the most succulent breast when it was cooked. I wanted to be fair. They said I should take the head. I was told to remove the beak and gouge out the eyes. After doing so, very proficiently I have to say, I was left with the skull. "What do I do with it?"

236

"Eat it."

"What, the whole thing?"

'Man,' they're thinking, 'this white guy has no idea - of course all of it.'

I popped it in like a boiled sweet and bit down. The brain oozed into my mouth.

Before I knew it, it was time to leave. They invited me to stay for a week next time. I was keen, very keen!

On the way back to the school, we had to avoid elephants again. This time I was on foot because the head teacher had taken my bike (after lowering the seat a lot), and was flying around like a kid at a fairground. His eyes were wide and his smile was bigger than ever. He came back to me and declared, 'This is sooooooo coooool!!'

'Luckiest man alive' doesn't come close to me.

With thanks

There are so many thank-yous to make. Below are just a few:

Firstly Mum and Dad who suffered more than I did during my trip, worrying incessantly, distressed, suffering sleepless nights and harrowing dreams. This manifestation of your love which you have lavished upon me my entire life is unfortunately what drives me to take up a challenge; to make a difference to others; to love unconditionally; to brighten the lives of those around me.

My sisters for partnering me on adventures from an early age. Who would have thought crawling up Prittle Brook tunnel in the pitch black, surrounded by rats, could lead to such an epic journey into the unknown? I felt you both with me at times on the expedition, and I thank you for the company.

Everyone at home, from friends to family, from my pupils to my teachers. Thank you for the kind words and kinder sentiments. Those few words on paper honestly kept this trip alive.

My sponsors: *Cotswold* for your invaluable advice and equipment; *Bicycle Richmond* for introducing me to Shirley; *Interhealth* for keeping me alive; and also *Nakd*, *Buff*, *Specsavers* and *Starbucks*. Without you, children who are now healthy and attending school, with a future ahead of them, would still be working the streets or, worse, would no longer be with us at all.

I have to thank the people I met on my trip, from the lady who blew the kiss (and I never even stopped to ask your name), to the thousands of people who waved but will forever remain anonymous smiling faces and waving hands, to the many friends I met on the way who kept me company and shared your own awesome adventures with me.

Thanks to Carina for creating and maintaining my website. Since I moved down south with my northern accent, sticking-out ears and freckles we have been on adventures, which generally entailed you getting me out of a scrap of bother or two with breathtaking grace.

And a special thank you to Sandra Rivaud for her amazing illustrations. I fell in love with your work in Ahmedabad and am honoured to have your pictures in my book. An illustrious career beckons you young lady!!

Thank you all from the deepest depths of my all-too-human heart. I will forever remain humbly in debt for the love and generosity I received.